Negotiating Asymmetry

China's Place in Asia

D1737268

Negotiating Asymmetry

China's Place in Asia

Edited by

Anthony Reid
Zheng Yangwen

UNIVERSITY OF HAWAI'I PRESS
HONOLULU

© 2009 NUS Press

First published by:

NUS Press
AS3-01-02, 3 Arts Link
Singapore 117569
www.nus.edu.sg/nuspress

Published in North America by:

University of Hawai'i Press
2840 Kolowalu Street
Honolulu, HI 96822
www.uhpress.hawaii.edu

Library of Congress Cataloging-in-Publication Data

Negotiating asymmetry: China's place in Asia/edited by Anthony Reid, Zheng Yangwen.
    p. cm.
Includes bibliographical references and index.
ISBN 978-0-8248-3412-8 (pbk.: alk. paper)
    1. China–Relations–Asia. 2. Asia–Relations–China. 3. China–Foreign relations–20th century. I. Reid, Anthony, 1939– II. Zheng, Yangwen.

DS33.4.C5N44 2009
327.5105—dc22
                                2009010276

Cover: A *Ch'onhado* ("Map of all under Heaven") from Korea, eighteenth or early nineteenth century, but based on much older Korean renderings of ancient Chinese cosmic ideas, complemented by some more recent names. The Central continent represents the known and civilised world with the Middle Kingdom, here depicted by the orange *Tsung Yuan* ("Central Plain") disk below the great wall. The Korean peninsula is depicted to its right, and Japan (*Riben*) as an island beyond that. The Yellow River in the north is matched by the Red River (of modern Vietnam) in the south. Siam (*Hsien-lo*) and Cambodia (*Chen-la*) are recognisable on either side of Red River's mouth. The more distant rings of places within and beyond the "four seas" are largely mythical (Courtesy of British Library, Maps 33.c.13).

Printed in Singapore

Contents

Part Three: The Long March from Empire to Nation

Preface

When the Asia Research Institute at the National University of Singapore began work in 2002, one of its first priorities was the long and increasingly critical relationship between China and Southeast Asia. A research cluster on "Southeast Asia China interactions" was established, which was convened by the then ARI Director Anthony Reid but took advantage of the wealth of expertise already in Singapore on this topic, including Wang Gungwu, Liu Hong, Ng Chin Keong, Leo Suryadinata, Huang Jianli and many others who would normally think of themselves as China or Southeast Asia specialists but were well-informed on the relationship simply because of Singapore's position. The cluster recruited Geoff Wade from Hong Kong in 2003, and Zheng Yangwen from Cambridge and Pennsylvania in 2004. It profited greatly from some valuable early visitors, including Sun Laichen, Momoki Shiro, Charles Wheeler, Wu Xiao An, and George Souza, and post-doctoral fellows such as Maung Aung Myoe and Kwee Hui Kian.

The cluster held several conferences essentially concerned with the historical dimension of this relationship. Some are now in the process of publication: on the Ming Factor in fifteenth-century Southeast Asia; on imperial expansions in Asia; and (with Osaka University) on "Offshore Asia" or the maritime connections between Northeast and Southeast Asia. As historians we knew, however, how much this past weighed on the present, and how much depended on a healthy appreciation of that past for the intense relationships now taking shape not only in Southeast Asia but all of China's neighbours.

This book is the outcome of that concern. It took initial shape in a Singapore conference on "Rationalising China's Place in Asia, 1800 to 2005" on 3–4 August 2006. Many contributed their critical ideas to that conference without being able to be directly represented in this book. We acknowledge particularly the contributions of Liu Hong, John E. Wills, Ignatius Wibowo, Richard Horowitz, Amitav Acharya, Liselotte Odgaard, William Callahan and Zhang Yunling, who wrote papers, and Bruce Lockhart, Leo Suryadinata, Geoff Wade and Kwa Chong

Guan who chaired sessions and contributed ideas. Wang Gungwu gave an insightful keynote address quite different from the closing chapter of this book, and provided invaluable guidance throughout. Geoff Wade, Sun Laichen and Maung Aung Myoe have been generous with their erudition, particularly for the Introduction.

We thank all of the ARI staff, especially Rina Yap, Valerie Yeo, Alyson Rozells and Henry Kwan for facilitating the conference, Valerie Yeo for continuing to assist the compilation of this volume, and Jiang Na and Kristy Won for helping Tony get through the work. In Manchester Yangwen thanks Laurence Brown, Steven Pierce, Paulo Drinot, Natalie Zacek, Anindita Ghosh and Till Geiger for reading and editing her chapter. Finally our thanks go to NUS Press, its two anonymous readers for their helpful critique, its Managing Director Paul Kratoska for much sympathy and guidance, and Lena Qua for final attention to the manuscript.

**Anthony Reid (Singapore) &
Zheng Yangwen (England)**
April 2009

Introduction

Negotiating Asymmetry: Parents, Brothers, Friends and Enemies

Anthony Reid

When the United Nations was formed in 1945 after the trauma of the Second World War, it declared as its first principle that "The Organisation is based on the principle of the sovereign equality of all its Members."[1] In a world still dominated by colonialism, in which the British monarch was sovereign over many kings and countries including several founder members of the United Nations, this was a radical statement. Nevertheless that "sovereign equality" dominated the international rhetoric of the following half-century. In the Cold War competition for the allegiance of weaker members, the superpowers constantly declared that they respected the sovereignty and territorial integrity of every state, and the principle of non-interference in one another's internal affairs.

Westphalia and Asymmetry

The system of international relations based on these principles is often referred to as Westphalian, despite the very different world represented in the European treaties of 1648. This is shorthand, also used in this book, for a European system of multiple states recognising one another's sovereignty and equal right to order their internal affairs in different ways. The Charter of the United Nations in effect proposed to extend to the world what had been the historical anomaly of a plural Europe which had exhausted itself in wars of legitimacy sparked by the Protestant Reformation. The nineteenth-century European system of a balance of power, even more than the Westphalia treaties themselves, was what

1

made this pattern of sovereign equality effective. Yet paradoxically it became an elaborate diplomatic doctrine during the very century when the European states expanded their authority over myriad existing polities in Asia and Africa. The system continued to be treated as normative through the colonial era only by means of the drastic limitation that only "civilised" states could be part of the club of "sovereign equality". Hence the determination of modernising Asian states such as Japan and Siam/Thailand to achieve this civilised status, however culturally biased its definition.[2]

The post-war international order represented by this sovereign equality principle was strikingly successful in ending formal relations of long-distance imperialism. Every part of the territory of Asia and Africa was reconfigured into the model of a nation-state and equal member of the United Nations. This was painful for peoples and polities that suddenly found themselves defined as problematic and peripheral subjects of a theoretically uniform sovereignty. People such as Tibetans, Karens, Shans, Ambonese, Assamese, Kashmiris and all manner of migrant minorities were the victims of a new world in which boundaries were supposed to be absolute and political affiliations singular. Cosmopolitan port-cities like Goa, Aden, Penang, Colombo and Hong Kong had difficulty adjusting to their new roles within nation-states of presumed internal homogeneity. But nevertheless the system, or what Vuving (below) calls the "myth" of the normative world-order, was largely unquestioned.

Paradoxically, one of the most vociferous champions of the new system of sovereign equality and non-interference in internal affairs after 1950 was China, the polity with the largest stake in an older system. Communist China was in the long term the most significant convert to these novel principles, adopted as the epitome of the Afro-Asian and Third World movements following the 1955 Bandung Conference. The enthusiasm of the new countries of Asia, including China, after 1950 ensured that it would be "Westphalia", and not any Asian system of international relations which dominated international discussion. Brantley Womack has made the point well that "Asia's experience and successes have had little effect on international relations theory, which remains rooted in the modern European experience of competitive nationalism."[3]

The experience of Europe demonstrates that "Westphalian" sovereign equality is no guarantee of peace. The contrary case would be easier to make, that unequal or asymmetric relations have historically been the more stable when accepted by both sides. In what Womack calls "asymmetric normalcy", "both sides manage their affairs with the confidence that the power of the larger side will not be challenged and the autonomy of the smaller side will not be threatened".[4] Although medieval Europe abounded with asymmetry of this type, in modern times it has been Asian experience that offers the most instructive examples, particularly in relation to China.

This book explores a past in which China's relations with its neighbours were inherently asymmetric, in the belief that this does have some lessons for a future also likely to present great challenges of in-equality in relationships. The niceties of sovereign equality will remain in the international order, since their advantages for small countries always sensitive to bullying cannot be gainsaid. Those same small coun-tries, however, have always had other means to manage their relations with giant neighbours, and they continue to do so within the conve-nient fictions of equality.

Elusive "Normality"

China's long history as a recognisable polity under successive dynasties, and an ancient written tradition favouring the authority of established texts over experienced reality, suggests a relatively high degree of conti-nuity and conservatism in China's worldview and external relationships. Imperial China appealed to centuries-old precedents, and conducted relations with distant polities that no longer existed in the form in which "tribute" had first been acknowledged. Nevertheless the notion of a "traditional Chinese world order" is elusive and even dangerous. Each of China's relationships with neighbouring countries was unique, these relations changed radically over time, and none can be said to have been understood in the same light on both sides.

Long before the Europeans, Japan had refused to play the game of "tribute" to the imperial centre. Japan opted out in the ninth century, insisting on its own imperial centre which was the equal of China's. The Ashikaga shoguns were the exception to this Japanese rejection in the fifteenth century, when like many Southeast Asian rulers they judged that the immense internal benefits for themselves of monopolising trade with China through the tributary mechanism, the sole legal access allowed by the Ming court, outweighed the private humiliation in the language of letters to Beijing. Other Japanese regimes endured the costs to trade which total boycott of the Ming/Qing system entailed. With the arrival of European competitive nationalism, extremely sensitive to indications of inequality, the tributary "order" was still less effective in regulating trade.

As the following chapters clearly show, the anomalies multiplied in the nineteenth century. Alexander Vuving refers to the long-term interaction of rival "myths that functioned as interface" between international actors with quite different world-views; while Kawashima Shin focuses on the "double standard" of the nineteenth century. Another analyst has described nineteenth-century Asian diplomacy as a prime case of "organised hypocrisy", whereby international actors systematically flout the rules they publicly profess.[5] In the twentieth century China nominally adhered to the Westphalian world order, signed treaties and appointed ambassadors. Yet the trauma of reinventing China through successive revolutions tended to invalidate the past completely. Treaties were denounced as "unequal" or "imperial", even though they had recognised the maximal definition of Qing eighteenth-century expansion. The isolation of China behind these boundaries during the Cold War caused another and more profound revolution, as porous border zones of ambivalent political affiliation were turned into absolute frontiers of unprecedented internal sovereignty. Internationally there could be no "normality" in conditions of war around China's frontiers in Korea, Vietnam, Laos and Burma, when even mutual recognition was in question.

Two books that could be seen as predecessors of the current volume, the collections edited by Fairbank as *The Chinese World Order* (1968) and by Rossabi as *China among Equals* (1983), while still valuable, are both limited to the imperial past and to a view essentially from China.[6] Because *Negotiating Asymmetry* seeks to give equal emphasis to the other side of the relationships, and to the twentieth century, it cannot take as comprehensive a view of China's Asian relationships as those volumes. We have deliberately limited its scope to the maritime Asian domain of Northeast and Southeast Asia, and sought to explicate the perspectives from Japan, Korea, and Southeast Asia as well as from China. There is already more than enough diversity here in both the past and the present to negate any arguments for an Asian "system" and to make clear how distinctive each relationship is.

Nevertheless it should be acknowledged that there were fundamental differences between neighbours by land, with whom warfare was always a major factor, and neighbours by sea, with whom military contacts in the Mongol and early Ming periods were a radical exception to the norm of imperial lack of interest. Among neighbours by land, only Korea, Vietnam and (northern) Burma are considered in this volume, and all these were sedentary rice-growers with varying degrees of respect for the Chinese civilisational model.

China's Central Asian neighbours were of a different kind — nomadic or semi-nomadic pastoralists and traders always ready to mobilise into formidable fighting and raiding units. Neither side was in much doubt that the essential relations between the empire and these neighbours were determined by force, nor that the major military threat to China came from this quarter. As Peter Perdue has made clear, "the role of expansive warfare in the expansion of the Qing state" to the westward was at least as important as cultural and commercial policies.[7] To regulate affairs on their western and northern borders, successive dynasties employed military means, both defensive and offensive, diplomatic endeavours "to control barbarians by using other barbarians", and the politics of bribery, by sending valued luxuries and trade goods as gifts to powerful neighbours. This did not stop the Confucian scholars of the imperial courts insisting on "the myth of world suzerainty [as] a useful ideological instrument for ruling China". Outside China, however, Chinese ambassadors accepted the equality of Herat, Lhasa, Kokand and Moscow with the Middle Kingdom as what Fletcher calls "the unseen side of a long-established tradition".[8]

Military factors might loom even larger, in other words, if this were a complete survey of China's relations with her neighbours. The empire's long-term lack of interest or capacity by sea (despite brief exceptions) made it easier for each side of a maritime relationship to pursue their own interpretation of its nature oblivious of the other.

This book shows an abundance of examples of asymmetric relations in Asia, and of the ideological, military, commercial and cultural means to manage them at both ends. Our closely-integrated contemporary world needs to draw on this experience as it faces a twenty-first century in which sovereign equality proves inadequate in practice, and misleading in theory.

Rival Ideologies in Asian Exchanges

As has been increasingly noted in the International Relations literature, Asia provides the principal challenge, by no means adequately realised, to the Eurocentric assumptions underlying most International Relations theory.[9] But in bringing this factor into play, the great diversity of Asia's systems must be remembered. Challenging Westphalian over-simplification with a "Chinese world order" simplification will not do. This book explores some of the variety of Asian systems that operated before and alongside the European norm.

If we can speak of a "Chinese world order", it operated only in Korea. There the purist Confucian assumptions embodied in the relations between exemplary imperial centre and respectful but autonomous tributary were most nearly approximated historically. As the most ancient, loyal and stable "tributaries" of the empire, Korean kings accepted that they derived their legitimacy from Beijing, conducted trade on a very large scale under the form of tribute, and entertained minimal political or economic relations with any other countries except China (and Japan in practice, if not admitted to the Chinese court). Korea was much more consistent and rigorous in carrying out these principles than China itself, and enforced the principle of isolation from any non-official interaction with neighbouring countries that seems totally at odds with the self-interest of a country with a very long coastline (and which today has one of the world's largest shipping fleets).

Already in Tang times the Silla kingdom which unified Korea was "perhaps the most exact and faithful of the many replicas in miniature of the great Chinese empire".[10] After the disruptions of Japanese, Ming and Manchu invasions of the half-century after 1590, Choson Korea settled into a particularly stable tributary relationship with Qing China, sending 12 tribute missions a year for most of the period up to 1872.[11] To its ruling regime, the benefits of asymmetry were in the strong support China's presence gave to Confucian orthodoxy, royal legitimacy, and Korean autonomy. As Seo-Hyun Park demonstrates below, the Korean elite was willing, as Japan and Vietnam were not, to accept the doctrine of *sadae* ("serving the great", or deference) towards China as "a strategic calculation of how best to guarantee Korean sovereignty". Yet even despite this normative deference, Korea's extensive trade and diplomacy with Japan's alternative "world order" throughout the Tokugawa period were a huge concession to realism.

Even if it was accepted only in Korea, the neo-Confucian orthodoxy that dominated the Ming and Qing dynasties in China has in some modern literature been elevated to an alternative "world order". As Alexander Vuving well demonstrates below, this doctrine should be understood essentially as the normative dimension of the view from the Chinese capital. As essentialised in Fairbank's 1968 book, it emphasised the civilisational centrality of the Chinese capital, a consequent hierarchic view of the surrounding "tributary" states, and a "disesteem of violence" in which the court was more interested in being respected beyond its borders than obeyed.[12]

Much as Japan and Siam were forced to adopt the trappings of European civilisation by the arrogance of nineteenth-century European assumptions about their world-order, Korea and Vietnam much earlier responded to Chinese arrogance by insisting that they had achieved the same level of civilisation as the empire itself. Since they wrote in Chinese, and read the classics, they shared most Chinese assumptions as to what civilisation meant. But their intellectuals were intensely aware, as Chinese literati were not, that civilisation was plural, with alternative capitals of equal worth and dignity.

The Vietnamese state had more intellectual and political options than the Korean, having intense diplomatic, military and cultural exchanges with Southeast Asian neighbours as well as sending tribute to the northern behemoth. Its rulers were judged by Confucian state chroniclers such as Le Van Huu and Ngo Si Lien by how far they had adopted correct Confucian principles on the one hand, and how far they had insisted on full political equality with China on the other.[13] The most celebrated statement of this equality was penned (in written Chinese) by Nguyen Trai in 1428, shortly after the successful expulsion of the Ming force that had been occupying Dai Viet.

> Mountains and rivers have demarcated the borders. The customs of the North [China] and the South [Dai Viet] are also different. We find that the Trieu, Dinh, Ly, and Tran [dynasties] built our country. Alongside the Han, Tang, Song and Yuan, the rulers [of our dynasties] ruled as emperors over their own part.[14]

Vietnam was Northeast Asian in its use of written Chinese (until the twentieth century) and acceptance of the centrality of the civilisation written in it, but was Southeast Asian in its pragmatic assumption that the paraphernalia of tribute was no more than another weapon to deploy in keeping Leviathan at bay. Vietnam insisted on the same titles and rituals as the Ming and Qing emperors, and conducted its own extensive relations with other states both as suzerain or equal. Yet after each showdown with Chinese forces sent against it (the latest in 1789), formal diplomatic relations were prudently re-established on the basis of tribute missions.

The remainder of Southeast Asia was protected from Chinese troops by Vietnam in the northeast, by Burma and by forbidding and malarial mountains in the northwest, and elsewhere by Imperial aversion to the sea. Unfamiliar with Chinese characters, their ruling courts depended on specialists (usually overseas Chinese or Sino-Southeast Asians) to operate the arcane diplomacy needed for trade with Ming and Qing China, and in most cases had little understanding of or interest in that world. Some rulers had similar relations with the tiny Ryukyu court of the fifteenth and sixteenth centuries, also authorising Hokkien traders to write the diplomatic letters in their name that made trade easier through the "organised hypocrisy" of tribute.

The Separate Worlds of Southeast Asian Diplomacy

Vietnam's extensive diplomacy within the Southeast Asian world was exceptional in its mimicking of China's "civilisational centrality" stance. Alexander Vuving sets out clearly below how Dai Viet saw itself as also a "central kingdom" (*trung quoc*, corresponding to China's *zhongguo*) of civilisation, surrounded by tributary "barbarians". Particularly as it hardened into a defensive dogma under Minh-Mang (1820–41), this model caused long-standing bitterness in "barbarian" Cambodia as the Vietnamese sought to assimilate and "civilise" them. Burma, France and England were listed among Minh-Mang's tributaries. As Womack remarks, at least as rigidly interpreted in this period, "Vietnam would have been better off without a Chinese model."[15]

The diplomatic and ideological world of maritime Southeast Asia, in which I include not only Archipelagos and Peninsula but Siam and Pegu (Mon-ruled southern Burma before 1600), was wholly distinct from that of Northeast Asia. The sacred written languages of external authority were not Chinese but Sanskrit and Pali, while Chinese reluctance to developing naval power (with the very brief exceptions of the early Mongol and early Ming dynasties), removed any practical threat from that quarter. "China", which appears routinely by that name in Southeast Asian sources from the fifteenth century, was perceived as a distant powerful kingdom not unlike Rome, Istanbul or ancient Indian kingdoms like Kalinga. Its name could be used to add lustre to a royal lineage, its court manipulated into offering privileged access to the Chinese market, and its subjects generally welcomed as unthreatening traders with (after 1450) no state power to back them up.

The political contrast between these Northeast Asian and Southeast Asian worlds is extreme, making any discussion of an "Asian" diplomatic model peculiarly inappropriate. In the civilisational pools of Eurasia,

China was at one end of the spectrum of "state-heavy", with a unique bureaucracy intimately tied to a literary tradition sustained by printing. Southeast Asian states were close to the other end of the spectrum of bureaucratisation, and many of its complex societies remained effectively stateless into the nineteenth century.[16] Chinese state memory was written, and highly conservative in following written precedent; Southeast Asian state memory was guided rather by strong personalities and court ritual, as well as oral tradition that was only incidentally written down. In dealing with the abundant European written sources of the sixteenth to nineteenth centuries for a relatively document-poor Southeast Asia, historians have long been aware of the danger of treating the European sources as normative simply because they are written. The same caution must be exercised in relation to Chinese state sources in an earlier period.

Religious and cosmic ideas supplied much of the social glue in Southeast Asia which bureaucracy and law did in China (or post-enlightenment Europe). The most substantial states of early maritime Southeast Asia — Pegu (southern Burma), Angkor (Cambodia), Champa, Siam, Sriwijaya (Sumatra) or Java — adapted Hindu-Buddhist ideological themes making their rulers into cosmic kings (*devaraja*) presiding over their own replica of Mount Meru. Diplomatic letters that have survived from the early modern period would devote much of their contents to establishing the supernatural assets and lineage of the king, which Jane Drakard has shown to be central to the claims of kings.[17] As Woodside noted, "The problematic relationship between their limited, unimperial sizes and their spiritually imperial universalising political-religious traditions is one of the most interesting features of their history."[18]

If the Ming and Qing imperial courts viewed trade as a marginal issue to be reluctantly accepted only as a means to expand the area of tribute, Southeast Asian kings took an almost opposite view of diplomacy as a handmaid of trade. These Malay kings lived by trade, and their success was judged by the abundance of ships in their ports. Traders coming from afar sought whenever possible to bring a letter from their own king or port-ruler, which would ensure a good reception at court. The trader would also bring gifts for the king, and in return would be "given great honour" at court, where "they eat and drink, all sorts of food and fruits are brought, they play, dance, with all sorts of entertainments, they play on the trumpet, flute, clarinet and *rebab*, and then the king asks for a garment of our local style to be brought, which he gives to the *nakhoda* [supercargo]".[19] A Dutch Company official described the way Siam frequently sent envoys to India, "with letters full of praisings and compliments and also with small presents. This is done only to promote trade."[20]

In contrast with these pleasantries with distant trade partners, relations with Southeast Asian rivals were more delicate. Unequal relations were more common and easy to manage, such as those between upstream chiefs or rajas of nearby districts and the ruler of the port on which they were dependent. But among the Malay-speaking states around the Melaka Straits there was intense rivalry for both status and trade. The chronicle of sixteenth-century Melaka seemed particularly concerned to explain how the more difficult relations of equality should be conducted. In an early passage it sets out the protocol for receiving royal embassies from greater or lesser states but adds the comment that the kings of Pasai and Haru (both in Sumatra) were regarded as "equal" (*sama*), "and however they might stand to each other in point of age it was 'greetings' (*salam*) they sent to each other". This doctrine was however contested, and the chronicle tells the stories of two cases where Pasai (as the older Islamic state) tried to insist on "homage" (*sembah*). One led to war between Haru and Pasai; the other was cleverly got around by the Melaka envoy.[21]

Tribute also played a role in relations between Southeast Asian states, particularly the more asymmetric ones. When Java or Sriwijaya were strong, surrounding rulers sent them a tribute. Almost all of the rulers of small rivers in the Peninsula sent the "golden flowers" (*bunga mas*) of tribute to Siam intermittently from the fifteenth century to the nineteenth. Yet these relationships never inhibited the state in question from pursuing independent trade and diplomatic relations with other states.[22] A Trengganu spokesman described his ruler in the 1890s as "like a child who had two parents" — a mother-like indulgent Siam, and a father-like frightening Britain.[23] This is the same engaging metaphor used in the sixteenth century by Ryukyu between China (father) and Japan (mother), and by Xishuangbanna (Sip Song Panna) between China (father), and Burma (mother).[24]

When Melaka was struggling to establish itself as the new entrepot in the early 1400s, it sent tributary missions to China, Java, and Siam, in an attempt to have them all as trading partners rather than enemies. By its mid-century peak, however, even though Beijing (and probably also Siam) continued to record occasional missions from Melaka as if they were tribute, Melaka itself appeared very concerned to assert its equality in friendship. Its chronicle tells of an exchange of envoys to make peace after warring with Siam in Sultan Muzaffar's reign (1446–59), when the Sultan ordered his ministers to write a letter to Siam that "must not be of homage (*sembah*), nor of greetings (*salam*), nor of friendship (*kasih*)".[25] The lengthy exchange with China was placed in the reign of Sultan Mansur (1459–77), Melaka's most successful king. While acknowledging in its fanciful descriptions that China was a mighty kingdom with innumerable subjects, the chronicle goes to some lengths to avoid any admission of inequality. It acknowledged that a letter was sent to China presenting *sembah* to its King, but only because the Emperor had already presented Sultan Mansur with his beautiful daughter as a bride, and thus had become entitled to the respect of a father-in-law. But when the envoys brought this letter of homage to Beijing, the Emperor was stricken with a disease, which a wise man interpreted as being caused by his sin in having accepted a letter of homage from Melaka. The Emperor duly repents, and sends a mission to Melaka to request the water in which Sultan Mansur's feet have been washed, which successfully cures his ailment. "So the Raja of China commanded, 'all my descendants, never demand homage from the Raja of Melaka but only an agreement of friendship (*muafakat berkasih-kasihan*)'."[26]

China in Southeast Asian Eyes

As these tales already suggest, China was known to all the political traditions of maritime Southeast Asia as a distant but wealthy empire, with innumerable subjects and advanced manufactures of ceramics, silks and metalware. Only once in public memory did it affect the region directly. The extraordinary irruption of Ming power and personnel into Southeast Asia in the period 1405–20 played a part in the rise of Siam (Ayutthaya), post-Angkor Cambodia, Melaka, Brunei, Manila and the Muslim Javanese states, as privileged centres for the China (tribute) trade. The chronicles, all written long after this period, usually contain at least one episode calculated to explain the importance of Chinese defectors from the imperial fleets and traders marooned in the south by the Ming bans on private trade in this period of history. Never is any political supremacy admitted of China over the Southeast Asian state. The favourite explanation of Chinese influence, occurring in Siamese, Malay (as above), Javanese, Bugis and Brunei chronicle traditions, is of a Chinese princess being bestowed on a founding local ruler, and arriving accompanied by hundreds of retainers. Although in reality the Chinese who settled in Southeast Asian ports in this turbulent period were almost exclusively male, only a few older chronicle traditions mention a Chinese male ancestor of a dynasty.[27]

Other traditions, of societies less affected by the Yung-lo Emperor's exceptional interventionism, still mention "China" as one of the world's great kingdoms. Minangkabau rulers in highland Sumatra, for example, proclaimed in chronicles and even their royal letters that they were brothers of the kings of China and "Rum" (Byzantium/Constantinople). Their legends insisted that the world-conquering Alexander the Great (Iskandar Zulkarnain in Islamic tradition) had three sons, who travelled to the Singapore area in pursuit of their destined kingdoms. There they quarrelled. The eldest brother went off to become the ruler of Rum in the West, the second brother to become the ruler of China in the East, while the youngest remained to generate the ruling dynasty of Minangkabau.[28]

Countries accessible overland to Chinese troops had a much more hard-headed view schooled on many battlefields. This applied particularly to the most consistently strong and bureaucratised states — Choson Korea, Dai Viet and Burma. For them, China was at all times before the nineteenth century the greatest potential threat. Playing its "tribute" game was a valued tactic, both to keep that threat quiescent and to confirm the legitimacy of a regime against its internal rivals. As the reality of European military power became apparent in the nineteenth century, that comparison became more marked. "In contrast to … western imperialism, China acted as the passive guarantor of a matrix of unequal but autonomous relationships rather than as an active metropolitan power. To go to Beijing was more reassuring than to have Paris come to you."[29]

Burma is a particularly interesting case, as the only major state in Southeast Asia having long-term diplomatic, military and commercial interactions with China but not sharing its written Chinese culture. There is a rich Burmese narrative of these transactions as well as a Chinese one, and the two have not yet been systematically reconciled. They demonstrate very clearly how wide the gap in official interpretation of the relationship was between the two sides. Unlike the Korea and Dai Viet cases, Burmese diplomatic letters had to be rendered into the appropriate Chinese by Beijing's Translation Bureau. The usual opportunities for altering the tone of messages in translation were heightened by this procedure, and many of the memorials from these culturally diverse "tributaries" enter Chinese records transformed into a deferentially stylised formula.

The Pagan kingdom which ruled most of present-day Burma was conquered and devastated by the Mongols in the 1280s. The following half-century was the only one when Burmese kings appear to have acknowledged a tributary relationship though the evidence for this is all on the Chinese side. More than 20 tributary missions were sent to the Yuan (Mongol) Dynasty between 1289 and 1339, two Burmese kings were invested by the Mongols, and several missions visited Burma in return.[30] Despite several attempts China never again succeeded militarily against the Burmese capital, which guarded its sovereign equality jealously.

In the early Ming period Burma was divided between the maritime and Mon Pegu kigdom and the interior and Burman Ava. The former behaved like other maritime polities, responding to the flurry of activity by Zheng He's fleets by sending five missions between 1407 to 1415. Ava in the north sent more frequent missions as part of its competition with the many chiefdoms to its north which had different kinds of relations with the Ming. Although we are dependent on Chinese sources for this period of the relationship, Sun Laichen has located enough evidence even there to show how different the Chinese-language tributary statements recorded by the Ming court were from what was written and practiced in Burmese. One Chinese traveller reported, for example, that the kings of Ava always referred to the Ming emperor as their elder brother — in marked contrast to the Ming self-image as father of all. Several Ming envoys to the two Burma states complained that their predecessors had been humiliated and forced to kowtow, partly in order to show how they, by contrast, had insisted on imperial precedence. When the unusually aggressive Chinese envoy Yang Xuan reached Pegu, according to his own account, he protested to King Rayadazit: "'The son of heaven of the great Ming is sending envoys to notify all the barbarians, why do not you kowtow to the edict bearer?' Rayadazit replied: 'Ruling this country, I only understand that others kowtow to me, how do I know to kowtow to others!'"[31]

Under the Konbaung (1752–1886), the last and one of the strongest of pre-colonial Burma dynasties, records are sufficient on both sides of the relationship to demonstrate more clearly the contrasting ideologies underpinning it. The Konbaung virtually ignored the Qing, as had their immediate predecessors, until conflicts in the border led these two expanding empires to war in 1765. For the next five years a bitter war was fought in the border hill tracts, with the Chinese armies having the worst of it both from battle casualties and disease. After what has been called "the most disastrous and devastating frontier war that the Qing had ever fought",[32] peace arrangements were agreed in 1769. Characteristically, the Chinese record of the agreement includes the sending of tribute, but it is clear from the Burmese records that they were by no means prepared to play the Chinese game for the sake of trade even to the extent of the equally victorious Vietnamese. What the Burmese kings agreed to was "good-will missions" every ten years. The negotiators appear to have conveyed different versions of the agreement to their respective courts, anxious for their own skins.

Since no tribute was forthcoming from Burma, the Qing closed the border until 1787, when Yunnanese traders, desperate to restore their lucrative business with Burma, sent a highly respectful bogus "Chinese" mission to the Burmese capital. Since China appeared to have taken the first step towards an equal relationship, Burma responded by resuming missions from Amerapura to Yunnan, and in several cases onward to Beijing. Myoe acknowledges 6 more, while Sun Laichen counts 14, though they agree on the dates of the last ones in 1843, 1853 and 1874.[33] Frequently the Yunnan authorities must have knowingly arranged the messages flowing to Beijing and Amerapura respectively to ensure that trade was not again interrupted. While the protocol of tribute, and due reverence for the symbols of Chinese authority are frequently recorded in the records of the Chinese court, these are never mentioned in the abundant Burmese sources. For example when a Chinese royal seal was sent to mark the investiture of a new king in 1792, the Chinese record emphasises that the correct protocol in Chinese eyes was observed, with much kow-towing before the symbols of imperial power. The Burmese one records a debate at court as to whether the seal should be accepted, concluding that it should because of its value in gold. But the King at the same time conferred flowery titles on the Qing ruler, as if to ensure there was balance for whatever was conferred from the Chinese side.

The countries closest to China were unsurprisingly the most realistic in developing the diplomatic weapons they needed to control the relationship. As Womack's politics of asymmetry suggest, both Burma and Vietnam were much more aware of the "China problem" than China was of them, fully aware that mishandling it could be fatal to themselves, though not to China.[34] Vietnam accepted China's perception of central civilisation versus peripheral barbarism, but used it to develop its own equal centre while using "tribute" as part of its diplomacy. Burma did not, and was particularly insistent on its own sovereign centrality in a different value-system, even while it gained from mediators who satisfied the structured hypocrisy of the Chinese system. Further south China was simply a trade opportunity, and tribute would be used as a key to that opportunity only when there was no other way in.

Asymmetry through Family

Much of the asymmetry in Asian diplomatic relations, particularly in its most stable formulations, was explained through the imagery of family. Wang Gungwu explains in the final chapter how China in contemporary times has often "preferred the softer hierarchy implied in terms like family and friends" to the legalistic fictions of sovereign equality. Sometimes the paternalistic claims of Chinese emperors had also been put in terms of a Confucian father's care for his children. We have seen that Southeast Asia's pre-colonial rulers accepted such formulations only in terms of a son-in-law's appropriate deference to his wife's father, their kinship systems being familiar with the ritual deference of wife-taker lineages to wife-givers.

But the imagery of brothers was developed historically not by China but by its neighbours, for whom it acceptably reflected the modest degree of primacy they were prepared to allow China. Many Asian languages assume that strict equality is uncomfortable, and intimacy best established once it is clear who should be treated in speech as the elder brother or sister, and who the younger. Personal terms of address reflect this presumption, providing few opportunities for a neutral and equal "you", but many for intimate inequality. Brothers, in particular, cannot be equal since the terms for them always distinguish between elder and younger. The formulations *Pauk-Phaw* (kinsmen, literally "born-together"), and at best *Nyi-Ako* (siblings), with which the modern Burmese statesmen discussed by Myoe below sought to designate their relations with the PRC, literally and necessarily refer to an "elder-younger" relationship, but an acceptable one.

In the case of Malay states, as examined above, the formulation that the "younger brother" greets the "elder brother" appeared natural even when envoys were prepared to die to resist deference in the salutation. Barbara Andaya has examined royal relationships in Sumatra through the lens of brotherhood. She concludes that despite the necessary hierarchy of elder and younger, "in ideal terms the relationship most approximating equals was that between siblings, particularly brothers".[35]

Sun Laichen has shown how conscious the Ming and Qing courts were of the necessary fatherhood of the Emperor towards the imagined family of "all under heaven". Although in 1627 the Manchus did refer to Manchuria and Korea as "brotherly states", once they had subdued Korea and still more assumed the role of Emperors of the Middle Kingdom, they insisted on being both suzerain and father to Korea.[36] Burma, like China, considered itself a "father" of its tributaries. But over several centuries up to the nineteenth, it appears to have been remarkably consistent in allowing China only the role of elder brother.[37] The letters received by Burma at decennial intervals after 1787, and purporting to come from the Chinese court, appear always to have used the formula that "the elder brother … addresses affectionately his younger brother … who rules over the great kingdoms to the westward".[38] The first such letter was evidently a bogus one drawn up in Yunnan in order to break the stalemate in relations in 1787, and it seems likely that subsequent letters of this type that arrived in Mandalay were also concocted in Yunnan to keep the relationship smooth. The Burmese court therefore believed it was responding to these missions with reciprocal missions of friendship, not sending decennial "tribute". The Burmese kings did not themselves use the younger brother formulation, but rather something like the following, from the last mission in 1874:

> The Suzerain of all Umbrella-bearing kings bearing rule over the Great Empires and kingdoms in the West, hereby lovingly address his Royal friend Tongzhi, the Emperor of China, the suzerain of all Umbrella-bearing kings bearing rule over the great Empires and kingdoms in the east.[39]

In Beijing, on the other hand, officials undoubtedly ensured that the Emperor received letters that corresponded with the Chinese view of tribute.

Junko Koizumi's chapter in this book shows how the idea of China as "elder sister" was taken up by Chinese diplomats of the transitional period as a means to retain some primacy within the new order. The socialist brotherhood of the 1950s and 1960s was a different matter again, aimed at creating a new type of international relations in defiance of the established order. Yet as Alexander Vuving and Maung Myoe show in the following chapters, both Vietnam and Myanmar believed that they could live with a Chinese "elder brother", provided it did not become a scolding "father".

Trade will Find a Way

Most of the above discussion, excessively reliant on state documents of both sides, relates to the attitudes of royal courts to each other. It must not be forgotten, however, that commercial relations did flourish even in the most unfavourable political circumstances. Although the Ming court in its Confucian theory opposed mere private trade with foreign countries, interpreting the purpose of international relations as spreading the civilisational influence and primacy of the middle kingdom, the country it ruled was the biggest importer and exporter in Asia. In its vast plurality, China was much less successful in preventing its subjects from trading abroad than Japan, Korea or even Vietnam. By 1800 there were almost a million Chinese in Southeast Asia, mostly engaged in trade, despite the continuing reluctance of official China to acknowledge, still less assist, them.[40] Kawashima Shin points to the debates among Japanese historians on these matters, with a new school pointing to what they call "mutual market trade", far more important than the officially sanctioned trade associated with tribute missions. The latter provided some additional perks for the official stakeholders who upheld it, but was by no means the main game of international commerce. The same is true across the land borders in the south. Traders paid off whoever they needed to at both ends of the trade relationship, and would not scruple to kowtow to any official if it helped their commerce.

The problems of negotiating asymmetry discussed in this book, therefore, are largely those of ruling elites. These elites, particularly in the larger landlocked countries, often seemed out of touch with the realities of business on the ground, and were no doubt kept so by court officials with a stake in the old order of things. The Ming and Qing courts, in particular, seemed usually content to appear to be "surrounded by distant deference … at minimal cost".[41] China's international merchants were further and further ahead of her rulers in adjusting to the new realities of the industrial age.

European Hegemony and the Re-imagining of Relations

The last Southeast Asian states to send "tribute" to China were Siam in 1852, Burma in 1874, and Vietnam in 1882. In each case it is too simple to ascribe the cessation to colonial conquest. Having lost their economic rationale once China was opened to trade through the Treaty of Nanking (1842), and their military one once there was nothing to fear from a decaying Qing regime, these relationships were in any case due for reformulation. Siam and Burma were aware of the European diplomatic system and its legal equality of "civilised" states. But it remained unclear whether a Chinese diplomatic card could be used to keep the European powers at bay, or whether sending tribute to China would reduce their chances of being accepted as a civilised state at the privileged table.

The Siamese case discussed by Junko Koizumi below is thus particularly interesting, as the only independent Asian state that moved very hesitantly from tribute to a Westphalian relationship with China during the century after 1840. The last mission sent was by King Mongkut (Rama IV), to announce his accession to the Siamese throne in 1851. The envoys had bitter experience of China's decline, being attacked on the painfully slow return journey by Taiping rebels. They described in their report how "tributary" states including Siam were treated as second class and made to wait while a French embassy was preferred. The envoys were told they could not enter the palace like European envoys because "you are envoys from small countries.... Only envoys from big countries such as Britain and France can be given an audience in the palace."[42] Finally, the envoys stopped in Hong Kong on their return journey for long enough to be given a lecture on Westphalia principles by the Governor, John Bowring. He argued that Siam's status was the same "as that of Britain, France and the United States. You should not go to pay tribute to China any more."[43]

Given this dismal experience, it seems unsurprising that King Mongkut, in one of the last decrees before his death in 1868, declared the "shameful" practice of paying tribute abolished and blamed Chinese traders and intermediaries for distorting Siamese letters into a form of tribute that had never been Siam's intention.[44] But, as Koizumi shows below, this was far from the end of the story. China continued to ask for tribute, and Siam to prevaricate, as both sides debated how to move from one system to another without losing face. Despite its modern treaties with Japan and the European powers, Siam/Thailand continued right up to World War II to evade China's requests for a treaty, chiefly out of concern that it might reduce the authority of the Thai government over immigrant Chinese.

Shortly before Britain conquered Mandalay and deposed the last Burmese king in November 1885, the Chinese Foreign Minister cabled London to say that "Burmah is our tributary state, and sovereignty will compel China to interfere."[45] This began a flurry of assertions from both sides, China and its British sympathisers quoting Chinese documents to show tribute, and British authorities in Burma and India citing Burmese documents to show the opposite. This gap in perception has not been entirely bridged since. At the time London compromised by signing a treaty with Beijing in July 1886, which in return for recognition of British sovereignty by China declared:

> Inasmuch as it has been the practice of Burmah to send decennial Missions to present articles of local produce, England agrees that the highest authority in Burmah shall send the customary decennial Missions, the members of the Missions to be of Burmese race.[46]

This remained a dead letter. Demarcating a border in Wa and Kachin territories over which neither Burma nor China had had effective rule took another 60 years, before Britain and the nationalist government in Chungking eventually agreed to the arrangements of a League of Nations-mandated commission in 1941.

Nevertheless, as Maung Aung Myoe's chapter below makes very clear, the gap in perception remained wide well into the 1950s and beyond. The communist government was inclined to take the view in relation to Burma that it was bound by no treaties of the colonial era. Because Burma had so few other friends after 1962, and a very exposed border, it was reluctant to make an enemy of China and made a virtue of playing the asymmetric relationship in ways that could help both states. The Burma-China relationship deserves the detailed attention he gives it, encapsulating most of the problems addressed by this book.

Vietnam in the nineteenth century adopted a very different approach. Where Siamese and Burmese courts began to see China as a declining factor and the traditional missions to Beijing as no longer appropriate, Vietnam's Emperor Tu-Duc (1848–83) moved closer to China than his stronger predecessors would have countenanced. Whereas reformers were beginning to demand abandonment of the ancient reliance on a written Chinese culture, he clung more rigidly to a Confucian world-view as the threat from France intensified. After humiliating treaties with France which ceded three southern provinces of Cochin-China in 1862, and the opening of the rest of Vietnam to French trade in 1874, Tu Duc appealed to China to help him control his disintegrating regime in the north. Chinese troops were sent to help suppress various rebels (many of them also Chinese). This allowed the Qing government to tell the French in 1880 that China had fulfilled its commitments as a suzerain to a vassal by suppressing rebellion in Vietnam, and that Tu Duc was a dependent king who had been invested by the Qing.

In 1882 France began its conquest of Tongking, brushing aside protests from China. Beijing responded robustly by sending troops across the border from Yunnan, leading to repeated clashes with French troops which escalated into a Franco-Chinese war in 1885. In the Treaty of Tientsin (June 1885) which ended it, China agreed to withdraw its troops from Vietnam, and to respect thenceforth all treaties made between France and the Vietnamese ruler. Ironically, as the "Chinese world order" died, the only Southeast Asian case that appeared to confirm China's view of it was Vietnam, which had fought so tenaciously for a thousand years for a completely different construction. By attempting to act in the 1880s like a European or Japanese imperial power sparring with rivals for territory, Beijing also laid the basis for both problems and opportunities in the future. Some Chinese nationalists of the twentieth century used the setbacks of the 1880s as a reason to reject the established international order, as discussed by Kawashima Shin below. Others re-imagined the struggle as an anti-imperial one in which Chinese and Vietnamese stood together against an aggressive West.

As Seo-Hyun Park shows in her chapter in this book, a similar transformation occurred in the ancient Korea-China relationship as it approached its demise. In 1882, she argues, "China interfered into Korean domestic affairs for the first time in their history of bilateral relations." Sino-Japanese competition created a different context from the Vietnamese case, however, and the reform party arguing for a strong assertion of Westphalia-style independence was relatively stronger in Korea, though their attempts also failed.

Revolutionary Comradeship and Cold War Hostility

The majority of this book is concerned with the adjustments of the twentieth century, as a Chinese civilisation and empire tried to find a new role as one nation-state within a nationalist Asia. The exceptional weakness and division of China before 1950 postponed this process of adjustment while internal disputes were fought out. Relations with independent Asian neighbours like Japan and Siam were strangely underdeveloped. The period of Maoist revolutionary politics postponed "normalisation" even further. As Prasenjit Duara suggests below, Maoist revolution represented a transformed "civilisational" goal of the Chinese state, replacing the Empire with the PRC as the virtuous centre of a world in need of moral guidance. But at the same time as this goal was pursued by the Party, including "socialist brother" relationships with North Vietnam and North Korea, the state apparatus developed pragmatic relations with India, Indonesia and Burma, advancing Chinese interests under the rhetoric of the Bandung principles of coexistence and non-interference. China was particularly successful in drawing Sukarno's Indonesia into a close alliance which appeared, until 1965, to be very helpful to the Indonesian Communist Party.

Such moderate gains were overwhelmed in the Cultural Revolution phase in the years after 1966. As Dr Myoe explains below, even Burma, which had been applauded by Beijing as the model for the kind of co-existence favoured by China, was attacked in words and actions. Until Nixon's visit and China's admission to the United Nations in 1971, relations with neighbours in Asia were anything but "normal".

China's Rise and Internationalism

Happily Asia has entered into a far more positive period since the 1990s. Not only have most countries in the region, led by China, come to regard rapid economic growth as a norm, relations between countries have at last begun to stabilise, effectively for the first time in the modern era. The expansion of ASEAN to embrace all the Southeast Asian countries formerly divided by the Cold War, together with China's engagement in the annual meetings of that body, create more favourable conditions in Southeast Asia. Prasenjit Duara, in his chapter on China and India, also sees an unprecedentedly benign international situation for India, in which China will be the major player. While Myanmar remains a sore point for the world, the engagement with it of both India and ASEAN, together with China's age-old asymmetric arrangements, remove it as a source of regional instability for China.

For most of Southeast Asia, concern over China's intentions has eased since the 1990s, as China placed less emphasis on imperial claims over the Spratleys and more on securing a share of Southeast Asia's energy resources. Vietnam will always be the most sensitive to per-ceived bullying, as demonstrations showed in December 2007 that un-precedentedly united domestic and diaspora Vietnamese to oppose China's establishment of an administrative district in the Spratleys.[47] The clouds on the horizon are darkest in Northeast Asia, and in the imponderables of China's own internal development. Paradoxically, the economic interdependence that has become such a feature of North-east Asia in the period of China's rise appears to have done nothing to dampen a rising rhetoric of nationalist distrust and even hostility. This centres not only on the Cold War flashpoints of Taiwan and Korea, but more profoundly on the centuries-old rivalry of China and Japan, with their very different world-views. As Wang Gungwu puts the danger in this volume, the post-ideology Chinese quest for roots and common values "could, if crudely handled, lead its people back to the nationalism that left China without family and friends". Shi Anbin's Chapter 8 reflects this quest accurately if somewhat chillingly, describing the vigorous reassertion of nationalism in China over the past decade in forms that insists on the peripheral status of the other countries discussed in the book. Alexander Vuving's Chapter 3 points out how quickly socialist brotherhood towards Vietnam was replaced during the hostile 1980s with the Middle Kingdom's moralistic rhetoric of "teaching Vietnam a lesson", a reversal well remembered in Vietnam and elsewhere.

In seeking to represent diverse perspectives on this critical issue, this book rightly retains an open verdict on the future. The degree to which China's emphasis on "soft power" should be welcomed or feared for its cultural nationalist acssociations was debated by the authors as by others. Dr Zheng Yangwen's chapter draws particular attention to the nationalist education which has tended to replace the Marxist one in Chinese schools. The disproportionate focus on China's historic victim-hood at the hands of the European powers and Japan, she points out, is far from reassuring as a mental preparation for the citizens of the new superpower. The world's only recent experiences of the attempts of authoritarian states to become superpowers have been decidedly nega-tive. Ultimately, the success of "China's peaceful rise" will depend on how far an open spirit of debate and self-criticism is able to flourish within China.

Notes

[1]   Charter of the United Nations, Chapter 1, article 2.

[2]   On Japan, see Shin in this volume. On Siam, Thongchai Winichakul, "The Quest for 'Siwilai': A Geographical Discourse of Civilisational Thinking in the Late Nineteenth and Early Twentieth-Century Siam", *Journal of Asian Studies* 59, no. 3 (Aug. 2000): 528–49.

[3]   Brantly Womack, *China and Vietnam: The Politics of Asymmetry* (Cambridge: Cambridge University Press, 2006), p. 23.

[4]   Ibid., p. 18.

[5]   Stephen Krasner, "Organised Hypocrisy in Nineteenth-Century East Asia", *International Relations of the Asia-Pacific* 1 (2001): 173–97. For a general statement of the theory see N. Brunsson, *The Organisation of Hypocrisy: Talk, Decisions and Actions in Organisation* (Chichester: John Wiley, 1989).

6   John King Fairbank, ed., *The Chinese World Order: Traditional China's Foreign Relations* (Cambridge, Mass.: Harvard University Press, 1968); Morris Rossabi, ed., *China Among Equals: The Middle Kingdom and its Neighbours, 10th–14th Centuries* (Berkeley: University of California Press, 1983).

7   Peter Perdue, *China Marches West: The Qing Conquest of Central Eurasia* (Cambridge, Mass.: Harvard University Press, 2005), p. 547.

8   Joseph Fletcher, "China and Central Asia, 1368–1884", in *The Chinese World Order*, ed. Fairbank, p. 224.

9   Barry Buzan and Richard Little, *International Systems in World History — Remaking the Study of International Relations* (Oxford: Oxford University Press, 2000); Yongjin Zhang, "System, Empire and State in Chinese International Relations", *Review of International Studies* 27 (2001): 43–63.

10   Edwin O. Reischaur and John K. Fairbank, *East Asia: The Great Tradition* (Modern Asia Edition, Tokyo: Tuttle, 1966), p. 411.

11   John K. Fairbank and Ssu-yu Teng, *Ch'ing Administration: Three Studies* (Cambridge, Mass.: Harvard University Press, 1960), pp. 193–8.

12   Fairbank, ed., *The Chinese World Order*. See the able summary and critique in Chapters 2, 4 and 8 of this volume.

13   Yu Insun, "Le Van Huu and Ngo Si Lien: A Comparison of Their Perception of Vietnamese History", in *Viet Nam: Borderless Histories*, ed. Nhung Tuyet Tran and Anthony Reid (Madison: University of Wisconsin Press, 2006), pp. 45–71.

14   Nguyen Trai, *Bingh Ngo dai cao* (1428), as translated by O.W. Wolters, "Historians and Emperors in Vietnam and China: Comments arising out of Le Van Huu's History, Presented to the Tran Court in 1272", in *Perceptions of the Past in Southeast Asia*, ed. Anthony Reid and David Marr (Singapore: Heinemann, 1979), p. 88.

15   Womack, *China and Vietnam*, p. 135. For Minh-Mang's "civilising" policy in Cambodia see Choi Byung Wook, *Southern Vietnam under the Reign of Minh Mang (1820–1841): Central Policies and Local Response* (Ithaca, NY: Cornell University Southeast Asia Program, 2004), pp. 135–59.

16   Anthony Reid, "Political 'tradition' in Indonesia: The one and the many", *Asian Studies Review* 22, no. 1 (Feb. 1998): 23–38; Tony Day, *Fluid Iron: State Formation in Southeast Asia* (Honolulu: University of Hawaii Press, 2002).

17   Jane Drakard, *A Kingdom of Words: Language and Power in Sumatra* (Kuala Lumpur: Oxford University Press, 1999).

18   Alexander Woodside, "The Relationship between Political Theory and Economic Growth in Vietnam", in *The Last Stand of Asian Autonomies: Responses to Modernity in the Diverse States of Southeast Asia and Korea, 1750–1900*, ed. Anthony Reid (Basingstoke: Macmillan, 1997), p. 246.

19   Frederick de Houtman's words put in the mouth of an Acehnese informant explaining the system in Aceh in 1601, as translated in Anthony Reid, *Southeast Asia in the Age of Commerce*, 2 vols. (New Haven: Yale University Press, 1988–93), II: 238.

20   Jeremias van Vliet, "Description of the Kingdom of Siam" [1636], trans. L.F. van
      Ravenswaay, *Journal of the Siam Society* 7, part 1 (1910): 93.
21   *Sejarah Melayu: The Malay Annals*, romanised edition compiled by Cheah Boon
      Kheng (Kuala Lumpur: MBRAS, 1998), pp. 124, 207 and 250. An English
      translation is in C.C. Brown, "Sejarah Melayu or 'Malay Annals'", *JMBRAS* 25,
      parts 2 and 3 (1952): 55, 120 and 154.
22   Reid, *Age of Commerce* II, pp. 234–5.
23   Clifford to Col. Secretary, Straits Settlements, 5 Sept. 1895, enclosed in Mitchell
      to Chamberlain, 29 Sept. 1895, CO273.
24   Sun Laichen, "Suzerain and Vassal, or Elder and Younger Brothers: The Nature
      of the Burmo-Chinese Historical Relationship", Paper presented at the 49th
      Annual Conference of the Association of Asian Studies, Chicago, 1997, pp. 17
      and 43.
25   *Sejarah Melayu*, p. 142. A different English translation is in Brown, p. 70.
26   Ibid., pp. 166–70 and 175–6 (quote from p. 176). An English rendering is in
      Brown, pp. 89–91 and 95–6.
27   Anthony Reid, "Flows and Seepages in the Long-term Chinese Interaction with
      Southeast Asia", in *Sojourners and Settlers: Histories of Southeast Asia and the
      Chinese*, ed. Anthony Reid (Sydney: Allen & Unwin, 1996), pp. 22–6. Anthony
      Reid, "Hybrid Identities in the Fifteenth-Century Straits of Malacca", in *Southeast
      Asia in the Fifteenth Century: The Ming Factor*, ed. Geoffrey Wade and Sun Laichen
      (Singapore: NUS Press, 2009).
28   William Marsden, *The History of Sumatra* [1811 edition] (reprinted Kuala Lumpur:
      Oxford University Press, 1966), pp. 338–42. Drakard, *Kingdom of Words*, pp.
      168–70.
29   Womack, *China and Vietnam*, p. 135.
30   Sun Laichen, "Suzerain and Vassal, or Elder and Younger Brothers", pp. 5–6.
31   Ibid., p. 10.
32   Maung Aung Myoe, "Sino-Myanmar Relations", forthcoming.
33   Ibid., Sun Laichen, "Suzerain and Vassal, or Elder and Younger Brothers", p. 15.
34   Womack, *China and Vietnam*, pp. 77–92.
35   Barbara Andaya, *To Live as Brothers: Southeast Sumatra in the Seventeenth and
      Eighteenth Centuries* (Honolulu: University of Hawaii Press, 1993), p. 26.
36   Sun Laichen, "Suzerain and Vassal, or Elder and Younger Brothers", p. 18.
37   Ibid., pp. 11–21.
38   This translation, rendered into English as early as 1837 by Henry Burney on the
      basis of Burmese records, is reproduced by Sun Laichen, "Suzerain and Vassal,
      or Elder and Younger Brothers", p. 15.
39   Cited in Maung Aung Myoe, "Sino-Myanmar Relations", forthcoming, p. 144,
      from a translation of the Burmese text by Ma Kyan.
40   T.J. Newbold, *British Settlements in the Straits of Malacca* (London, 1839),
      Vol. I, p. 9.
41   Womack, *China and Vietnam*, p. 141.

42 Masuda Erika, "The Last Siamese Tributary Missions to China, 1851–1854 and the 'Rejected' Value of *Chim Kong*", in *Maritime China in Transition 1750–1850*, ed. Wang Gungwu and Ng Chin-keong (Wiesbaden: Horowitz, 2004), p. 37, translating from the Thai report of the mission.

43 Ibid., p. 37, translating from the Thai report of the mission.

44 Ibid., pp. 38–9.

45 Cited Maung Aung Myoe, "Sino-Myanmar Relations", forthcoming, p. 1.

46 Convention Between Her Majesty and His Majesty the Emperor of China Relative to Burmah and Thibet (signed at Peking, 24 July 1886), as cited in Maung Aung Myoe, "Sino-Myanmar Relations", forthcoming, p. 3.

47 David Koh, "Sino-Vietnamese Relations: Hanoi's Catch-22 situation", *Straits Times*, 23 January 2008.

PART ONE

Alternative Asian
World Orders

Chapter 1

Small States and the Search for Sovereignty in Sinocentric Asia: Japan and Korea in the Late Nineteenth Century

Seo-Hyun Park

Introduction

Studies of East Asian international relations (IR) tend to assume that the introduction of the Westphalian state system in the late nineteenth century similarly pressured regional actors into adopting new standards of state behaviour based on sovereign equality. This view, however, does not give due credit to the possibility of influence emanating from the existing Sinocentric state system with its own rules and norms, which had guided East Asian interstate relations. Instead, it is presumed that East Asian states experienced the same "shock", precipitating similar outcomes in response to the common challenge presented by Westphalian sovereignty to the traditional regional order. In fact, Japan and Korea showed contrasting responses to the European state system, with Japan fully accepting it and striving to become part of the Western "international society", while Korea sought to maintain the *status quo*, as an autonomous-yet-dependent kingdom in the China-centred world.

In this chapter, I argue that the alternative paths taken by Japan and Korea since the 1860s can be traced back to their previous positions within the traditional Sinocentric order, reflecting their different conceptions of state sovereignty. Sinocentric hierarchy was not a homogeneous normative order; it allowed different types of interest formulation in each country based on its own understanding of how best to achieve security and to strengthen state sovereignty. Smaller states such as Japan and Korea have historically strived to protect their sovereignty, through different security strategies ranging from isolation to deference, while learning to deal with political penetration and pressures, either real or imagined, from powerful regional "hegemons" such as China.

While Japan in the Edo period had conducted foreign relations based on autonomy and insulation from China, the Korean kingdom of Chosŏn had tried to assert and achieve its sovereign status by revering China (*sadae*) and integrating itself into the Sinocentric world order. In the late nineteenth century, Japan and Korea switched courses. Japan turned to a status-achieving integration strategy within the European state system, but Korea was less successful in asserting autonomy from China due to its incomplete internalisation of Westphalian sovereignty. In sum, different sovereignty norms affected Japanese and Korean political strategies for asserting their sovereign autonomy amidst the duel between two state systems, led by China and the European great powers respectively.

State Sovereignty in the Traditional East Asian State System

The Westphalian system was not the first state-based model in East Asia, unlike in other regions. The difference was of course in the organising principles of the two systems — Sinocentric hierarchy versus Westphalian anarchy.[1] The variability of state sovereignty and its historical context have been noted by empirically-oriented constructivist work in IR theory, which tend to view sovereignty as "politically contested and [having] variable political effects" (Katzenstein 1996: 515). For example, authors writing on non-European nations, which attained sovereign statehood in the aftermath of decolonisation, have described the different understandings and claims of sovereignty. For the small states of Southeast Asia, Westphalian sovereignty entailed strong norms of noninterference, which were institutionalised into the form of ASEAN to keep each other out of their own domestic affairs (Acharya 2001). In Africa and other Third World countries, sovereignty is asserted not against one another, but *vis-à-vis* the "West". The "empty vessel" analogy is frequently employed in discussions of African sovereignty — how many African states lack empirical indicators of sovereignty (such as domestic authority, control over territorial borders, etc.) but cling onto their international legal status as sovereign states (Jackson 1990) and indulge in various "sovereignty expenditures" such as defense spending, building airports, and maintaining disproportionately large cabinets (Van de Walle 2001: 101–9).

In East Asia, the actual practice of state sovereignty in terms of both domestic rule and conducting foreign relations preceded the concept of Westphalian sovereignty. By the time the Western powers arrived, the centralised state bureaucracy of the Chosŏn dynasty in Korea had administered a relatively stable realm for over 400 years, and a sense of territory had already developed even before their direct encounters with Western powers in the nineteenth century (Schmid 2002: 18). Intellectuals recognised and asserted Chosŏn Korea's separate and particular national identity *vis-à-vis* the universalist *hwa-i* or Sinocentric order (Hamashita 1997: 123–4; H. Kim 1997).[2] Japan, too, existed as an independent state within Sinocentric Asia. After the establishment of the military *bakufu*, Tokugawa Ieyasu, in a letter to a Chinese official, claimed the legitimacy of his rule on the grounds that he had unified the country of Japan.[3] In addition, Masaru Kohno (2001) argues that the Meiji Restoration "occurred not because of the absence of sovereignty, but rather because Japan was already a developed and internationally recognised sovereign state" (p. 267).

The states of East Asia were organised into a hierarchical order, ideologically based on Confucian "rules of propriety" (*li*) and institutionalised into the ceremony of tributary relations. In foreign relations, as well as in domestic order, the ruling ideology in East Asia was the principle of hierarchy, in contrast to sovereign equality in the European system of states. As the suzerain, China granted investiture to its vassal kingdoms as official approval of succession and provided help to its vassals in times of emergency. Surrounding vassal states in response acknowledged the suzerainty of China by regularly offering tribute to the Chinese emperor, through which they could claim to be "civilised", while those outside the Sinocentric order were deemed to be "barbarians" (Y. Kim 2001: 7–8; Nelson 1946: 7–8; Larsen 2000: 13–4; Hong 1993: 43).

Relations between Asian countries were also described as a "family of nations" in the Confucian discourse. Ties between China and Korea were often presented by both sides in the high-flown moral rhetoric of Confucian fraternalism: China was the elder brother, Korea the younger.[4] In Japanese discourses during the early Tokugawa period, China functioned as a paternalistic authority figure, a metaphorical standard of morality and civilisation. Kumazawa Banzan, a Confucian scholar, wrote in *Shūgi washo* (1672) that "*chūka* [Chinese civilisation] was the parent to the children, who were the eastern, southern, western and northern barbarians, as the mountain was parent to the river's children".[5]

Types of Strategies in Strengthening State Sovereignty in Hierarchical Orders: Insulation versus Integration

In regional hierarchies such as the traditional China-centred system in East Asia, small states conceptualised their sovereign capacity and authority in regard to the region's dominant power.[6] China was a reference point against which weaker states such as Japan and Korea sought out the most effective ways of asserting their sovereignty.[7] They could either: (a) seek autonomy and *insulation* from external powers through an indigenous source of legitimacy or (b) pursue external legitimation by *integrating* or "ingratiating" themselves with the region's dominant power, relying on the latter's benign leadership.[8] In terms of foreign policy choices, while insulation-oriented states seek to "hide"[9] from the dominant power, integrationist conceptions of sovereignty urge states to increase their regional or international legitimacy and prestige through close alignment with the dominant power.[10] In addition to affecting policy behaviour, a particular definition of state sovereignty based on its choice of a sovereignty-strengthening strategy gives a particular framework of legitimacy to the ruling regime. For instance, when domestically weak or lacking in legitimacy, a state can turn to international relations or diplomatic success for recognition and status as a member of international society or civilisation. On the other hand, elites can prop up their legitimacy by using tradition and nationalistic symbols, thereby mobilising the public with calls for autonomy and self-reliance.

State sovereignty then becomes an ideological frame of reference, which can involve certain tradeoffs for ruling elites. When elites strive to strengthen sovereignty through outward integration, they may enhance the state's prestige and security but are accused of compromising their sovereign autonomy by inviting foreign influence into domestic politics.[11] For instance, the Korean practice of *sadae* ("serving the great") during the Chosŏn period was criticised by reformers in the late nineteenth century as perpetuating dependence on an outside power, even though the initial decision to accommodate China was motivated by a pragmatic assessment of the best way to guarantee both security and autonomy for a militarily weak Korea (Yi 1994; Ledyard 1968; Larsen 2000: 19). Similarly, in Japan, Ashikaga Yoshimitsu, who had entered the Ming tribute system in the late fourteenth century in order to trade with China and enhance his prestige, was criticised later for compromising Japan's sovereignty (Toby 1977: 331–2; Fujimura 1977).

Elites immersed in ideas of autonomy-oriented sovereignty, in contrast, are able to highlight their "nationalistic" credentials, unimpaired by pressure from an outside power, but run into the potential problem of rhetorical entrapment. Due to their limited menu of options for garnering legitimacy, insulation-minded elites are often forced to fend off foreign influences altogether or scapegoat them for policy failures or domestic ills, which may deepen the state's diplomatic isolation and harm its security. The demise of the Tokugawa *bakufu* in the latter half of the nineteenth century is an example of the delayed consequences of "hiding" from its neighbours.[12]

Japan and Korea during the seventeenth and eighteenth centuries provide clear examples of contrasting conceptions and practices of sovereignty, seeking insulation versus integration *vis-à-vis* Qing China.[13] Chosŏn Korea was very much a leading player in the Sinocentric tributary and "family of nations" system or in other words, geared towards an integrationist, status-achieving sovereignty conception (K. Kim 1980; Chun 1968; Nelson 1946). In comparison, Tokugawa Japan adopted a policy of maintaining informal and weakly institutionalised contact with its East Asian neighbours, using Tsushima and Ryukyu as intermediaries for trade with Korea and China (K. Kim 1980: 22–5). The *bakufu* (military government) rulers, preoccupied with centralising domestic control, preferred to maintain a low profile on the international stage to insulate themselves from China.[14]

The variation in sovereignty conceptions shown by Japan and Korea in regional history demonstrates that the traditional state system in East Asia was not a homogeneous normative order, as implicitly assumed in existing analyses of the introduction of Westphalian sovereignty to the region. Even though on surface it was ordered on rules of proper conduct, East Asian interstate relations were not strictly played out according to Confucian principles. Relatively free from the deep intrusion of Confucianism and with access to more pervasive Western knowledge, Tokugawa Japan was able to build its own legitimacy. Even in China and Korea, Confucian thought and the Confucian order were subject to change and compromise (D. Kang 2004: 8). The ruling elites in each country had some degree of manoeuvreability to contemplate and choose a sovereignty-strengthening strategy, supported with either internal or external sources of legitimacy, which best met their security interests.

Tokugawa Japan

Tokugawa diplomacy and ideology stressed solidification of internal rule and national autonomy, taking the route of non-participation in the Chinese world order (Toby 1984: 235; Fujimura 1977: 423–4).[15] The Tokugawa *bakufu* initially considered the possibility of formal relations with China but concluded that the cost was too high; acceptance of a tributary role in China's East Asian order was incompatible with its dignity and with Japan's sovereign independence (Jansen 1992: 2). After taking power, Tokugawa Ieyasu had hoped to gain admission to the Chinese world order, but this could not be achieved without his succumbing to the rules of *sadae* (*jidai* in Japanese). For example, he would have had to call himself a subject of the Ming emperor and use the Ming calendar in official documents. Ieyasu and his advisors decided that they could not compromise the very platform of legitimacy — sovereign autonomy and independence — that he was seeking to establish and instead, turned to a symbol of domestic legitimacy, his Japanese imperial appointment as *shogun* (Toby 1984: 56–60).

With the severing of diplomatic ties with Ming China, the Tokugawa *bakufu* created its own ideological centrality and attempted to establish the *Nihon gata kai-i chitsujo* (Japan-centred civilisation) in East Asia (E. Kang 1997: 150). The Tokugawa *bakufu*'s most potent self-legitimation tactic was the manipulation of relations with Korea (via Tsushima) and the Ryukyus. In order to enhance the authority and legitimacy of the Tokugawa regime, the *bakufu* leaders worked strenuously to resolve the diplomatic crisis with Korea in the aftermath of Hideyoshi's invasions (E. Kang 1997: 141–2; see also Toby 1984, Pak 1980). Contrary to the generally accepted image of *sakoku* (closed country), extravagant Korean embassies were sent to Japan and bilateral trade flourished through the *waegwan* (Japan House; *wakan* in Japanese) in Pusan during the Tokugawa period (E. Kang 1997: 137).[16] Korean and Ryukyuan diplomatic missions to the *shogun*'s court, which continued into the nineteenth century, played important roles in the structure of the *bakufu*'s legitimacy, "both in the *bakufu*'s policy calculations and in the response of the political public" (Toby 1984: 8).[17]

The structure of Tokugawa foreign relations was established by the mid-1630s through the intermediaries of Tsushima and Ryukyu. In another move that set Japan apart from Korea, the *shogun* Yoshinari used the title "great prince" (*taikun*) for the first time in diplomatic correspondence with Chosŏn Korea in 1636.[18] As summed up by Ronald Toby (1984), the choice of "great prince of Japan" was a declaration of independence from the Sinocentric order, a "declaration of a new, self-sufficient domestic legitimacy structure willing to meet with others autonomously in the diplomatic arena" and "the establishment of an alternative order, a 'great prince' order, a Japan-centred order of international relations (88–9)".

The establishment of the structure of Tokugawa foreign relations can be linked to the maturation of the idea of "Japan-as-central-kingdom" (Toby 1984: 82–7). Upon the construction of the Tokugawa diplomatic order, the Tokugawa *ka-i* ideology of Japan-centred civilisation also matured. Hayashi Razan, Ieyasu's advisor and Tokugawa ideologue, unified Neo-Confucian doctrine with the indigenous Shinto ideology for the first time to create a Japan-centred ideology, which was endorsed by ethnocentric Shintoism of Tokugawa intellectuals (Toby 1984: 160).[19] In sum, the Tokugawa *bakufu* succeeded in establishing an alternative self-reliant presence within the Asian region by insulating itself from the Chinese civilisation and capitalising on an indigenous source of legitimacy. The result was a low degree of internalisation of Confucianism and Sinocentrism in Tokugawa Japan (Pak 1980).

Chosŏn Korea

In contrast to Japan's domestically-driven sovereignty conception, in large part due to its chronic domestic instability and relative insulation from the continent, Korea had a long history of foreign, especially Chinese, penetration.[20] Throughout its history, Korean rulers opted to accommodate the militarily stronger China, but also engaged in acts of defiance at times. It was with the founding of Chosŏn by Yi Sŏng-gye in the fourteenth century that the policy of showing deference to the Chinese civilisation became solidified as a tool for guaranteeing long-term peace. In order to bolster the authority and legitimacy of the new regime as well as its security, the founders of Chosŏn sought recognition and approval from Ming China.

To justify their externally-induced sovereign authority, Chosŏn's ruling class propagated the *sadae* (literally, serving or revering the great) principle. Chosŏn rulers claimed their sovereign legitimacy by claiming to have attained regional and civilisational status as an integral part of the Sinocentric world. China was depicted as more than a militarily superior Great Power; it was the center of civilisation and the only legitimate source of authority in the regional order. The *sadae* order was also a reciprocal relationship, in which the smaller state showed deference to the suzerain (*sadae*) in exchange for protection and benign leadership, or *chaso*, which literally means benevolence and concern for the small neighbour (Chun 1968; Hara 1998; Pak 1982).[21]

Although the *sadae* order was rich with ideological principles and rhetorical propriety, Korea's *sadae* policy toward Ming China originated as a strategic calculation of how best to guarantee Chosŏn's security as well as establishing stability and legitimacy of domestic rule. While Korea's *sadae*-based foreign policy has been widely treated as having been culturally and normatively-informed, and as a hindrance to the assertion of Korean sovereignty, the basic motivation behind *sadae* was survival and security (Yu 1987: 204–5). As Etsuko Kang (1997: 170) notes: "For the ruling classes of militarily weak countries, sadae diplomacy was a wise policy to avoid military violation by a stronger country and at the same time to secure internal dominance, since a rebellion of the ruled classes might occur with the military intervention of a stronger country." In fact, elaborate rhetorical formalities and seeming intimacy at the abstract-level notwithstanding, China and Korea sought to limit mutual contact as much as possible in reality (Ku 1988: 6). The Korean court was guaranteed autonomy in its domestic affairs and virtually left alone to do as it pleased as long as it declared fealty to China (Larsen 2000: 13–5). In practice, the Sinocentric hierarchy system contained considerable normative flexibility, allowing self-interested behavioural practices such as restricted interaction and benign neglect based on mutual understanding, rather than imposing strict adherence to its stated rules of propriety.

Such context-richness of Ming-Chosŏn bilateral relations is why the rise of the Manchus and the founding of Qing China in the early seventeenth century posed a foreign policy dilemma for Chosŏn Korea. The Manchus were considered barbarians and not deserving of *sadae*, as opposed to the great civilisation of Ming China.[22] When King Kwanghaegun and the Puk'in faction chose a pragmatic foreign policy initiative by accommodating the increasingly powerful Manchus, the opposition Sŏin faction used this opportunity to replace Kwanghaegun with a new king (Injo) and take power in a *coup d'etat* known as the

Injo revolt. Kwanghaegun was charged with violating the rules of *sadae* and ungratefully forsaking Chosŏn's sworn loyalty to the Ming, especially when the latter had come to the aid of Korea during the Japanese invasions in 1592–98 (H. Kim 1997: 28; E. Kang: 174–7). The takeover by the Sŏin faction also meant the reign of neo-Confucian purists, who continued to revere the Ming even after the latter's demise and prided themselves on being the sole legitimate heirs of the great Sinocentric civilisation (see, for example, Chung 1998; Watanabe 1977). Anti-Qing sentiments were heightened even further after the Qing invasion of Chosŏn in 1636, during which King Injo was forced to kowtow to the Qing emperor and send his three sons as hostages to China.

Although the "strike the north argument" (*pukpollon*) ran rampant in the immediate aftermath of Chosŏn's defeat against the Qing, the policy of *sadae* and tributary relations continued until the late nineteenth century. The *sadae* doctrine did, however, undergo a qualitative change *vis-à-vis* the Qing, with its concept changing from "serving China", the center of civilisation, to "serving the great", a militarily powerful country (Watanabe 1977: 414). The tributary mission to Qing China was relabeled as the "mission to Peking" (*yonhaeng*) instead of the former "going to court" (*choch'on*) (K. Kim 1980: 28).

Yet, the *sadae* order based on Sinocentric hierarchy persisted without much interruption due in large part to the continued guarantee of Korean autonomy under the tribute system. Investiture was never used as a political leverage by the Qing, whose policy toward Korea had non-interference as its basic principle (K. Kim 1980: 8–9). In fact, the Qing practised even more of a benign neglect policy than the Ming, and by the nineteenth century, Chosŏn elites began to recognise as legitimate the Qing-led Sinocentric order.[23]

Sovereignty Crises in Late Nineteenth-century Asia: Divergent Responses to Westphalian Sovereignty in Japan and Korea

The two types of sovereignty conceptions, as shown by Japan and Korea in the traditional Sinocentric interstate system, became identifiable during systemic crises when existing beliefs and behavioural patterns were politically contested. When Western imperialist expansion into Asia in the nineteenth century introduced a fundamental challenge to the physically and normatively closed regional order, existing understandings of sovereign statehood in both Japan and Korea were disrupted and reversed. The challenge of Westphalian sovereignty set off debates about the choice between opening up, or integrating with the "enlightened" world, on the one hand, and seclusion and defending national tradition, on the other, as ways of asserting sovereignty. It was the outcome of this domestic political contestation, informed by existing conceptions of sovereignty, rather than the degree of ideological inflexibility in Korea compared to Japan, that led to different behavioural paths for Tokugawa Japan and Chosŏn Korea. In this section, I show how elites in Japan and Korea reacted differently to the Westphalian sovereignty system, followed by a discussion of what accounts for the divergence in their responses.

Japan's Reverse Course Policy: Modernisation and Re-entering International Society

The first thing to note in the comparison of Japan and Korea in the nineteenth century is the fact that they did not experience the exact same "shock" of Westphalian sovereignty since they had different starting points. Japan's "shock" came in 1860 when Peking was besieged by British and French forces. The significance of this incident is that it clearly revealed China's weakness *vis-à-vis* the West, which posed a threat not only to the regional order, but significantly to Japanese sovereign autonomy. The Tokugawa *bakufu*'s accommodation of Commodore Perry's demands in 1853–54 had exposed the vulnerability of Japan to external pressures and questioned the validity of the previous policy of national seclusion. By the 1860s, *bakufu* leaders faced a counter-coalition that pointed out the backwardness of the state's position compared to other powerful competitors and was able to consolidate widespread support for "catching up" to the advanced states.[24] Anti-*bakufu* forces exposed the weakness of the Tokugawa regime by rallying around the slogan, "revere the emperor and expel the barbarians" (*sonnō jōi*).

Following re-centralisation and faced with a sense of crisis created by China's succumbing to Western forces, however, the Meiji oligarchs reversed courses and instead took the integration route in the European state system and adopted the Western civilisation-emulating "rich country, strong army" (*fukoku kyōhei*) doctrine. The Meiji government forcibly carried out new reforms, persuading its citizenry that Japan must adopt Western institutions and culture in order to rival their power (Toyama 1985: 36). In sharp contrast to the Qing's *status quo* aspirations, the worldview of Japanese elites changed dramatically since the late 1860s until the 1870s, owing in large part to Western learning (D. Kang 2004: 27). Modernisation and "civilisation and enlightenment" (*bunmei kaika*) became symbols of security and sovereignty for the Japanese state.[25] Accordingly, the achievement of status in the international community based on the European "standard of civilisation" became Japan's primary foreign policy goal (Gong 1984: 175).[26] The Meiji leaders went to great lengths to accommodate the rules and mores of the international system, pressing for the adoption of Westernised legal codes in order to impress on the powers the civilised progress of Japan and to hasten the revision of unequal treaties (Pyle 1989: 688).

Within Asia as well, Japanese leaders began to put to use the institutions and diplomatic tactics they themselves had learned from their encounters with Western powers, beginning with the forced opening of Korea at Kanghwa in 1876 and the signing of an "unequal treaty". Japan's real security concern, however, was China and its diminishing role in maintaining regional order. Japanese leaders, having closely observed China's gradual downfall since the Opium War, contemplated whether they should focus on usurping China's position atop the regional order to create a new revisionist coalition or distance itself from the traditional system to achieve greater "civilisation" — above and beyond China and Korea.[27] Following the sweeping modernisation reforms as a result of the Meiji Restoration in 1868 and victory over China in the war of 1894–95, Japan opted for the latter position, seeking respect from the Western powers as a great power itself in Asia. This was reinforced by the experience of the Triple Intervention in 1895, when Britain, France, and Russia "took away" some of Japan's gains in China (Kim 1980; Suganami 1984; Kohno 2001).

Korea's Quest for Reclaiming Sovereign Autonomy

In Korea, the shock of Westphalian sovereignty came a bit later and for a different reason. Although wary of the Manchu rulers of Qing China, Korean elites were deeply deferential to the systemic norms of Sinocentric hierarchy that originated from its relations with the Ming and viewed themselves as the most "civilised", even more so than the Qing to some. Korean scholar-officials (*literati*) disapproved of the Chinese court's associating with those outside the "civilised world" since the early nineteenth century and in fact maintained a fierce seclusion policy for a decade while still maintaining close ties with the Qing (K. Kim 1980; Deuchler 1977).[28] Still relying on Chinese power and guidance and accommodating the Qing policy to integrate the "treaty port system" into the Sinocentric order, the Korean government allowed a Chinese official to negotiate treaties on its behalf with Japan in 1876 and the United States in 1881 (Kim and Kim 1967: 18–23). In 1882, however, when China interfered with Korean domestic affairs for the first time in their history of bilateral relations (K. Kim 1980: 326–7), fierce debates between the reformers and the ruling elite followed on how to deal with the Western powers amidst the unraveling of the Sinocentric system (Nahm 1988: 180–95; Nelson 1946: 215–6).[29]

Since opening up the country in the 1876 treaty with Japan, government-led reforms were slowly taking place in Chosŏn Korea under Qing influence. China's *de facto* foreign minister Li Hungchang advised the Korean government to conclude treaties with Western powers in the advent of Japanese influence "to check the poison with an antidote" (Kim and Kim 1967: 18). In 1882, however, China took a more direct interventionist stance in the domestic affairs of Korea and dispatched troops to help quell the Imo rebellion as well as kidnapping the Taewon'gun (King Kojong's father). China's military intervention effectively ended the policy of "benign" leadership by China.[30]

This presented an opening for anti-government mobilisation as progressive reformists split from the gradualists in their frustration with the pace of and Qing influence over domestic reforms. Against the government elites, led by Queen Min's relatives, emerged an opposing coalition of the so-called "Enlightenment leaders" who formed the Enlightenment (or Independence) Party and stated as their policy objective "independence" from the Qing and reforms modeled after the Western civilisation and Japan. These young and modernisation-advocating officials, and later Western-educated elites, sought to reform the corrupt and anachronistic literati, anchoring their movement in anti-*sadae*-ism. The Enlightenment party members above all strived to free Chosŏn from its "humiliating" vassal status by leaving the defunct Sinocentric order and its accompanying *sadae* relations (Y. Chung 2004: 113–4). By labeling those who called for gradual reforms, such as China's self-strengthening movement and still maintaining traditional *sadae* relations with the Qing the Conservative or Sadae party, these progressives politicised the direction and validity of Korea's hitherto integration-oriented sovereignty-achieving strategy (Y. Chung 2004: 112–3; Y. Kim 1989: 72–3).

In doing so, what used to be a sign of propriety in the traditional East Asian order transformed into a position of repressing independent tendencies (D. Kang 2004: 96–103).[31] The principle of *sadae* and the logic of civilisation in promoting state security and sovereignty were now stigmatised as compromising Korean sovereignty and independence by autonomy and reform-promoting Enlightenment leaders (Hahm 2006).

The Shadow of the Sinocentric Order

The different responses by Japan and Korea against the thrust of the Westphalian sovereignty system, as shown in the opposition movements' criticism of existing sovereignty-strengthening strategies, can be explained by their previous positions within the Sinocentric order, reflecting their different conceptions of sovereignty. Japan had been "outside" the Sinocentric *sadae* order and had its own particularistic worldview and indigenous source of legitimacy in the form of the *tenno*. Korea in contrast was entrenched within the Sinocentric hierarchical system. This variation in the degree of prior socialisation into the traditional state system had significant impact on the role of China and perception of its leadership in the foreign policy of its smaller neighbours in the late nineteenth century.

Since each of the three East Asian countries operated differently under the traditional order, each interpreted concepts such as "autonomy" (J. *jishu*; K. *jaju*) and "vassal" (J. *zokuhou*; K. *sokbang*) differently. Around the time of the signing of the Sino-Japanese treaty in 1871, *jishu* and *zokuhou* were translated into "independence" and "vassal state" respectively, while in Chinese the words were interpreted as the traditional "subordinate-yet-autonomous" relations between Qing China and Chosŏn Korea. In short, the Japanese equated autonomy with independence, while treating vassal countries, of which Chosŏn Korea was an example, as a province or a colony of a larger power. This differed from the views of the Chinese and the Koreans, who maintained that a vassal state had autonomy of rule and foreign policy in the Sinocentric order (D. Kang 2004: 26–33).

Japanese elites were able to accept the Westphalian sovereignty principle of "equality" among states with relative ease based on their own particularistic Japan-centric worldview (D. Kang 2004: 24–5). As Takashi Inoguchi observes, "Because the Japanese had long envisioned a separate world order, distinctive and apart from the Sinocentric one, which put Edo at the center, Japan was perhaps more successful than Korea at relinquishing what remained of a traditional East Asia" (Inoguchi 2006: 8). The Meiji leaders quickly made the Western world its principle reference and replaced earlier references to the Chinese world order (pp. 8–9). It is also significant that Japan was relatively free from external pressure after Perry's arrival in 1854 and in the immediate aftermath of the Meiji restoration, allowing fast-paced implementation of reforms.

Unlike Japan's speedy departure from its Sinocentric ties, Korean officials consistently tried to handle foreign incursions (e.g., during the French attack of Kanghwa Island in 1866) within the framework of traditional Sino-Korean relations until the 1880s. After the signing of treaties with Western powers, Korea existed within a dual structure, which allowed relations between East Asian states to continue under the traditional hierarchical system, while principles of Westphalian sovereignty governed relations with the West. While Japan sought to revoke its "unequal treaties", Korea however clung to its treaty with the United States and other European powers as a security guarantee.[32]

Moreover, there is evidence that Korean officials viewed the United States as a replacement of the "elder brother" after China's "defection" from traditional bilateral relations.[33] To repay the United States according to the principle of mutual "moral obligation", King Kojong awarded American businessmen over other foreign competitors with lucrative concessions.[34] Due to years of socialisation into the hierarchical view of interstate relations, Chosŏn elites mistakenly believed that Western powers would also guarantee Chosŏn's autonomy as long as Chosŏn paid its respects (Ku 1988: 17–8). In other words, autonomy from China did not conceptually translate into sovereign "independence" for Korea. Rather, Korean foreign policy continued to be bogged down by its paradoxical dependent-yet-autonomous *sokbang* status of the Sinocentric era (D. Kang 2004; Ku 1988). Only with the political participation of the Enlightenment leaders were autonomy and independence recognised as the same concept, as in Westphalian sovereignty (Y. Chung 2004: 166).

By the time that efforts to strengthen sovereignty shifted towards the promotion of autonomy and self-reliance, Korean self-strengthening and reform movements were marred by heavy penetration of foreign pressures. China changed its long-standing principle of non-interference and attempted to transform Korea into a Western-style protectorate, and Japan lent its hands to the progressive reformers in Korea (Fujimura 1977: 426–7; Larsen 2000).[35] It was such continued foreign involvement in

Korean attempts at reform that considerably influenced Chosŏn Korea's failure at strengthening its sovereign autonomy. Yong-jak Kim (1989: 176–7) argues that Chinese self-strengthening movements owe their failure to political opposition by conservatives but in the case of Korea, the reform movement collapsed due to China's military intervention.

The lack of domestic consolidation is another reason why Korea's "sovereignty crisis" ended in turmoil. The degree of consensus reached on the state's new course of sovereignty-strengthening strategy depends on the strength of the challenging coalition. In Japan, the Meiji leaders were able to not only consolidate and centralise their power but also added legitimacy to their rule by aligning with the *tenno*. In Korea, however, the pro-autonomy reform movement was divided between proponents of full-blown modernising reforms like Japan and anti-Japanese moderates who advocated gradual change.

Conclusion

In this paper, I have addressed the question of why the arrival of the modern European state system elicited such different responses in China's two smaller neighbours. Eschewing the inaccurate dichotomy of treating the traditional Asian state system as a normative order and the Westphalian state system as a power-based one, I have shown how Japan and Korea pursued different interests under Sinocentric hierarchy. In particular, I argue against the notion that the Sinocentric system was inflexible and unable to adapt to environmental changes; in fact, it was highly contextual and at times paradoxical. Despite the demise of the traditional Sinocentric system in East Asia, the legacy of the hierarchical worldview can be found in the sensitivity towards "Great Powers" shown in the political debates of contemporary Japan and Korea. Anti-*sadae*-ism is a powerful mobilising tool in contemporary Korea (as evident in today's anti-American movements), while Japan's on-going quest for seeking international status are reminders of patterns of sovereignty conception in secondary states.

Notes

I would like to thank participants at the Conference on *Rationalising China's Place in Asia, 1800 to 2005* hosted by the National University of Singapore's Asia Research Institute on 3–4 August 2006 for their helpful comments. I am also grateful to the Japan Foundation for providing me with funding for conducting my research in Japan.

1   The traditional East Asian system of interstate relations has been characterised as the "Chinese world order", the Sinocentric tribute system, the "*sadae* order", the *hwa-i* (or *ka-i* in Japanese; literally, civilian-barbarian) order, and the *kaikin* (or *haegum* in Korean; Maritime Prohibition) system, to name a few examples. See Fairbank 1968; K. Kim 1980; Y. Kim 2001; E. Kang 1997; D. Kang 2004.

2   It is in this sense that Heaseung Kim (1997: 19–20) argues that Korean nationalism did not begin as a response to Western pressure in the late nineteenth century, but can rather be traced back to the Chosŏn period.

3   Unification of the country was a key criterion in the legitimation of a new regime according to the classical Chinese texts. See Toby 1984: 56–9.

4   Chandra 1988: 17.

5   Cited in Harootunian 1980: 12.

6   In his portrayal of routinised asymmetrical relations between Vietnam and China, Brantly Womack (2006: 82–4) refers to such hegemon sensitivity as the "politics of overattention", in which vulnerability to the larger power makes the smaller state sensitive to all possibilities of the former's actions.

7   While some would argue that Japan does not belong in the same category of "small states" such as Korea and Vietnam, Japan in its history was not a "great power" in the conventional sense of the word as we use it now. Territorial expansionism and outward ambition was nearly absent (with the exception of Hideyoshi's invasions in the sixteenth century) until the late nineteenth century. More importantly, both Japan and Korea recognised the power and influence of China, although they sought varying degrees of distance from the "centre of civilisation".

8   On the "ingratiation effect", as an alternative to the balance-of-power mechanism, see Healy and Stein 1973.

9   On "hiding" strategies, see Schroeder 1994; Deudney 1996.

10   Gilpin (1981) also speaks of prestige as the international currency among states.

11   Vital (1967) and Morrison and Suhrke (1978) also note the potential sacrifice of autonomy in small states in exchange for allying with larger powers.

12   Ronald Toby (1977, 1984) argues that Japan was not really closed off from the outside world and that that the *sakoku* (closed country) policy was only against Christianity and not against its neighbours in East Asia. While I am not disagreeing with this view, Japan was considerably less engaged in state-to-state relations within the Sinocentric order and interacted only indirectly with its neighbours.

13   Geography played a role in the formation of Japanese and Korean security strategies. Greater distance from the Chinese mainland and the ocean as a natural barrier allowed Japan greater autonomy than Korea, which shared a border with China. At the same time, geographical differences did not solely determine outcomes. Earlier Korean kingdoms, such as Koryŏ, did not always "revere" China or even necessarily accommodate the various dynasties on the Chinese mainland, sometimes balancing against one kingdom or tribe by aligning with its rival.

14   A major reason for minimising contact with outsiders was the fear by the Tokugawa *bakufu* of domestic rivals forming anti-regime alliances with foreign allies (K. Kim 1980; Toby 1977).

15   Throughout the Tokugawa period, and until the beginning of the nineteenth century, the focus of Japan's foreign policy was with its neighbouring countries. In contrast, the "*sakoku* (seclusion)" versus "*kaikoku* (opening up)" debates in the early nineteenth century shifted the focus to relations with the West (Mitani 2006).

16   Past research has tended to overlook the significance of the *waegwan*, as if Tokugawa foreign relations only operated in Nagasaki where Dejima and *Tōjin yashiki* handled Dutch and Chinese ships respectively. Recent research on the *waegwan*, however, reveals that it maintained important economic, political and social functions between Korea and Japan. In fact, the scale of the *waegwan* was much larger than Dejima and *Tōjin yashiki*; "the *Waegwan* was one hundred thousand tsubo in area compared with the ten thousand tsubo of *Tōjin yashiki* and four thousand tsubo of Dejima. Furthermore, the volume of trade conducted at the *Waegwan* surpassed that of the trade in Nagasaki during the mid-Tokugawa period" (E. Kang 1997: 147)

17   Hidetada's reception of a Korean embassy at Fushimi Castle in 1617 was one of the clearest cases of the use of diplomacy as propaganda (Toby 1984: 64).

18   Until then, the Japanese shogun was addressed as the "King of Japan" (despite the existence of the *tennō* in Japan) by both China and Korea, as was the custom in addressing rulers of vassal kingdoms.

19   On the Tokugawa Ieyasu's use of Confucianism as an indoctrination and legitimation tool, see also Maruyama 1974, especially pp. 16–7.

20   On Japan's oscillation between withdrawal and engagement from the Asian continent, see Inoguchi 2006.

21   Interestingly, only "sadae", and not "chaso", is in usage in contemporary political language.

22   On the development of Chosŏn's worldview since the mid-sixteenth century, see Pak 1982; Hong 1993; Chung 1998; Haboush and Deuchler 1999.

23   Possible reasons include: the Qing's demonstration of benevolence (read: non-interference) befitting a suzerain toward Korea, the Chosŏn elites' attempt to bolster their weak legitimacy through their relations with the Qing, and the view that China and Chosŏn shared the same fate in the advance of the Western powers since 1840. For details, see D. Kang 2004: 14–5.

24   This catch-up mentality is still displayed by Japanese and Korean elites and motivates state behaviour in the post-1945 period. See, for example, Woo-Cumings 1999; Leheny 2003.

25   In the late nineteenth century context, modernisation referred to accepting modern European institutions as the "global standard" (Y. Chung 2004).

26   An important reason for Japan's successful Westernisation was the recognition of the link between foreign relations and domestic order. Indiscriminate attacks against foreigners were banned and violations were severely dealt with in order to prevent diplomatic incidents and the undermining of the government's stature in the international arena. The Meiji government also improved its system

of law enforcement and embarked on an extensive propaganda campaign to inform the public that anti-foreign attacks were against "the laws of the world". Such strategies were calculated to consolidate the government's authority and prestige — both domestically and internationally (Iriye 1989:734–5).

[27] The latter idea was the precursor of the theory of *datsua*, or leaving Asia.

[28] It should be noted that the disagreement with the Qing policy of accommodating the West was not because Korea wanted more autonomy, but because Korean officials thought increasing contact with "uncivilised barbarians" would disrupt regional stability since foreigners did not understand the appropriate rules of state conduct.

[29] While the existing literature tends to emphasise Korean "rigidity" in dealing with the West in the late nineteenth century, there was in fact much debate in the Korean court even in the 1870s over the diplomatic overture from the new Meiji government in Japan, which was seen as no better than the Western "barbarians" (Hara 1998: 390).

[30] The heavy involvement of China in Korean affairs began after Japanese annexation of the Ryukyuus in 1879 and the increasing threat from Russia (Y. Chung 2004: 161).

[31] Dong-kuk Kang (2004) also notes that *sadae/jidai* and *sadaejui/jidaishugi* are terms created and used by Enlightenment intellectuals in Japan such as Fukuzawa Yukichi and later in Chosŏn to portray Sinocentric traditions as backward and undesirable.

[32] In a telling example of their misunderstanding of Western law and institutions, Korean officials took the "good offices" clause stated in the 1882 Korean-American treaty as "a firm commitment on the part of the United States to come to Korea's assistance if Korean sovereignty and independence were threatened", as had been the moral principle guiding the *sadae* order (P. Hahm 1984: 30).

[33] In 1897, the Korean king is reported to have told Horace Allen, the newly-appointed American minister in Seoul, "We feel that America is to us as an Elder Brother" (Wilz 1985: 249; see also Swartout 1980).

[34] Examples include the timber extraction from Ullung Island, providing electricity, the building of the Incheon-Seoul railroad, the Unsan gold mines in North Pyongan province, and building streetcar lines in Seoul. See Lee 1970; Simons 1995.

[35] In October 1882, the Chosŏn-Qing commercial treaty was signed to promote Chinese commercial activities and to strengthen its influence in Chosŏn (Choi 1993: 128–9). On China's commercial activities in Korea as an "informal empire", see Larsen 2000.

Chapter 2

Between Tribute and Treaty: Sino-Siamese Relations from the Late Nineteenth Century to the Early Twentieth Century

Junko Koizumi

Introduction

Given the long and close historical relations between Thailand (Siam) and China, the fact that the two countries did not have any formal diplomatic relations for more than a century after 1854 is seemingly a paradox. In 1852, King Rama IV (or King Mongkut, r. 1851–68) sent a tributary mission to Beijing to inform the Chinese court of the demise of King Rama III (r. 1824–51) and his own accession to the throne. But on their journey back from Beijing to Canton, bandits robbed the gifts from the Chinese emperor, killed a Chinese interpreter and assaulted the envoys. Siam never sent any tribute to China again after this mission returned to Bangkok in 1854.[1]

This chapter aims to examine Sino-Siamese relations during the several decades after the return of Siam's "last" tributary mission to Qing China in 1854. The relations between the two countries during this crucial period of time has been neglected by historians, as the alleged abolition of tributary missions to China with the conclusion of the Bowring treaty of 1855 is regarded in retrospect as a shift in the Siamese inter-state relationship from the obsolete Chinese tributary system to the modern Westphalia system.[2] Scholarly interest in post-1854

Siamese diplomacy has been centred on her troubled relations with the Western colonial powers, while studies concerning the Chinese in Siam as well as Sino-Siamese relations are focused on a few specific topics, such as the role of the Chinese in Siamese capitalist development and the nationalist movements in both Siam and China, which serve the regnant paradigms of national history and modernisation.

As a result, many important questions such as how Siam and China, two of the few countries in Asia that remained independent in the period of high colonialism, related to each other in the late nineteenth and early twentieth centuries when many turbulent events affected the region, and how these two countries managed to cope with the various problems stemming from the growing Chinese immigration into Siam without any formal channel for negotiation, are left unexplored.

Interestingly, China requested tribute from Siam at least a few times between the 1860s and mid-1880s, and tried to negotiate a treaty several times from the late 1880s to the early twentieth century. Despite the pressures exerted by China, however, Siam successfully avoided China's requests. Why did Siam never clearly declare the abolition of tribute to China, while it severely criticised China's arrogant attitude toward Siam as a vassal state? Why and how did Siam, on the other hand, persistently refuse a treaty with China, if modern treaties were understood as an agreement between two nations based upon the principle of sovereign equality?

Based on Thai archival records, this chapter examines the various issues involved in the negotiations between Siam and Qing China from the late nineteenth to the early twentieth centuries. The negotiation processes will reveal the far-reaching effects of the "China problems" on Siam, and raise questions about the clear boundary drawn between domestic and regional/international affairs as well as the contrast between the Western treaty arrangement and the Sino-centric tributary relation.

Tribute Question after 1854

Requests from Canton Officials

It was ten years after the dispatch of the "last" tributary mission to China that China, or perhaps more precisely, the officials in Canton, sent envoys to Siam to remind them of tribute missions. Two Chinese officials from Canton arrived in Bangkok on a junk named the *Senghin*[3] in April 1862 bearing the following three royal letters: a proclamation of *bansiu* (*wanshou*) ceremony on the occasion of the thirtieth birthday of Emperor Xianfeng and the announcements of the death of Emperor Xianfeng and of the enthronement of the Emperor Tongzhi from Emperor Xianfeng and one from Emperor Tongzhi.[4]

Interestingly, these imperial letters were accompanied by several letters from the local officials in Canton: four from the Governor-General of Canton (*chongtok kwangtung*) to *Chaophraya* Phrakhlang Senabodiphuyai [henceforth abbreviated as Phrakhlang], the Siamese Minister in charge of the royal treasury and foreign affairs; two from a Canton official named *Chin Seng Chong*, who was ranked as *nai hang punkang* in charge of affairs concerning royal letters from Bangkok, addressed to both Phrakhlang and *Phraya* Chodukratchasetthi [henceforth abbreviated as *Phraya* Choduk], the official in charge of affairs concerning the Chinese community in Siam and trade with China, respectively; and another letter to Phrakhlang from an official named *Yu Lim*. Yu Lim was also explained as *nai hang punkang*, allegedly in charge of tax affairs regarding the ships from Siam and Vietnam.[5]

While the letters from the Governor-General of Canton concerned the ceremonial matters in the imperial court, Yu Lim's letter to Phrakhlang was a strong reminder of Siam's unpaid tribute missions since 1852; he also detailed the five occasions for tribute which Siam had missed.[6] Chin Seng Chong's letter to Phrakhlang, dated 23 February 1862, was on the other hand a request for tax exemption for the junk that carried the imperial letters and envoys to Bangkok. The letter read:

> When the junk *Senghin* reaches the port of Bangkok, please kindly grant it exemptions of tax and commission just as in the case of the junk *Poseng*. It is reminded that when *Chin An Pun* was the master of that junk *Poseng*, which carried the imperial letters to Bangkok on previous occasions, it was granted with tax and commission exemption on their return.[7]

Moreover, Chin Seng Chong also mentioned that he himself had granted Siamese junks visiting Canton a favour of tax exemption during the past few decades and promised that the same favour would be given to Siamese junks in the future.

Phrakhlang responded to these letters by writing three letters to the Governor-General of Canton on 25 June 1862.[8] The first letter was acknowledgement of the receipt of letters. It explained that Phrakhlang had reported the contents of the letters from the Chinese emperors and Canton officials to the King and that the King ordered the officials to arrange a procession to carry the letters both by waterway and by land according to the proper customs for receiving imperial letters from the Chinese emperors to pay high respect. The second letter was a reply to the request for tribute. It pointed out first that as the letter requesting the overdue tribute was merely from *nai hang*, the Siamese officials decided the matter should be consulted upon only among the ministers. After elaborating the situations which had prevented Siam from sending envoys since 1852, such as the failure for Canton officials to punish the bandits who had assaulted the Siamese envoys in 1854 by bringing them to trial and the outbreak of battles with the British and French in Canton and Beijing, he informed the Chinese the decision for this as follows: Siam would appoint envoys and send them to promote friendship with the Emperor of Beijing if and when the ministers at Beijing could suppress rebels/bandits and the country could be peaceful and united.

Regarding the matter of granting tax exemptions to the junk *Senghin*, Phrakhlang and *Phraya* Choduk wrote to the Governor-General of Canton and Yu Lim respectively, informing them that the *Senghin* was given the same privilege of tax exemption as the one given to the junk *Poseng* on the following conditions: both the three per cent import tax, totalling 1,953.375 bahts and the tax on rice presumably for export from Siam to Canton, which amounted to 1,200 bahts, were exempted, while the measurement duty was not imposed as it had already been abolished.[9]

Seen from the customary procedures concerning the tributary relations between the two countries, the request for tribute this time seemed rather unusual since local officials in Canton such as *nai hang punkang*, who had, as far as existing Thai records are concerned, never appeared in the correspondence between China and Siam on previous occasions, was taking active roles. Considering that these officials seem to have been interested in inviting Siamese envoys to Canton and obtaining tax exemption on their cargo, the dispatch of the envoys to request tribute in 1862 could have been initiated by those local officials at Canton with a strong motive for promoting trade with Siam.[10]

However, it seems that the officials in Canton were not satisfied with such an ambiguous answer from Phrakhlang. Another letter from *nai hang punkang* in Canton to Phrakhlang dated 6 July 1863 to request tribute was brought to Bangkok with additional letters from the Qing emperor and the Governor-General of Canton.[11] However, even though *nai hang punkang* reconfirmed the safety of the route to Beijing and generously offered a discount in the number of the overdue tributary missions from five to three, he failed in persuading Siam. *Phraya* Choduk replied to *nai hang punkang* that it would be impossible to send envoys at present as the monsoon season for the year was already over and the ships that were used for carrying the tribute in former times were all rotted, and that they would make an arrangement to meet the request when new vessels were prepared.[12]

Before arriving at such a dilatory response, there had been a consultation between the King and high officials on how to deal with this request for tribute.[13] The discussion focused on the following four points and possibilities. The first concerned the possibility of sending envoys via Canton. The problem was that those who were to be envoys would still be too afraid to go because of the expected danger of bandits and rebels, and forcing them to go should be regarded as inappropriate as such trepidation by the envoys would contradict the absoluteness of Thai kingship: anyone who was under royal discipline should go wherever ordered by the king. The second was the idea of sending tribute via Tianjin. But this was also dismissed. It was feared that if China approved the proposal, it would become necessary to prepare a large sailing boat or a steamship to carry the envoys to that destination, which would incur a considerable investment, too large to be offset by the return gifts from the Chinese emperor. In addition, it was also suggested that it would not be appropriate to make a huge investment in "*kong*" (*gong*), for sending tribute should not be regarded as an opportunity for seeking commercial profit any more.

The third question concerned the discrepancy in texts between the Siamese royal letters written in Thai and their translation in Chinese. There was a proposal to announce the original texts publicly to let the Europeans know the distortions the Chinese translator introduced when rendering the Chinese version. But it was decided that publishing the royal letters would not be appropriate. The last point was the problem of governing the Chinese population in Siam. It was feared that if Siam stopped tribute to China, Chinese merchants who sent vessels to trade in China would complain at the loss of their profits and a large number of the Chinese residing in Bangkok might cause problems. These arguments suggest the complexity of sending tribute to China. But perhaps because this last danger seemed more real, they ultimately decided to respond in the form of proposing a postponement rather than termination of tribute.

Request for the Tianjin Route

While the initiative of the local officials in Canton was notable in the case of requesting tribute from Siam in 1862, it was the Siamese Phrakhlang and Fujian officials who took the initiative in resuming the negotiation over tribute several years later. In 1869, when officials from Fujian arrived in Bangkok to purchase teak for shipbuilding, Phrakhlang received the envoys and handed them a letter addressed to officials in Fujian to be delivered on their return with the following contents.[14] In the letter, after emphasising his efforts in facilitating the purchase of teak for the Fujian officials despite the recent price hike caused by the shortage of teak, Phrakhlang expressed dissatisfaction at the way in which the Chinese had dealt with the attack by bandits on the Siamese envoys in 1853, and pointed out the recent outbreak of turmoil in China. Phrakhalng then expressed his wish to send tribute to ask for investiture from the Chinese court on the occasion of King Chulalongkorn's enthronement in 1868 and proposed a new tributary route to enter Beijing via Tianjin. The reason for proposing the Tianjin route was that it would be safer and take less time in comparison with the overland route from Canton.

The Fujian officials conveyed the message to Emperor Tongzhi. The Emperor however rejected the proposal on the ground that the customary route via Canton was already safe since the bandits had all been suppressed, while the sea route to Tianjin would be subject to the dangers of large waves, strong winds and no proper officials to guard the envoys from such danger.[15]

Despite the refusal by the Chinese Emperor, however, Siam continued to propose sending envoys via Tianjin. In early 1876, soon after the enthronement of Emperor Guangxu, a Canton official named *Ngo Seng Chiang*, who claimed to be in charge of affairs relating to Siam and Vietnam, sent a letter to Phrakhlang with eight imperial proclamations and nine letters from the Governor-General of Kwangtung regarding imperial affairs. *Ngo* requested that Phrakhlang inform the Siamese King of these matters and send him the acknowledgement of their receipt.[16] Phrakhlang, in his reply dated 15 April 1876, again raised the issue of sending a mission via Tianjin. Referring to the fact that the Emperor had opened the port of Tianjin to commercial ships coming from various countries and allowed foreign envoys to enter Beijing via Tianjin, Phrakhlang expressed his deep regrets about being obliged to take a long and troublesome route to Beijing from Canton. This would be dishonouring Siamese envoys in the face of other envoys that were allowed to enter Beijing from Tianjin. However, the Governor-General of Canton rejected the Tianjin route without informing the Emperor as the same request from Siam had already been rejected in 1869.[17]

Ngao Siang Chiang, allegedly *nai hang punkang* in Canton and presumably the *Ngo* mentioned above, wrote to inform Siam of the decision to reject the Tianjin route. When the letter reached Bangkok in April 1877, King Chulalongkorn consulted with his ministers and the members of the Council of State about the question of sending tribute to China.[18] Among the 13 consulted, 4 supported the continuation of sending tribute, 4 proposed its discontinuation and the remaining 5 proposed a further wait-and-see strategy.[19]

The points in question, which were similar to the ones discussed in previous cases, could be summarised as follows. The first issue was the value of maintaining the royal tradition from ancient times. This was cited as a reason for continuing the practice of sending tribute and also for taking a further wait-and-see policy.[20] The second issue, which was relevant to the first one, was what sending tribute meant to the sovereignty of Siam and the authority of Siamese kingship. Many were negative about sending tribute to China as they saw it to be a symbolic expression of submission to China. Some expressed concern about the problem of textual distortion made at the translation of the royal letters from the Thai version into the Chinese version which emphasised the submissive attitude toward the Chinese Emperor excessively. It was feared that if the royal letters translated into Chinese came to be known to the Western envoys who were visiting Beijing, they might also demand the same submissive attitude from the Siamese King when they sought to conclude treaties with Siam.[21]

Whether or not Siam should accept the request for tribute to China depended on how one would evaluate the power of China; and this was the third point at issue. Even though one would admit China had been a great power in the past, evaluations on the degree of China's recovery from the recent turmoil and confusion varied. One pointed out, for instance, that now that China was regaining power, it would be difficult to choose whether or not Siam should send tribute, and suggested pursuing a wait-and-see policy by proposing the Tianjin route. Another proposed sending tribute as he admitted that China was so powerful that Siam would either be forced to accept China's request, be it tribute or a treaty, or have to depend on other foreign powers to resist China and might thus have to follow a fate similar to the Khmer, if foreign powers were invited to intervene.

In this regard, what seemed particularly difficult was the question of concluding a treaty. It was feared that China would demand a treaty with extraterritoriality like other Western powers, which would possibly make all the Chinese in Siam "foreign subjects". Theoretically, the Siamese government could refuse China's demand for a treaty if Siam found it disadvantageous.[22] But egalitarianism and mutual agreement seemed too idealistic in the face of the apparent difference in power between the two countries. It also seemed realistic to expect that China would send a commissioner to supervise Siam as China's "tributary state" [*muang bannakan*] if Siam refused to send tribute. Some even supported the idea of sending tribute in order to avoid the possibility that China might request the establishment of consulate in Siam if Siam refused to send tribute. To cope with the situation, building up the military forces to enforce order among the Chinese in Siam was also proposed.

In fact, the question of extraterritoriality was a difficult one because it was directly linked to the problem of governing the Chinese in Siam. Since the mid-nineteenth century, uprisings of Chinese "secret societies" known as *ang-yi* frequently occurred. In the mid-1870s when the demand for another tribute mission arrived from China, large scale problems among the Chinese in the south were being reported to Bangkok.[23] Caught in a deep dilemma for which no simple solution seemed possible, most of those consulted presented their conclusions after giving due consideration to both pros and cons that might result from either a refusal or an acceptance of China's request. After considering all these points, *Phraya* Choduk replied to *Ngao Siang Chiang* by simply stating that the Siamese King wished friendship between China and Siam and regretted the decision of China not to allow the Siamese envoys to take the Tianjin route.[24]

From "Tribute" to "Treaty"?

Despite the repeated evasive responses from Siam, China did not stop her requests for tribute from Siam. It was less than three years after the request of 1877 that China sent another reminder to Siam. This time, the request was made under the name of *Loei po* (*libu*) in Beijing. A letter from *Loei po* addressed to the King of Siam concerned a Siamese sailor named *Asan* who arrived in China in early 1880. Asan, who was on board an American ship, got drunk in Amoy and stabbed a Chinese to death in 1873. He was first given a death sentence, and was later discharged by a pardon upon Emperor Guangxu's accession in 1875. However, since there was no one to look after him after his release, the Chinese authorities wanted to send him back to Siam with Siamese envoys if Siam agreed to resume tribute.[25]

Siam however decided not to dispatch envoys to receive Asan. The letter from *Phraya* Choduk dated 20 April 1880 was addressed to *Ngo Siang*, "*punkang* in charge of Siamese and Vietnamese affairs in Canton". It stated clearly that Siam had no intention of accepting Asan and pointed out that if a Siamese committed any crime in the land of the emperor of Beijing, he/she should be punished by the Chinese law. *Phraya* Choduk also mentioned the Siamese intention to promote a "friendly relationship" with China, and stated that Siam would wait for an opportunity to be allowed to visit Beijing via Tianjin as were envoys from many other countries.[26]

What happened to Asan after that is unknown from the Thai records. But this refusal did not discourage China from requesting tribute from Siam. In fact, the tone of Canton officials in demanding for tribute seems to have become stronger toward the mid-1880s. In August 1881, an imperial proclamation to announce the demise of the Empress Dowager and addressed to the King of Siam arrived in Bangkok. This was accompanied by letters from the Governor-General of Canton and an official named *Ngo Seng Siang*,[27] who had allegedly "assumed the position of *punkang* in charge of Siam, Vietnam, and Ryukyu affairs at Canton"; these letters were brought to Bangkok by a son of Ngo Seng Siang named *Ngo Hun Yong*. Ngo Seng Siang's letter to Phrakhlang requested Siam to resume sending tribute via Canton.[28]

Phrakhlang's reply to Ngo Seng Siang sent at the end of September 1881 conveyed the deep condolences of the King of Siam on the demise of the Empress Dowager and regretted the repeated rejection of Siam's proposal to take the Tianjin route; his letter to the Governor-General of Canton did not mention sending tribute.[29] Behind such a reply were the following two considerations. First, it was merely a letter from *punkang* that requested tribute and the real intention of China was not clear. Second, it was possible that China would in turn request a treaty like other European countries. But conclusion of a treaty should be avoided because of the situation in which a large number of Chinese had long established roots in Siam.[30]

The replies from Ngo suggest that he stiffened his attitude and even intensified the request. Writing to Phrakhlang, Ngo criticised

Phrakhlang, stating that his letter was impolite in putting Siam on an equal footing with China and in using expressions improper in letters addressed to Chinese officials.[31] Writing to *Phraya* Choduk, he demanded that Siam prepare a golden boat and musical troops and fire a salute in order to receive the imperial proclamation, and he also demanded that he accommodate the Chinese envoys at a special guesthouse for foreign envoys visiting Bangkok so that the customary practices for receiving guests from abroad should properly be observed.[32]

A similar strong attitude was also found in the reaction of Ngo Hun Yong. While emphasising Siam's status as a vassal of China, he pointed out that the letter of the Chinese Emperor should be received with due ceremonial procedures such as firing a salute to demonstrate the highest respect so that other foreign envoys would not look down upon the Chinese Emperor. Explaining that China had already suppressed all the rebels and had been making efforts in building up armament, and that the Chinese Emperor had always demonstrated deep mercy and high virtue toward his vassal states by sending armies to help protect them, Ngo Hun Yong again requested Siam to send tribute via Canton without insisting upon the Tianjin route. He even mentioned that China had raised an army to help Vietnamese in their struggle against France and to check Japanese intervention in Korea and Ryukyu.[33]

Siam, obviously offended by the arrogance of Ngo Hun Yong, received him according to the customary practice without meeting Ngo's request for a royal audience and firing a salute. The reply letters from Phrakhlang to the Governor-General of Canton and Ngo Siang Chiang simply acknowledged the receipt of the letters from China, informed them that the contents were conveyed to the Siamese King properly, and warded off the criticism on impoliteness by saying that Siam had just followed Siamese custom without any intention of being impolite.[34] After this, Siam declined yet another request of tribute demanded by Li Hongchang in 1884; it expressed deep regret that China did not wish to promote friendship with Siam like with other countries.[35] The next negotiation took place in London on 6 March 1886. The Siamese minister, Prince Nares Varariddhi, met with the Chinese minister, Marquis Tseng (Zeng Jize) at the Siamese Legation in London. The meeting lasted for 50 minutes; the details of the conversation were recorded in both Thai and English.[36]

The main point at issue was how to (re)open official relations between the two governments. Although both agreed that it was important for China and Siam to be on good terms with each other as they used to be and expressed their desire for a resumption of diplomatic relations between the two, their views on the nature of the relationship to be realised were not quite in accordance with each other. Regarding the historical relations between Siam and China, Prince Nares expressed his understanding that their past relations were characterised by the exchanges of envoys and "presents", not tribute, according to the customary practices of the East. He criticised those who regarded Siam as a tributary state of China as being ignorant of the customs of the East, not knowing the fact that the Chinese Emperors had also sent "presents" to Siam. Prince Nares also proposed "a commencement of diplomatic relations between the two countries precisely on the same footing that such relations now exist between European nations". In his view, it would be appropriate to have a treaty of commerce and friendship with China as two friendly and independent sovereign powers rather than resuming the old Asiatic way. Although Prince Naret had to admit that Siam was smaller than China, he could not yield on the point that "the independence of Siam was in no way compromised".

The Marquis Tseng, on the other hand, expressed his general approval of Prince Nares's view on the past relationship between the two and agreed that to view the presents sent from Siam in the nature of tribute, or a token of suzerainty of China over Siam, was erroneous. However, he, at the same time, expressed his hope that "the Siamese would regard China as being in the position of an elder sister and show her some respect which such a position naturally entailed" because China was "an enormous country". He also told Prince Nares that he should "remember that China was a very big country, peopled by men of very different opinions which the Chinese Government could not neglect, and that some of them would consider entering on such a course of negotiations was doing what was against her dignity"; this implied that treaty negotiation could be difficult to achieve. Although they also talked about how to open negotiations formally, both had to admit that they had to consult their respective governments before starting a direct negotiation; and the meeting ended by both expressing the intention to make efforts to influence the governments in favour of realising such negotiations.

Yet it seems Siam was still cautious about China's move. In January 1888, a mission of inquiry headed by the General *Ong Eng-Ho* (Wang Ronghe) visited Bangkok. Commissioned by the Emperor, this visit was part of a trip to survey various Chinese communities in Nanyang regions including Java, Sumatra, the Straits Settlements, and Australia.[37]

Having received a prior notification of their visit with some information on how they had been received in Singapore from Tan Kim Cheng, the Siamese consul stationed in Singapore, the Siamese authorities decided to receive them by following the customary practice for receiving Chinese officials visiting Siam: *Phraya* Choduk provided the accommodations in Bangkok and royal audience was not granted. The envoys met the foreign minister of Siam and obtained information on exports and imports, the population census, as well as the situation of the Chinese population in Siam. Regarding the question of concluding a treaty, they inquired about the recent treaty between Japan and Siam, criticised France as oppressing China, and expressed the necessity of studying international law.[38] It seems both sides were becoming positive toward concluding a treaty in the Western style. However, the actual negotiation processes in the following years proved difficult as historical relations formed under the tributary system still provided the premises to condition the negotiation on both sides.

Negotiation for Avoidance: Yang Shiqi's Visit in 1907[39]

From the late 1880s to the early twentieth century, Siam witnessed an influx of Chinese immigrants. While these Chinese immigrants came to play important roles as labourers or artisans or entrepreneurs in the growing export-oriented industries in Siam, problems such as conflicts among Chinese secret societies and, later political movements related to revolutionary causes also became serious.[40] To the Siamese authorities' annoyance, moreover, some European consulates, especially the French one after the Pak Nam Incident of 1893, abused extraterritoriality by issuing certificates of registration to the subjects of non-treaty countries such as China and other Asian populations, for instance, the Lao and Khmer, residing in Siam. If registered with the European consulates, they could enjoy such privileges as consular jurisdiction and tax exemption.[41] The Siamese government, while negotiating with these European powers to stop the improper registration of Asiatic subjects, had to hasten their efforts to introduce modern legal codes, the prerequisite for abolishing extraterritoriality. It was under such circumstances that China resumed her request for treaty negotiation with Siam in the mid-1900s.

In the beginning of November 1907, the Chinese minister in Paris, Liu Shixun, visited Prince Charoon (*Momchao* Charunsak), the Siamese minister in Paris. Liu told the Siamese Prince that Yang Shiqi,[42] the

"Under Secretary of State for the Ministry of Commerce" in Beijing, was appointed as head of a mission to "visit the towns [of] countries in the neighbourhood of China where there are important Chinese commercial relations".[43] The Chinese minister asked the Prince to inform the Siamese government of Yang's intention to visit Bangkok and requested that the mission would be granted a favourable reception with due protection and customs facilities. He also impressed on Charoon that the purpose of the mission would be neither diplomatic nor political. Charoon presented the matter to the Siamese government and proposed welcoming the mission as "guests of His Majesty's Government" so it would show the Chinese government that even without a treaty, "the Chinese are received as one of us".[44]

The Siamese government held a cabinet meeting on 25 November, and discussed plans to receive the mission. King Chulalongkorn expressed his view that even without a friendship treaty, China should be respected as other powerful countries with which Siam maintained a close friendship. But he rejected the idea of establishing a Chinese consulate in Siam on the grounds that the Chinese in Siam were already being treated as well as Siamese subjects.[45] On 27 November, Yang's mission, which came from Saigon with two first-class cruisers, landed in Bangkok. For about a week until their departure on 2 December, Siam welcomed and politely hosted the mission. What is implied in the Thai sources, which recorded every detail of their visit, is that both sides were well aware of the fact that the implicit purpose of the mission was diplomatic and political, and yet because of the sensitive nature of the mission, both sides deliberately avoided taking up the issue of concluding a treaty openly. Instead, they probed indirectly to find out the ideas of the other party, while trying to demonstrate power through non-verbal means.[46]

For instance, the Chinese mission made inquiries on such topics as the situation of the foreign consulates in Bangkok, the size of the Chinese community in Bangkok, and the relations between Russia and Japan. At one time, they even hinted at their interest in appointing a Chinese consul in Siam, but it seems that a Siamese official to whom this was addressed met the question with deliberate neglect. In addition, the mission also talked about the current situation in China by pointing out that China was a big country, being rich in money and human power but currently lacking knowledge and training. Based on the observation that China was recovering from the recent confusions and making progress toward prosperity and that the Chinese and the

Siamese could be regarded as relatives, they even suggested that if China and Siam made progress together, both could collaborate in firmly maintaining Eastern countries.[47]

It is noteworthy that the local Chinese in Bangkok welcomed the mission by decorating the streets in the Chinatown area, collecting contributions from the local Chinese, and holding banquets and dinners for the mission on various occasions. It was even reported that some Hakka were secretly planning to petition the mission for establishing a Chinese consul in Bangkok.[48] Even though the envoys' stay in Bangkok was very short, it was regarded as an epoch-making event in the history of Siamese relations with China. Siam's reception of a Chinese mission as a formal guest of the government was a change in its policy, as the government had always entrusted the reception of such visitors to the Chinese in Bangkok. King Chulalongkorn even granted a private audience on 29 November , which gave the mission great satisfaction.[49] Writing to Prince Charoon in Paris, King Chulalongkorn stated as follows:

> With regard to the visit of the Chinese to Bangkok, it has passed off well. On my return, I have found that the policy here was to keep them at arms length, only ordering the Chinese to receive the Chinese, but I have changed all that according to the policy that we have spoken to the Chinese minister, which, I am glad to say, was generally approved…. Yesterday I gave them a private audience. They expressed a great satisfaction at the reception given to them. Not a word was spoken about politics.[50]

Replying immediately to this King's telegram, Prince Charoon expressed his views as follows:

> As events turned out there is nothing to fear. I donot [sic] understand the policy of avoiding them so ostensibly which would have the reverse of the desired result. I think that the policy of Your Majesty is the best for the present. It must not be forgotten that the Chinese are important factors in the Siamese life, and this question will be one of our most important and difficult questions to solve one of these days.[51]

Agreeing with Prince Charoon's view, King Chulalongkorn called for another cabinet meeting on 5 December 1907 and discussed the Chinese question with the ministers. The king saw the possibility that China would demand for the establishment of the consul in a more decisive manner was real because there was a constant need among the Chinese in Siam to have someone to act as their administrator due to the several conditions that had recently emerged. First, after France had agreed to hand their [jurisdictional] power over Asiatic subjects to Siam, the Chinese in Siam had to seek alternative authorities to replace France. Second, the introduction of more direct ways of tax collection resulted in the fall of influential tax farmers who had been leaders of the local Chinese communities in Siam. Third, the newly emerging leaders of the Chinese in Siam were primarily owners of rice mills and merchants with fewer connections to the Siamese government than the old influential tax farmers. Unless the Siamese government provided some protective measures, it appeared inevitable that the Chinese would increasingly feel like foreigners and continue to request the establishment of a Chinese consul as their protector in Siam.[52]

This observation was not groundless as news that some Chinese in Bangkok were attempting to establish associations or supporting the growing revolutionary movements in China and other overseas Chinese communities in Siam's neighbouring regions was reported. The local Chinese in Bangkok, for instance, proposed the establishment of a Chinese Chamber of Commerce in the beginning of 1908. But the Siamese authorities, suspicious of its implicit political purposes and possible influence of the Chinese government, were unwilling to give approval for its establishment.[53] In the same year, the Hakka, who had allegedly requested Yang's mission to establish a Chinese consul in Siam, formed the Khek Association of Bangkok.[54]

In the meantime, the negotiations between China and Siam regarding the conclusion of a treaty continued in Europe. On 14 April 1908, the Chinese and Siamese ministers in France met in Paris again. There, the Chinese minister, Liu Shixun, expressed the wish for concluding a treaty with Siam and asked the Siamese minister, Prince Charoon, to propose the matter to the Siamese government. Charoon, while agreeing to convey the matter to the Siamese government, told the Chinese minister his personal view that it would be not yet appropriate to conclude a treaty between China and Siam, and he cited King Chulalongkorn's view that the Chinese in Siam had already been treated as equally as the Thai and there would be nothing to worry about the state of the Chinese community in Siam. In addition, Charoon also explained that since the Siamese government was in the process of negotiating the revisions of the treaty conditions on extraterritoriality with various countries, it would be better to wait until the revisions were complete because it would be regarded as "embarrass" [*sic*] for Siam to have another treaty with China presumably with extraterritorial conditions. Emphasising that the Chinese in Bangkok "hold an exceptional position" in "Thailand" (*muang thai*) for they were regarded as of the same party [as the Siamese] and were enjoying "the same rights and privileges as the Siamese", Prince Charoon also insisted that if a treaty should ever be concluded, it should include special provisions suitable for the "special position enjoyed" by the Chinese in Thailand.[55]

The question of concluding a treaty with China affected the treaty negotiation with Switzerland in progress at that time. Even if there was a possibility that Switzerland might offer to negotiate the conditions for concluding a treaty without extraterritoriality, it was still feared that "if the Swiss government would agree to a treaty without extraterritoriality", "it will be a precedent for China to do the same", and that if that happened, "there are large advantages to be gained by China under a treaty with Siam, while Siam has very little to hope from such an agreement".[56] Siam still needed to pursue a dilatory policy. King Chulalongkorn, writing to Prince Charoon in mid-June 1908, admitted that sooner or later China would make another move to demand a treaty with Siam, and stated his ideas about how to cope with the situation. Seeing that having a treaty with China, unlike the case with Switzerland, would be disadvantageous to Siam even without extraterritoriality, the King emphasised that Siam should not accept a treaty with China. The King also considered possibilities that might arise from not accepting China's request for a treaty. First, China might put obstructions in the way of the commercial activities of Siamese merchants; second, China might also obstruct coolies from entering Siam; third, China might incite the Chinese in Siam against the Siamese government; fourth, if China built up enough naval power, she might use force like the Western powers.[57]

King Chulalongkorn's prospect that all the above four were not yet an immediate threat was soon proven to be too optimistic. A large-scale strike to protest the increase in the amount of the poll tax levied on the Chinese was staged by the Chinese in Bangkok from 1 June 1910, which seriously hindered the commercial activities of the city. The incident deeply shocked the Siamese government and made them fear that intervention by China could happen at anytime.[58] A few months after the strike, King Chulalongkorn again consulted his ministers on the issue of concluding a treaty with China. Three ministers, Prince Damrong, the Minister of Interior, Prince Nares, the Minister of Public Works (and the former Minister of the Capital), and *Phraya* Wongsanupraphat (the Minister of Agriculture), gave their views.[59] Given the long historical relations between Siam and China, all three had to admit it impossible and not beneficial to halt Chinese immigration into Siam. The ideas proposed were primarily concerned with how to evade China's request or mitigate its undesired impact on Siam without harming the benefits that Siam could enjoy from maintaining relations with China and without offending both China and the Chinese in Siam.

Prince Damrong, for instance, observed that China did not possess enough force to compel Siam to conclude a treaty at the moment; he also pointed out, however, that there was a possibility for the Chinese government to use manoeuvres to gain power in two ways: first by uniting the Chinese in Thailand (*muang thai*) in showing disloyalty to the (Siamese) authorities and soliciting help and support from the Chinese government; and second, by entrusting the protection of the Chinese to the care of the foreign powers which had concluded friendship treaties with Siam. Regarding the first case, Prince Damrong saw that the Chinese government had already made a move by encouraging the Chinese in Siam and in other places to establish commercial associations. But observing that the Chinese ways of managing such associations were likely to have internal problems, Damrong expected that they would pass as a temporary phenomenon if the Siamese government kept a fearless attitude. As for the second case, Damrong pointed out that the French and Japanese governments had already proposed offering protection for the Chinese in Siam but the Chinese government refused both. Seeing such possibilities would still exist, he insisted that the Siamese government should oppose any foreign powers acting as protector for the Chinese in Siam.

While confirming that the present policy of giving the Chinese the same treatment as the Siamese without a treaty would be beneficial to the Chinese in Siam themselves, Prince Damrong did admit that such a situation would also be a temporary one. Expecting that the time would come before too long when Siam would really have to conclude a treaty with China, Damrong also examined and assessed the possible circumstances under which Siam might be obliged to negotiate a treaty.

The first case was that China would gain enough power to force Siam into a treaty. But Prince Damrong deemed it negative as he saw there would be intervention by other nations that would wish to prevent China from gaining greater power. The second scenario he examined was the possibility for the Chinese in Thailand to unite sufficiently to request a treaty with China. Prince Damrong was also negative about

this possibility based on the class differences within the Chinese themselves. By citing the case of the recent strike in Bangkok, Damrong
observed that the Chinese in Thailand were mostly temporary sojourners
and lower-class labourers with no political interests. The upper-class
Chinese, on the other hand, could further be divided into two groups:
those who had already established themselves; and those who were
ambitious but could not yet fulfill their own wishes. It was those in
the second group who were likely to have deep dissatisfaction and
thus be a cause of political disorder. To prevent the outbreak of future
disorder, Prince Damrong proposed building up enough military power
to control the Chinese in Siam and to govern them properly so that
their satisfaction should be guaranteed and their united action should
be prevented.

The third scenario was that the Thai government and the Chinese
government would reach a mutual agreement to conclude a treaty. The
crucial point to be taken into consideration in this case was to ensure
that the Thai government would maintain the controlling power over
the Chinese residing in Siam. What was especially important was to
cultivate the sense of being "Thai citizens" among the Chinese in Siam.
Unless such a condition was fully secured, it would be impossible to
have a treaty with China.

Prince Nares also paid attention to class differences among the
Chinese population. Based on his observation of the recent strike, Prince
Nares pointed out that those who were most likely to complain about
their hardships to the Chinese government through such channels as
commercial associations were poor small-scale shopkeepers. He therefore pointed out the importance of promoting cooperation between
rich and powerful Chinese merchants and government officials so that
their support for the Siamese government would be secured.

Like Prince Damrong, *Phraya* Wongsanupraphat also saw that
the second-generation Chinese born in Thailand were in the process of
becoming "Thai". Based on his analysis of the recent political movements and developments in China and East Asia, he emphasised the
importance of facilitating the process of transforming the Chinese into
Thai in two ways: through marriages with local Thai women; and by
promoting the progress and prosperity of the county. Unlike other
colonial states, he observed, the Chinese in Thailand were likely to get
married to local women, particularly women of lower class, and become
Thai. Thus it would be important to educate those women so that they
could exercise good influence over their Chinese husbands and children.

Similarly, promoting prosperity and progress was also important as this would make it attractive enough for Asiatic subjects to become Thai. In other words, unless those Chinese were securely internalised, it would be impossible for Siam to meet China's request for a treaty.

Concluding Remarks

Siam and China did not have any formal diplomatic relations for a century after 1854. However, this does not mean that there was no contact between the two countries. Indeed, as the examination above has revealed, negotiation between the two countries to seek formal diplomatic relations, be it tribute or a treaty, continued throughout the late nineteenth and early twentieth centuries. Despite the repeated efforts, mainly initiated from the Chinese side, however, re-establishment of formal diplomatic relations was never realised during the period examined here. Or more precisely, Siam, facing the dilemma of being not allowed to either reject or accept any formal relations with China, had to pursue a dilatory strategy against China throughout that time.

Behind the deep dilemma that Siam had to face in her relations with China were the close and longstanding relations with China cultivated under the Sino-centric tributary system and, particularly, the existence of a large number of Chinese in Siam formed from the period before the early nineteenth century. Sino-Siamese relationship thus formulated was not simply the relationship between the Siamese King and the Chinese Emperor, but was a multi-dimensional, multi-lateral complex embracing diverse channels and actors on different levels interacting with one another across the boundaries.

The "China factors" in Siam were so manifold and deeply embedded in the society that Siam had to avoid choosing either clear acceptance or rejection of the treaty (or tributary) relation with China when problems concerning the Chinese rose in Siam. Discussions on how to deal with China's requests for tribute or a treaty among the Siamese elites suggest that an ambiguous response was indeed inevitable as they saw either an acceptance or a refusal would pose serious problems in one way or another due to the fact that relations with China were not merely a matter of economic gain but concerned many other issues that were critical to the authority of the monarchy, the stability of society, and the question of "Thai" identity. In addition, such a problematic situation was reinforced by the fact that the historical concept of Chinese suzerainty continued to haunt the Siamese elite with reality, as it was repeatedly voiced and brought to mind by the Qing officials even in the beginning of the twentieth century.

The perspective of looking at Siamese diplomacy since the late nineteenth century as a shift from tributary relations to modern Western diplomacy by assuming a clear dichotomy between the two systems needs critical reconsideration. With "China factors" firmly embedded in Siamese society, the boundary between domestic and foreign and the principle of sovereign equality under the European state system had to remain as a theory in Siamese diplomacy toward China.

Notes

[1]   See, for example, Sarasin Viraphol, *Tribute and Profit: Sino-Siamese Trade, 1652–1853* (Cambridge [MA]: Council on East Asian Studies, Harvard University, 1977); Suebsaeng Promboon, "Sino-Siamese Tributary Relations, 1282–1853", PhD dissertation, University of Wisconsin, 1971; Jennifer W. Cushman, *Fields from the Sea: Chinese Junk Trade with Siam during the Late Eighteenth and Early Nineteenth Centuries* (Ithaca: Southeast Asia Program, Cornell University, 1993); and Masuda Erika, "The Last Siamese Tributary Missions to China, 1851–54 and the 'Rejected' Value of *Chim Kong*", in *Maritime China in Transition 1750–1850*, ed. Wang Gungwu and Ng Chin-keong (Wiesbaden: Harrassowitz Verlag, 2004), pp. 33–42.

[2]   The proclamation of King Mongkut on "Sending the royal embassies to promote friendship", published as one of the royal proclamations issued in the last year of his reign, is usually understood as the official declaration of Siamese intent to stop sending tribute to China [*Prachum prakat ratchakan thi 4* (Collected proclamations of the Fourth Reign) (Bangkok: Khurusapha, 1985), vol. 4, pp. 155–84]. However, the following observation seems to indicate further examination is necessary before concluding it to be King Mongkut's proclamation issued in 1868: this royal proclamation, both published and unpublished archival versions, is undated; and the expressions used to address the king and *Chaophraya* Rawiwong in the beginning of the text seem unusual if compared with their expressions used in other contemporary proclamations. The unpublished version is in the National Library of Thailand [abbreviated as NL], *Chotmaihet* [abbreviated as CMH] (administrative records), *Ratchakan thi si* [abbreviated as R.IV] (the Fourth Reign), *mai prakot pi cho.so* (documents without a year of issuance indicated), no. 154.

[3]   Names of the Chinese officials that appeared in those Thai administrative records were a phonetic transcription of their pronunciation written in the Thai alphabet. It is understood that they were expressed in one of those dialects, such as Cantonese and Fujianese, suggesting that the Chinese translators serving the Siamese court were speakers of those dialects rather than mandarin Chinese.

4   The description here is based on unpublished archival copies of the Thai translations of the correspondence preserved at the National Library of Thailand: NL.CMH. R.IV. *chunlasakkarat* (the Siamese lesser era) [abbreviated as C.S.] 1222, no. 201; and The National Archives of Thailand [NA], Ekkasan yep lem, chut Krasuang Kantangprathet [KT (L)] (Bound Volumes, Series for the Ministry of Foreign Affairs) 1: 38–40. *The Dynastic Chronicles of the Bangkok Era (Fourth Reign)* also recorded the incident by giving a slightly different account. See Thiphaakorawong, *Cawphrajaa, The Dynastic Chronicles, Bangkok Era, the Fourth Reign, B.E. 2394–2411 (A.D. 1851–1868)*, translated by Chadin (Kanjanavanit) Flood (Tokyo: The Centre for East Asian Cultural Studies, 1966), vol. II, pp. 280–5. For the Thai text, please see Thiphakorawong, *Chaophraya, Phraratchaphongsawadan krung rattanakosin ratchakan thi 4*, (reprint, Bangkok: Cremation volume for Anong Thiankharat, 1964), pp. 142–4.

5   "*Nai hang*" means head or manager or master or owner (*nai*) of a store (*hang*). As for *punkang*, I am grateful to Professors Bruce Lockhart, Geoff Wade, and Ch'en Kuo-tung for kindly pointing out to me that it would probably be *bengang* (*hang*), which is explained in, for instance, Cushman, *Fields from the Sea*, Chapter 2, particularly pp. 29–32; Viraphol, *Tribute and Profit*, Chapter VI; and Anthony Ch'en Kuo-tung, *The Insolvency of the Chinese Hong Merchants, 1760–1843*, Monograph Series, No. 45 (Nankang, Taipei: Institute of Economics Academia Sinica, 1990), Chapter 1. We also find the phrase "*pungkang chao tha*" to be one of the local high officials listed among the Canton officials who attended the send-off dinner for the Siamese envoys of 1852 leaving for Beijing. *Chao tha* in Thai means the chief or head of port affairs. See "Raya thang ratchathut thai pai krung pakking prathet chin" (Journey of the Royal Thai embassy to visit Beijing, China), *Thalaeng ngan prawattisat ekkasan borannakhadi* 8 (1974): 20.

6   NL. CMH. R.IV. C.S. 1222, no. 201.

7   NL. CMH. R.IV. C.S. 1222, no. 201.

8   NA. KT (L) 1: 38–43.

9   NA. KT (L) 1: 44–7. The Bowring Treaty of 1855, for instance, abolished the measurement duty prescribed by the Burney Treaty and introduced new import duties at the rate of "three per cent", "calculated upon the market value of the goods" as well as a new set of export duties. Rice for export was to be taxed at the rate of four bahts per koyan (*kwian*, meaning ox cart, approximately 2,000 litres). See John Bowring, *The Kingdom and People of Siam* (Kuala Lumpur: Oxford University Press, 1969), vol. 2, pp. 219–21, 224–5.

10   The fact that Chinese scholars who used the Chinese dynastic chronicles as their source did not mention this mission of 1862 may lead us to wonder if the dispatch was a result of the decision of Canton officials rather than by the imperial order. See, for example, Yu Dingbang, "1852–1890 nian de zhong tai jiaowang" (Contacts between China and Siam from 1852 to 1890), *Journal of Sun Yatsen University: Social Science Edition* 3 (1992): 58–65. I am grateful to Mr. Naoto Mochizuki who kindly brought this article to my attention.

11   NA. KT (L) 1: 47–57, 59–60.

12   NA. KT (L) 1: 59–60.

13   NA. KT (L) 1: 57–8. Promboon, "Sino-Siamese tributary relations", pp. 290–4,
     gives an account of the same consultation based on Thiphaakorawong, *The Dynastic
     Chronicles, Bangkok Era, the Fourth Reign.*

14   NA. KT (L) 1: 150–3. The letter was addressed to the following officials: (1)
     Sae (family name) Bun, allegedly the Fujian Governor in charge of taxes and
     military affairs; (2) *Sae* Eng, allegedly the Governor-General of Fujian and Chit-
     kang (*Zhejian*); (3) *Sae* Bian (?), allegedly the Vice-Governor of Fujian; (4) *Sae*
     Sim, allegedly in charge of ship affairs. Another document, on the other hand,
     mentioned the names of the two officials who visited Bangkok as *Bun Yok* and *Eng
     Kui.* See NA, Ratchakan thi ha [R.V.] (the Fifth Reign), Krasuang Kantangprathet
     [T.] (the Ministry of Foreign Affairs) 21/28 [hereafter abbreviated as NA. R.V.
     T.21/28]. Based on relevant Chinese sources, we may speculate these officials
     could be Wen Yu, Ying Gui, and Bian Baodi. See Yunnansheng lishi yianjiusuo,
     ed., *'Qing shi lu' yuenan miandian taiguo laowo shiliao zhaichao* (Extracts from
     Qing shi lu regarding Vietnam, Burma, Thailand, and Laos) (Kunming: Yunnan
     renmin chubanshe, 1985), pp. 933–4; and Qian Shifu, ed., *Qingdai zhiguan
     nianbiao* (Chronological Tables of Offices and Officials during the Qing Dynasty)
     (Beijing: Zhonghua shuju chuban, 1980), vol. 2, pp. 1480, 1711.

15   NA. KT (L) 1: 153–8. See also Yunnansheng lishi yanjiusuo, ed., *'Qing shi lu'*,
     pp. 933–4.

16   NA. KT (L) 1: 71–96.

17   NA. KT (L) 1: 96–9; 102–7.

18   NA. R.V. T. 21/28; and Kong chotmaihet haeng chat, Krom Sinlapakon,
     ed., *Samphanthaphap thai-chin* (Thai-Chinese Relationship) (Bangkok: Krom
     Sinlapakon, 1978), pp. 210–34.

19   According to the unpublished archival version, the number of the persons
     consulted was thirteen, whereas the published version listed opinions from
     fifteen with *Phraya* Phatsakorawong and *Phraya* Thammachanyanukunmontri as
     additional members. See NA. R.V. T.21/28 and Kong chotmaihet haeng chat,
     Samphanthaphap thai-chin, pp. 223–34. At the end of the archival version, there
     is an anonymous and undated statement that appears identical with the one cited
     as the opinion given by *Phraya* Phatsakorawong in the published version. This
     statement was an extensive argument on various points concerning the question of
     tribute and treaty; and it denied sending tribute even via Tianjin on the ground
     that tribute was an expression of being a vassal state of China and that Siam,
     having had concluded treaties with Western powers, should be regarded as a fully
     independent state.

20   While some found positive value in sending tribute as a proper practice for the
     monarchy, others saw it as an expedient not to provoke China for the time being.

21   In this regard, there was a proposal that if Siam still wished to send tribute to
     China, she should declare in the royal chronicles that the reason why she had

sent tribute to China was because she, never being a "vassal" [*muang khun* or *muang bannakan*] of China, wished to promote the supreme rank of King.

22 One also expressed a hope that other European powers would not allow the Chinese emperor to "force" Siam into a treaty with China.

23 Suparat Lertpanichkul, "Samakhom lap ang-yi nai prathet thai pho.so. 2367–2453" (Triad societies in Thailand 1824–1910), MA thesis, Chulalongkorn University, 1981, pp. 155–95. While it was pointed out that refusing tribute would cause difficulties in administering the Chinese in Siam, there was an opinion that the past experiences of uprisings in Chachoengsao and Nakhon Chaisi could be evidence to suggest Chinese uprisings would occur even if Siam sent tribute to China. Although most agreed that extraterritoriality would make it difficult for the Siamese government to govern the Chinese in Siam, there also was an opinion that the Chinese consulate, if established in Siam, would find it troublesome to administer the Chinese subjects in Siam based on the observation that recent turmoil in China would suggest the Chinese would never wish to uphold one's *chat* ("nation").

24 NA. KT (L) 1: 109–10.

25 NA. KT (L) 1: 111–4.

26 NA. KT (L) 1: 124–6.

27 Ngo Seng Siang might be the same person as Ngo Seng Chiang or Ngao Siang Chiang who appeared in previous correspondence with Canton officials.

28 NA. KT (L) 1: 162–7. Ngo's proposal this time was that Siam would send tribute via Canton first and then the Governor-General of Canton and Kwangsai would forward the Siamese wish to take the Tianjin route to the Emperor in Beijing.

29 NA. KT (L) 1: 169–72.

30 NA. R.V. T.21/28.

31 NA. KT (L) 1: 182–4. Here Ngo's name is expressed as Ngo Siang Chiang.

32 NA. KT (L) 1: 176–7.

33 NA. KT (L) 1: 185–95.

34 NA. KT (L) 1: 193–211.

35 NA. KT (L) 1: 214–6.

36 The following explanation about the meeting is based on NA, Krasuang Kantangprathet [KT] (the Ministry of Foreign Affairs) 24/1. The record of the meeting in Thai is much more detailed than that given in English.

37 The details of the mission based on the Chinese sources were revealed in a series of article by Aoyama Harutoshi: "Shincho seifu ni yoru 'nanyo' chosadan haken (1886–88nen) no haikei: Shinmatsu 'nanyo' ryoji setchi mondai tono kanrende" (The background of sending a Chinese mission of inquiry on the overseas Chinese in 'Nanyang' (Southwest [*sic*] Asia and Australia) by the Qing Government [1886–88]), *Bunkenkai kiyo: The Journal of the Graduate School of Humanities, Aichigakuin University*, no. 13 (2002): 8–28; "Shincho seifu ni yoru 'nanyo' chosa (1886–88nen): Kajin hogo no jisshi to ryoji setchi no yobi chosa" (The Inquiry on 'Nanyang' (Southeast Asia and Australia) by the Qing Government

[1886–88]), *Bunkenkai kiyo: The Journal of the Graduate School of Humanities, Aichigakuin University*, no. 14 (2003): 1–24; "Shincho seifu ni yoru 'nanyo' kajin no hogo to seiyo shokoku tono masatsu: 1886nen no 'nanyo' chosadan no haken kosho wo chushin ni" (Protection of Nanyang Chinese by Qing Government and friction between China and Western countries), *Higashi Ajia Kindaishi* (*Modern East Asian History*) 6 (2003): 52–69. Some difference is indicated between the Chinese records cited by Aoyama and the Thai records, which deserves further examination.

38   NA. KT (L) 1: 128–33, 218–41.

39   The following discussion of Yang's visit is based on the following files from the National Archives of Thailand: NA. R.V. T.21/13; and NA. R.V. Krasuang Nakhonban [N.] (the Ministry of the Capital) 8.1/464.

40   For instance, it was reported that Sun Yat-sen visited Siam in June 1903 and from late November to early December 1908 [NA. R.V. T.21/10].

41   Chariyavan Apornratana, "Panha khong ratthaban thai nai ratchasamai phrabat somdet phra chunlachomklaochaoyuhua thi kieo kap khon esia nai bangkhap angkrit lae farangset" (The problems of Thai Government concerning the Asian British and the Asian French subjects during the reign of King Rama V), MA thesis, Chulalongkorn University, 1982; Koizumi Junko, "Tai ni okeru kokka kaikaku to minshu" (State reform and the people in Thailand), in *Minzoku to Kokka: Jikaku to Teiko* [Nations and the State: Awakening and Resistance], Rekishigaku Kenkyukai, ed. (Tokyo: University of Tokyo Press, 1995), pp. 327–51; Iijima Akiko, "Tai ni okeru ryojisaibanken wo megutte" (On the consular jurisdiction in Thailand — A Preliminary Note), *Southeast Asian Studies* 14, no. 1 (1976): 71–98.

42   Between 1906 and 1911, Yang was Vice-President of the Board of Agriculture, Industry and Commerce (nong gong shang bu shi lang). See Qian, ed., *Qingdai zhiguan nianbiao*, vol. 4, pp. 3059–64, 3068–9, 3076–78, 3112, 3243.

43   Telegram from Prince Charoon, 3 Nov. 1907 [NA. R.V. T.21/13].

44   Telegram from Prince Charoon, 3 Nov. 1907 [NA. R.V. T.21/13].

45   Report of the cabinet meeting, 25 Nov. 1907 [NA. R.V. T.21/13].

46   For instance, arriving on cruisers rendered the Chinese mission a tone of gunboat diplomacy; and Siam responded to it by sending a gunboat of the Navy to meet the mission at the bar off the mouth of the Chaophraya River. King Chulalongkorn also mentioned in his instruction to Prince Boriphatsukhumphan in charge of the Royal Navy that the Navy should receive the mission fully according to the Western (*farang*) customs. Seeing the Chinese boats equipped with the latest facilities from the West, on the other hand, the Siamese officials read it as an effort to awaken the Chinese community in Bangkok by showing them the progress of China. See King Chulalongkorn to Prince Boriphatsukhumphan, 25 Nov. 1907; Prince Boriphatsukhumphan to King Chulalongkorn, 26 Nov. 1907; Prince Devawongse to Prince Sommot-amonphan, 27 Nov. 1907; *Phra* Montri-photchanakit to Prince Devawongse, 28 Nov. 1907; Prince Devawongse

to Strobel, 29 Nov. 1907; *Phra* Montri-photchanakit to Prince Devawongse, 2 Dec. 1907 [NA. R.V. T.21/13].

47   Prince Devawongse to Prince Sommot-amonphan, 27 Nov. 1907; *Phra* Montri-photchanakit to Devawongse, 28 Nov. 1907; Prince Devawongse to Strobel, 29 Nov. 1907; *Phra* Montri-photchanakit to Prince Devawongse, 2 Dec. 1907 [NA. R.V. T.21/13].

48   Prince Naret to King Chulalongkorn, 29 Nov. 1907; *Phra* Montri-photchanakit to Prince Devawongse, 2 Dec. 1907 [NA. R.V. T.21/13]. See also NA. R.V. N. 8.1/464.

49   Prince Devawongse to Prince Sommot-amonphan, 27 Nov. 1907; *Phra* Montri-photchanakit to Prince Devawongse, 28 Nov. 1907; Prince Devawongse to Strobel, 29 Nov. 1907; *Phra* Montri-photchanakit to Prince Devawongse, 2 Dec. 1907 [NA. R.V. T.21/13].

50   His Majesty's telegram to Prince Charoon, 30 Nov. 1907 [NA.R.V. T.21/13].

51   Prince Charoon's letter to His Majesty, 1 Dec. 1907 [NA. R.V. T.21/13].

52   Report of the cabinet meeting, 5 Dec. 1907 [NA. R.V. T.21/13]. See also NA. R.V. N.1.1/260. What was proposed in the meeting was the abolishment of *Krom Tha Sai* (the Department of Left Port) and the transfer of administration of the Chinese in Bangkok from the Ministry of Foreign Affairs to the Ministry of the Capital. *Krom Tha Sai* used to be one of the administrative units that had constituted *Krom Tha* (the Department of Port) and was in charge of the maritime trade with China and the administration of the Chinese in Siam. *Phraya* Chodukratchasetthi, one of the major figures in the correspondences with China mentioned above, was the head of the *Krom Tha Sai*. Through the administrative reforms in the late nineteenth century, it came to be placed under the Ministry of Foreign Affairs. However, when the administration of the Chinese became an issue, its existing affiliation with the Ministry of Foreign Affairs came to be questioned for such an arrangement would appear that they were treating the Chinese as foreigners [NA. R.V. N.1.1/260].

53   See, for example, NA. R.V. N.1.1/260; NA. R.V. N.8.7/11; NA. R.V. N.8.7/27; NA. R.V. N.8.7/32; NA. R.V. N.8.7/33.

54   NA. R.V. N.20/27.

55   Prince Charoon to Prince Devawongse, 17 April 1908 [NA. R.V. T.8/4].

56   Prince Charoon to Prince Devawongse, 9 May 1908; Westengard to Prince Devawongse, 15 May 1908; Prince Devawongse to Westengard, 9 June 1908; Memorandum by Westengard, 12 June 1908; Prince Devawongse to Prince Charoon, June 1908 (undated draft) [NA. R.V. T.8/4].

57   King Chulalongkorn to Prince Charoon, 16 June 1908 [NA. R.V. T.8/4].

58   NA. R.VI.N. 25/2. In 1909, the Siamese government, following the revision of the conditions of taxation on the Asiatic subjects prescribed by the treaties with France and Britain, abolished the triennial *phukpi* tax on the Chinese and decided to apply the newly introduced annual capitation tax on the Siamese to the Chinese as well. When this was introduced to Bangkok in 1910, the Chinese protested

severely, since this change meant a sharp increase in the amount of tax on them. See Koizumi, "Tai ni okeru kokka kaikaku to minshu", pp. 341–4; and Sonsak Shusawat, "Phukpi: Kanchatkep ngoen kharaeng thaen kanken raeng-ngan chak khon chin nai samai rattanakosin" (Pookpee: The poll tax collection from the Chinese during Bangkok period), MA thesis, Chulalongkorn University, 1981. Involvement of the Chamber of Commerce in Shantou was strongly suspected in the incident.

59 The following views are based on NA. R.V. T.6, file no. 2, cited in Polagool Angkinuntana, "Botbat chao chin nai prathet thai nai ratchasamai phrabat somdet phra chunlachomklaochaoyuhua" (The Chinese Movement in the Reign of King Rama V), MA thesis, Witthayalai Wichakansuksa, 1971, Appendix *kho khai*.

Chapter 3

Operated by World Views and Interfaced by World Orders: Traditional and Modern Sino-Vietnamese Relations

Alexander L. Vuving

Introduction

How do states interact? What guides the states' foreign policy and shapes international relations? These questions often involve a discussion of world order, in which the world order is variably defined as the framework for action, the patterns of activities, or the structures of relations, between states.[1] The concept of world order is used to denote the framework that shapes international relations and interaction.

It is widely accepted that modern international relations are based on Westphalian principles such as sovereignty of and equality between states. In the modern international system states are thought to be sovereign equals and act in accordance with these principles. Thus, the modern international system is also referred to as the "Westphalian system". As the Westphalian order first emerged in late medieval Europe, other world regions are supposed to have lived under their own distinct world orders in the pre-modern times. For decades, the "tribute system" or the "Chinese world order" has been regarded as the framework of traditional East Asian international relations. Unlike the Westphalian system, which is characterised by equality between states, the Chinese world order is a hierarchical system in which China is the suzerain, the world centre, and the superior state, while other states are its vassals, tributaries, and subordinates. These two beliefs constitute the conventional wisdom that the tribute system had been the traditional world order in East Asia and this Chinese world order was replaced by the Westphalian system in the modern times.

Sino-Vietnamese relations offer an ideal site to witness both world orders. Having been the world centre in the tribute system, China in the modern era is a fierce supporter of the Westphalian principles. A central element in the People's Republic of China's doctrine on international relations is the Five Principles of Peaceful Coexistence, which are essentially the entrenchment of the Westphalian principles of sovereignty, equality, and non-interference. Pre-colonial Vietnam is seen as a loyal member of the tribute system, whereas post-World War II Vietnam is a vigorous fighter for sovereignty, self-determination, non-intervention, and equality between nations. It is widely believed that the Westphalian system is, and before it, the tributary system was, the framework that guides and shapes relations between China and Vietnam.

This chapter challenges these conventional beliefs. Examining Sino-Vietnamese relations during the pre-colonial and the post-World War II periods, the chapter finds that it is not the world orders that guided the actions and formed the ties between China and Vietnam. In fact, there is a wide gap between the normative frame and the actual nature of the Sino-Vietnamese relationship. The reason for this discrepancy is the fact that ruling elites in the two countries pursued conflicting visions of the world, which utilised or ignored, and promoted or violated, the normative world order in ways that suited their own ambitions. The normative world orders turn out to be myths that functioned as interface — sometimes user-friendly, sometimes not — in the communications between the two international actors. The real operating systems — to use the computer metaphor again — that guide and shape their relations are not the shared world order but the actors' different world views.

The chapter begins by critiquing the "Chinese world order" paradigm, which is to date the most influential approach to traditional East Asian international relations. I argue that this paradigm provides a distorted picture of international relations in pre-modern East Asia. Central to this paradigm is the concept of the "Chinese world order" elaborated by John King Fairbank. This concept collapses the normative, strategic, and actual levels of international relations into one. The conflation of these ontologically different levels is a major reason for the paradigm's failure. Learning from the failure of Fairbank's model, I propose instead a three-way distinction between world order, world view, and world pattern, which refer to the normative, strategic, and actual levels of world configuration. This three-way distinction will serve as the conceptual basis for the subsequent examination of traditional and modern Sino-Vietnamese relations.

World Order and the "Chinese World Order"

The "Chinese world order" paradigm is hitherto the most influential approach to traditional international relations in East Asia. A product of Western study of Chinese foreign affairs, this paradigm is part of the larger project of constructing China by Westerners. Western authors from the Jesuits in the seventeenth century to Voltaire in the eighteenth century and Max Weber in the twentieth century helped to construct a Chinese other that was Confucian in essence.[2] Focused on the Sino-Western encounter and based on the belief that traditional Chinese thought and government were deeply influenced by Confucianism, modern authors in both China and the West have advanced two theses about the Chinese way of war and diplomacy. These were succinctly formulated by Fairbank as the "disesteem of violence" and the "tribute system".[3] These two components constitute the "Chinese world order" paradigm.

The popularity of the notion of a Chinese disesteem of violence is probably rooted in the symbolic power of the Great Wall of China and the belief that Sun Tzu's *Art of War* exerted heavy influence on Chinese strategic thought and practice. Sun Tzu is famous for sayings such as "The best policy is to attack the enemy's mind, the worst is to attack the enemy's forts." Thus, authorities in military history from Basil Liddell Hart to John Keegan readily adopted this notion.[4] The association of the Chinese world order with the tributary system can be explained by the fact that for more than three centuries, European merchants who sought to trade with China were constrained by the Ming and Qing courts to agree on tribute as a condition of trade and diplomacy. From a concept of the Qing tributary system, it then became a framework for the Western understanding of the timeless Chinese foreign policy.[5] By the late 1960s it became one of the dominant schools of thought in the study of Chinese foreign policy — traditional and modern alike — with Fairbank's "tribute system" being its master concept.[6]

The core assumptions of the "Chinese world order" paradigm can be stated as follows:

1. China lies at the centre of a basically stable world.
2. The stability is to be achieved not by means of a balance of power but by the recognition of a hierarchical order reflecting China's superiority.
3. This is because China seeks status rather than territories or domination. In return, China's neighbours are willing to accept its pre-eminent position in exchange for China's non-intervention and for trade privileges.
4. The relationship between China and the other states is regulated by the "tribute system", which is a set of rituals such as tribute-paying, investiture, kowtow, etc. performed to express China's supremacy and the other states' acknowledgment of this supremacy.

The Chinese world order is assumed to have prevailed for most of imperial China's history, from the Qin to the Qing dynasties (221 BC–1911 AD). Yet a closer look at the power configurations of the East Asian world reveals that the Pax Sinica, including the Mongol hegemony, existed only less than a half of the whole period. During this 2132-year period, the East Asian world was unipolar in 993 years, while in 1138 years, it saw two or more major powers contesting for dominance.[7]

The "Chinese world order" paradigm is based on Fairbank's description of China's foreign relations and especially his model of the "tribute system". These concepts — the Chinese world order and the tribute system — found their clearest statements in Fairbank's introduction to the volume *The Chinese World Order*, published in 1968.[8] It is worth distinguishing between Fairbank's richer description of the Chinese world order and his distilled model of the tribute system. While Fairbank's description of the Chinese world order mixes up elements of the shared norms and principles of East Asian international relations, the Chinese view of world order, and the actual patterns of China's foreign relations, his model of the tribute system describes the ideal Chinese outlook on the world rather than the actual patterns of China's foreign relations. As Fairbank himself recognises, "The Chinese world order was a unified concept only at the Chinese end and on the normative level, as an ideal pattern."[9] In fact, Fairbank's model does not match the evidence of most chapters in the same volume.

An apparent bias of the model is its Sinocentrism. It adopts the view of the Chinese court at the expense of other actors' perspectives. Most protagonists in the East Asian world shared with the Chinese the notion of a universal ruler, who obtained his mandate from heaven, their supreme god. But it was the Chinese who "acquired from the nomads north of them the notions of star-worship that made Heaven the supreme god".[10] As recorded by Sima Qian in the *Shi Ji*, the sovereign of the Xiongnu called himself at one time "set up by Heaven", while at another time represented himself as "born of Heaven and Earth and ordained by the Sun and Moon".[11] The Turkish Heaven-God (*tengri*) not only made the Turkish people independent but also enthroned their ruler, the Khaghan.[12] As David Farquhar has pointed out in the same Fairbank volume, the Manchus maintained their own view of nation and ruler and they considered the Chinese country and emperor on an equal footing with their own.[13] Under Japan's *ritsuryo* system, Japan alone was the centre of its world order, and the Tang were regarded as "barbarians".[14] In late tenth-century Korea, Koryo king Kwangjong styled himself "emperor" (*hwangje*) and named his capital Kaegyong "imperial city" (*hwangdo*). By these acts, he declared his country to be an independent "empire" of its own.[15]

Another limitation of the tribute system lies in the fact that it covers only one portion of China's foreign relations. For example, intermarriage played an important role in Chinese foreign relations, especially in the Han, Sui and Tang periods and in China's relations with Inner Asia. Tang, Song, and Qing engaged in treaties with other powers. The blood-oath was another common practice in Chinese foreign relations.[16] Because the model is biased toward trade and diplomatic ceremonies, it ignores war as an important practice of Chinese foreign relations. In two millennia of imperial China, times of war outweigh times of peace. During the Ming dynasty, which is one of the most peaceful periods in Chinese history, 308 large-scale external wars, or 1.12 wars per year on average, were recorded.[17]

The limitations of the "tribute system" model and, more generally, the "Chinese world order" paradigm are rooted in the conflation of different levels of world configuration. At the normative level, world configuration consists of the principles of international relations and norms of international conduct that are shared by international actors. World configuration at this level can be properly called world order. World order denotes the normative structure that is to guide the conduct of actors in international relations and frames their relationships.

At the strategic level, there are the actors' visions of the world. World configuration at this level is the structure of the world as seen through the perspective of an actor. Such a vision includes typically the actor's interpretation of world order and her conception of the division and dynamics of the world. These visions are separate from the actual patterns of the world, which include particularly the patterns of actual interaction and practices between actors in world affairs. Usually, the visions reflect the desired state of world affairs while the patterns feature the actual state.

In order to avoid confusion, I call these normative, strategic, and actual levels of international relations respectively "world order", "world view" and "world pattern". These levels refer to three realms that are ontologically distinct though operationally interrelated. World order refers to the realm of norms, world view to the realm of strategy, and world pattern to the realm of interaction. World order is shared by the minds of the actors. Each actor's mind is home to a world view. World patterns are located between the actors, in the field of their interaction. The following study of Sino-Vietnamese relations will be based on these distinctions.

Traditional Sino-Vietnamese Relations

In the first decade of the tenth century, the collapse of the Tang dynasty ushered into a period of disunity in the Chinese world. Within a few decades, Vietnam regained its autonomy after more than ten centuries under Chinese rule. Except for a 20-year interlude under Ming rule (1407–28), Vietnam was an independent kingdom from the tenth century until the late nineteenth century, when the country was conquered by the French. In this study, I confine my discussion of traditional Sino-Vietnamese relations to this period, which will be called, for the sake of simplicity, the Dai Viet era, after the name of the Vietnamese state during most of this period.

The emergence of a literate and state-building, Vietnamese-speaking society was a result of the southward expansion of Chinese empire and civilisation. After ten centuries under Chinese rule, the Vietnamese were well versed in the Chinese discourse of world order. An independent kingdom from the tenth century on, Vietnam shared with China the same vocabulary of world order and foreign relations. The two also shared the same set of fundamental principles and norms of inter-national relations. Thus, as much as modern nations invoke international law and the U.N. Charter, pre-colonial Vietnam cited precedents from Chinese history and invoked Chinese classical texts both in its diplomatic communications with China and in its domestic discussion on foreign relations.

The Vietnamese adopted the Chinese concepts of world affairs and the values associated with them. For the Chinese as well as the Vietnamese, "all under heaven" (Chinese: *tianxia*, Vietnamese: *thien ha*), or the world, was divided into domains (Chinese: *guo, bang*, Vietnamese: *quoc, bang*), whose relationships to each other were defined in hierarchical terms. This order was one of the central domain and its peripheries, of the superior state and its subordinates, of the suzerain and his vassals. In this world order the centre (*zhong*) represented civilisation (*hua, wenxian*) and the peripheries (*fen*) barbarism (*yi*). The centre was not a closed circle, but the middle of a vivid, pulsating, stream that was unfolding outward. In the peripheries there were contrasts and contradictions; and it was the centre that was to transform the peripheries into harmony.[18] This world order was based on the notion of a universal ruler who obtained his mandate to rule all under heaven from heaven himself, who was the supreme authority. This concept of universal rulership was probably invented by the nomads of Inner Asia, who spread it to sedentary people in South and East Asia.[19]

China and Vietnam both subscribed to these principles, but they interpreted them differently. As a result, despite sharing the same principles of world order, the two international actors held fundamentally different world visions. In the Chinese vision, China was the central state and all other states were China's vassals. Accordingly, the Chinese called themselves the "splendid" (*hua*) people and their country the "central kingdom" (*zhongguo*); they called the non-Chinese the "barbarians" (*yi*) and their countries "peripheral" (*fen*) or "subordinate" (*shu*) domains. In other words, China was the domain of civility and outside China the domain of barbarity. From the Chinese perspective, Vietnam, being non-Chinese, was barbarian and belonged to the world's peripheries. However, from the Vietnamese perspective, Vietnam also belonged to the world's centre. The Vietnamese called themselves the "metropolitan" (*kinh*) people and regarded their country a "domain of manifest civility" (*van hien chi bang*).[20] For example, the Vietnamese court employed the hallowed term *trung quoc* (central state), which was identical with the Chinese term *zhongquo*, to refer Vietnam.[21]

The Vietnamese world vision contradicted the Chinese world view at a crucial point.[22] In the Chinese view, the Chinese emperor was *the* universal ruler. He alone ruled the entire world in heaven's name, and "nobody else could claim the title of emperor".[23] The Vietnamese, however, asserted that the world was naturally divided into north and south and each domain was ruled by its own emperor. According to the Vietnamese view, the Vietnamese emperor was the legitimate ruler of the south, while the Chinese emperor the legitimate ruler of the north.[24]

There was a subtle but important change over time in the Vietnamese court's world view during the ten centuries of Dai Viet. Ly-Tran Vietnam perceived itself as the centre *of* the south, whereas Le-Nguyen Vietnam perceived itself as centre *in* the south. In the Ly-Tran era (eleventh to fifteenth centuries) the emphasis was on the division of the world into two separate hemispheres — the north and the south. The south was the domain of the southern emperor or the Vietnamese king, and the north the domain of the northern emperor or the Chinese ruler. In the Le-Nguyen era (fifteenth to nineteenth centuries), the emphasis was on the division of the world into two different zones — one of civility and one of barbarity. In the Le-Nguyen view, both Vietnam and China belonged to the zone of civility.[25]

This difference was reflected in the ways the Vietnamese court dealt with China and built the Vietnamese state. The Ly dynasty (1010–1225) maintained at times an offensive posture toward China. In the late eleventh century, Ly Vietnam launched preemptive strikes and invaded southern China. But in the fifteenth century, Le Vietnam supplied Ming Chinese troops with food and carriages and sent them unharmed back to China after having defeated them in Vietnam. Le-Nguyen Vietnam (1428–1885) never harboured the idea of invading China. The only exception during this later period was King Quang Trung (Nguyen Hue) of the Tay Son dynasty, who supported pirates in the Tonkin Gulf raiding the Chinese coasts. But Quang Trung came from Dang Trong (Southern Vietnam, which considered itself a separate domain from the North) and laid emphasis on the territorial separateness rather than the cultural unity between China and Vietnam. The Tay Son state-building resembled that of the farther Ly and Tran dynasties more than that of the nearer Le and Nguyen dynasties, which were the Tay Son's predecessor and successor. Unlike the Le and the Nguyen, which saw in China the only source of culture, the Ly, the Tran, and the Tay Son were open to cultural influences from both the Chinese and the Southeast Asian worlds. Ly-Tran court culture bore the mark of both Chinese and Cham influences.[26]

Vietnam shared with China the basic norms of foreign relations. These included the principle of hierarchy between states and the practices that were to regulate their relationship. These practices included tribute-paying, investiture, and kowtow, but also punitive war. Besides their material functions (tribute was a form of trade, while war was a means of conquest), these practices were to express the lord-vassal relationship between rulers. Despite its infrequency, war played a crucial role in hierarchical international relations. War is the time when "the stakes of the parties involved are most intensively expressed".[27] War was the measuring of relative power, and in its aftermath it functioned as the reminder of it. The Chinese cited their past defeats by the Vietnamese to warn themselves about the possible fatal consequences of intervention in Vietnam. The Qing court argued against an expedition to punish Vietnam in 1789 by stating that "the history of past dynasties has demonstrated that Chinese occupation of that country has never lasted for more than one or two decades".[28] On their part, the Vietnamese cited their past victories over the Chinese to bolster their confidence in preparation for possible Chinese attacks. Peace in traditional Sino-Vietnamese relations was the aftermath of war rather than the harmony of things. It was the institutionalisation of the memories of war rather than the institutionalisation of imperial virtue. War and its aftermath embodied the clash and compromise of the competing world views of Vietnam and China.

Toward its non-Chinese neighbours, Vietnam asserted its lordship and imposed their vassalage. It expected and forced them to pay tribute to it or waged war to punish the intransigent.[29] In its relations with China, however, the Vietnamese conduct was "*trong de ngoai vuong*" (literally: inside as emperor, outside as king). This posture is illustrated by the fact that the first act of a Vietnamese ruler was to proclaim himself "emperor", while his second act was to seek investiture as "king" from the Chinese ruler. Also, the Vietnamese strategy toward China was a combination of military resistance and diplomatic deference. Military resistance and "inside as emperor" reflected the Vietnamese view of the world that emphasised Vietnam's separation from and parity with China. But diplomatic deference and "outside as king" reflected the Chinese view that stressed China's superiority.

The nature and practices of Sino-Vietnamese relations were interpreted by the Chinese and the Vietnamese in conflicting ways. As Brantly Womack notes, the normalcy of traditional Sino-Vietnamese relations established during the Ming and Qing dynasties (fifteenth to

nineteenth centuries) was between "unequal empires", with "China dwelling on the 'unequal' and Vietnam emphasising 'empires'".[30] While the
Chinese annals conveniently considered the Vietnamese court's tribute-
paying, investiture, kowtow, etc. as expressions of China's superiority
and Vietnam's vassalage, the Vietnamese literature emphasised Vietnam's
successes in breaking or avoiding the norms imposed by the Chinese to
manifest the hierarchical nature of their relations. A major symbolic act
that expresses Vietnam's subordination to China is the performance of
kowtow by the Vietnamese king when receiving the edicts sent by the
Chinese emperor. Refusal to kneel and touch the forehead to the ground
when receiving Chinese imperial edicts may provoke China to wage
a punitive war. Though aware of this consequence, many Vietnamese
rulers nevertheless refused to comply. The Vietnamese kings also declined
China's request that they come to the Chinese capital in person. These
refusals during the second half of the thirteenth century created serious
crises in relations between Tran Vietnam and Yuan China.[31] China
traditionally required Vietnamese kings who had opposed the Chinese
to visit the Chinese emperor to beg for pardon. However, Vietnamese
rulers usually declined such an invitation, sending in their stead a golden
statue of a man. The only time when a Vietnamese king accepted the
invitation and visited the Chinese emperor was in 1790. However,
Vietnamese records invariably reported that the king himself did not
go to China but he sent his double instead.[32]

The hierarchical nature of the bilateral relationship also found its
expression in the sitting order at diplomatic receptions. The Chinese
required that the Vietnamese king face north and the Chinese envoy
face south when the king received the envoy. The north-south direction
was to symbolise Vietnam's subordinate status. The Vietnamese court
suggested, however, that they sit along the east-west axis, thus implying
equality. According to Vietnamese records, the east-west sitting order
prevailed with only one exception.[33]

War between the two courts was also a practice of this relationship,
and the Vietnamese successful resistance to Chinese invasions was seen
in Vietnam as a sign of the prevalence of the Vietnamese world order. In
a sense, history-writing and -telling was also a practice of international
relations. Thus, the Chinese historical records, upon which much of our
narratives on East Asian past are based, also played a role in China's
foreign relations. They reflected Chinese interests and asserted the world
order as viewed from the Chinese capital. The same can be said of the
Vietnamese historical records.[34]

From a third person's perspective, the practices of relations between China and Vietnam neither expressed Chinese supremacy, nor did they indicate some equality between Vietnam and China. Rather, they embodied the encounter and interplay of the two countries' conflicting worldviews, and reflected the actual balance of power between them. Whether Vietnam asserted its own view of world order or it accepted the Chinese one was not so much a matter of domestic vs. international, of ideal vs. pragmatic, or of military vs. diplomacy, but a matter of circumstances, of relative capabilities, and of expediency.

Modern Sino-Vietnamese Relations

During the nineteenth and twentieth centuries, Western powers became the master of the East Asian world. A consequence of this process was that the traditional East Asian world order, which was Chinese in origin, was replaced by the Westphalian system, which was the Western framework of international relations. In the post-World War II era, both China and Vietnam were re-established under the Westphalian framework of international relations.[35] The Westphalian system is constituted by a set of principles. Central among them are the principle of the sovereignty of states and the fundamental right of national self-determination, the principle of equality between states, and the principle of non-intervention of one state in the internal affairs of another state.

The ideas and values associated with the Westphalian order were both imposed on the Asians and adopted by them. At the turn of the nineteenth to the twentieth century, both Chinese and Vietnamese societies underwent a transformation of their self-perception. Instead of thinking the world in terms of a hierarchy of domains, they began to perceive it as a society of equal nations. Although their highest aspiration might still be to become a domain of manifest civility and the world's centre, but their stated ambition was to become a sovereign nation and an equal member of the international society. The concept of a nation-state has replaced that of a domain of civility in Chinese and Vietnamese self-definition; and nationalism replaced culturalism as the primary form of expression in Chinese and Vietnamese foreign affairs.[36] The highest aspiration of Chinese nationalism was China's equality with the Western powers; its trauma was the "unequal treaties" that West powers forced upon the Chinese empire during the last three centuries. The highest aspiration of Vietnamese nationalism was Vietnam's independence from foreign powers; its trauma was the country's conquest and colonisation by the French.

The struggle of the Chinese and Vietnamese people for sovereignty and independence and to become an equal member of the international community also brought the Communists to power. From their respective inception, the Chinese Communist Party and the Vietnam Communist Party subscribed to the framework of Marxist-Leninist analysis of the world. They identified imperialism as their fundamental enemy and a united front of anti-imperialist forces was the central strategy in their fight against imperialism. Imperialism was defined as a relationship of domination and exploitation, and the West was the embodiment of imperialism in the contemporary era. It is on the basis of an analysis of imperialism that communist China and communist Vietnam developed their world views.

The Vietnamese Communist world view during the Cold War was the theory of "two camps, four contradictions, and three revolutionary forces (or currents)", which they adopted from the Soviet Union. This theory claimed that the world was divided into a socialist and democratic camp, led by the Soviet Union, and a capitalist and imperialist camp, headed by the United States. Underlying the dynamics of the world were four contradictions: between the socialist countries and the capitalist system, between the bourgeoisie and the proletariat, between imperialism and colonial and dependent states, and among imperialist countries themselves. The world trends were marked by three world revolutionary forces or currents, which were identified as the world socialist system, the communist and working-class movement in the capitalist countries, and the national liberation movement. In this vision of the world, Vietnam saw itself as the "outpost of socialism in Southeast Asia" and the "spearhead of the world national liberation movement".[37]

While the Vietnamese world view remained relatively consistent throughout the Cold War, the communist Chinese view of the world underwent a number of major transformations. As early as 1946, Mao Zedong put forward the view that the world consisted of three zones: the United States and its sphere of influence, the Soviet Union and its sphere of influence, and an intermediate area that included China and belonged to neither power's sphere. He predicted that the struggle against imperialism and for democracy would be waged in the third zone. The three-zone theory thus suggested that once the Communists assumed power in all China, the new state would play a very important role in world affairs while pursuing a foreign policy independent from the world powers. As Mark Mancall has noted, "On the one hand, it prefigured the concept of a First, a Second, and a Third World; on the other, the theory reflected China's position in the world and remained a major point of departure for all Chinese foreign policy thinking down to the present."[38]

In the early days of the People's Republic, circumstances required that the new state seek an alliance with the Soviet Union. This gave rise to the policy of "leaning to one side", the idea that an alliance with the Soviet is the mainstay of China's foreign policy. At the same time, as the three-zone theory suggested, China did not seek membership in the Soviet bloc, though it recognised Soviet leadership in the anti-imperialist camp. Also, China began to regard itself and not the Soviet Union as the third zone's natural leader. "Leaning to one side" was thus an appropriate policy for the reemerging state to adopt in a specific circumstance in the three-zone world.[39] Indeed, the three-zone theory foresaw the collapse of the Sino-Soviet alliance and the PRC's rapprochement with the United States.

In the early to mid-1960s, with the Soviet Union now becoming China's enemy, China invented a new world view, which divided the world into two parts: "world cities" and "world countryside". In this vision, China was clearly the model and natural leader of the world countryside, which consisted of the developing countries in Asia, Africa, and Latin America. As an industrialised country, the Soviet Union was grouped together with the United States and other advanced industrial nations in the West. The world trend, or "world revolution", as Lin Biao proclaimed, was taking the form of "surrounding the cities from the countryside".[40]

The third Chinese world view during the Cold War period was the "three worlds" theory. Announced by Deng Xiaoping in 1974, it marked the return of Chinese foreign policy to pragmatism. The theory was a summary of new strategic changes China had made since the late 1960s. It categorised the two superpowers — the United States and the Soviet Union — as the "first world", grouped the industrial nations in the West and Eastern Europe into the "second world", and classified the developing countries as the "third world". China would take the leadership role in the third world, which would join forces with the second world in opposition to the superpowers, particularly the Soviet Union.[41] The Three Worlds Theory provided guidance for a foreign policy that was aimed at forming the largest possible international front against the Soviet Union. In this vision of the world and contrary to the theory of "world countryside surrounding world cities", an alliance of China with the United States against the Soviet Union and closer cooperation with other advanced industrial countries in the West were again possible. The Three Worlds Theory thus anticipated the reestablishment of diplomatic relations between China and the United States and the policy of "reform and opening up", which was initiated in late 1978.

As the Cold War approached its end, China began to reassess the world situation. In the mid- to late 1980s, Huan Xiang, Deng Xiaoping's national security adviser, recognised that the old world order had already disintegrated and the new world order was now taking shape, giving rise to a new, multipolar, world.[42] In the post-Cold War era, China became a lead advocate of multipolarity. Multipolarism also helps to formulate the new Chinese ambition: to become a pole of the future multipolar world.

Multipolarism also features prominently in post-Cold War Vietnamese vision of the world. Vietnam after the Cold War was torn by two different world views. These two world views provide the basis for two competing grand strategies, which I call anti-imperialism and integration. Anti-imperialism is based on the orthodox two-camp theory, now in an updated form that stresses the fundamental contradiction between socialism and imperialism while abandoning the concept of three revolutionary currents. This new-old world view provides the rationale for the alliance on an ideological basis with China that Hanoi persistently pursued throughout the 1990s despite repeated Chinese refusals. The integrationist world view emphasises national interests as opposed to class struggles as the motive force of world politics. According to this view, globalisation and multipolarity are two central characteristics of the contemporary world. The new two-camp view also incorporates elements of multipolarism. It recognises that the world revolution is in the defensive and multipolarisation serves as one of the strategies of opposition to U.S. imperialism.[43]

The Chinese and Vietnamese Communists shared the same orthodoxy of world politics. After communist control was established in mainland China and northern Vietnam, the relationship between the two countries was defined as between "comrades plus brothers" and "as close as lips and teeth". This indicated that besides the principle of national self-determination, the principle of socialist internationalism also applied in relations between China and Vietnam. But while the Vietnamese preferred the formula "comrades plus brothers", the Chinese favored the metaphor of lips and teeth. The phrase "as close as lips and teeth" (*chun chi xiang yi*) is a Chinese saying, which communist China also used to characterise its relations with North Korea. The phrase "comrades plus brothers" is a Marxist-Leninist concept and it was the late Vietnamese President Ho Chi Minh who first brought it into the context of Sino-Vietnamese relations. Although the Vietnamese recognised that they were the younger brother and China was the elder, what Vietnam expected was assistance and generosity rather than a hierarchical relationship. The metaphor of Vietnam and China as lips and teeth would remind the two countries of Chinese proximity and power rather than their interdependence because China is too large to be dependent on Vietnam. Socialist internationalism can thus be differently interpreted, and each of the two international actors favoured the interpretation that suited its own interests more.

Despite being comrades plus brothers and as close as lips and teeth, Sino-Vietnamese relations deteriorated in the late 1970s, after Hanoi gained control in all previous Vietnamese territories. In February 1979, China invaded Vietnam in what it called a "punitive war to teach Vietnam a lesson". The vocabulary of socialist internationalism was suddenly replaced by that of the pre-modern Chinese world order. The formulae of "lips and teeth" and "comrades plus brothers" were abandoned in the 1980s when open hostility dominated relations between the two countries.

In 1999, a new guideline was endorsed to provide a foundation for the re-normalised Sino-Vietnamese relationship. This time again, the Chinese and the Vietnamese versions are different. The Chinese version of the guideline reads "long-term stability, future orientation, good neighbourliness, all-round cooperation". In the Vietnamese version, good neighbourliness and comprehensive cooperation comes first, preceding long-term stability and future orientation. With their version, the Chinese convey the message that the Vietnamese should give priority to the long-term stability of their relationship and not look back to its past. With their own emphasis, the Vietnamese signal that they prefer to see in China a friendly neighbour and to see China engage in a comprehensive cooperation with Vietnam.

Conclusion

This chapter investigates traditional and modern Sino-Vietnamese relations in order to ascertain how far different normative world orders such as the tributary system, the Westphalian system, and socialist internationalism have worked in this corner of the world. The three systems provided the normative constitution of the pre-modern East Asian world, the modern world, and the socialist world, respectively. The tributary system is based on the principle of hierarchy between states, the Westphalian system on the principle of equality, and socialist internationalism on solidarity. In the tributary system, international relations were characterised by lordship and vassalage. In the Westphalian system, states are sovereign equals. Under socialist internationalism, states are bound by comradeship and brotherhood. Chinese and Vietnamese states, both in the traditional and the modern ages, invoked the normative constitution of the world to form their ambitions and define their relationship. Nevertheless, they invoked it selectively and according to their own interpretation. In the traditional ages, China asserted its world overlordship and treated Vietnam as its vassal. But Vietnam did not conformed to this Chinese world order. It strived to become another world overlord, thereby breaking the Chinese world order. In the modern ages, both China and Vietnam have fought for sovereignty and equality. In this sense, both are ardent supporters of the Westphalian order. As two communist states, they are also bound by socialist internationalism. Thus, no Chinese or Vietnamese leaders would deny that they should respect the sovereignty and equality of the other country and that the two countries should be bound by mutual solidarity. But the shared normative principles have served to promote communications between the international actors rather than guided their conduct and shaped their relations. China and Vietnam acted in conformity with their different goals, which were not directly derived from the normative constitution of the world. As a result, the Sino-Vietnamese relationship underwent different forms, which at times reinforced and at times violated the normative world orders.

There is a gap between the norms and principles of world affairs shared by international actors and the actual patterns of their interaction and relationship. Sometimes, this gap is insignificant, but at other times, it is huge. The reason lies in that international actors interpret the shared concepts and shared principles that constitute the world order according to their own interests. The tributary and the Westphalian systems, as well as socialism internationalism, were in reality "eroded" by the different interpretations and conflicting world views to the extent that they were no more than sets of generic codes that remained to be filled with contents by the actors. Previous studies that embrace the tribute system as the model of traditional East Asian international relations or assume the practical validity of Westphalian principles such as sovereignty and equality in modern international relations are bound to ignore these phenomena and misconceive world order.[44]

An adequate study of world order must not conflate the normative, the strategic, and the actual levels of world order. Actual patterns of world affairs diverge from the normative constitution of international relations because actors pursue different strategies based on their own world views. The three-way distinction between normative world order, strategic world views, and actual world patterns enables us to shed light on the functions of world orders and world views. The tribute system, the Westphalian system, and socialist internationalism are myths. They are myths because in reality they are not what they are said to be. Yet these myths are useful and necessary. To use a computer metaphor, the normative world orders serve as interface — sometimes user-friendly, sometimes not — in the communications between international players. Without these myths, diplomacy would collapse and the messages of war could not be understood. The "operating systems" — to use the computer metaphor again — that drive the players are their own world views. The world views talk in the language of normative world orders but pursue their own purposes that are not directly derived from the latter.

Notes

[1] For different but influential concepts of world order, see Hedley Bull, *The Anarchical Society: A Study of Order in World Politics* (New York: Palgrave, 1977); Kenneth N. Waltz, *Theory of International Politics* (New York: Random House, 1979); Robert W. Cox, *Approaches to World Order* (Cambridge: Cambridge University Press, 1996).

[2] D.E. Mungello, *Curious Land: Jesuit Accomodation and the Origins of Sinology* (Honolulu: University of Hawaii Press, 1989); Jonathan Spence, "Looking East: The Long View", in Jonathan Spence, *Chinese Roundabout* (New York: W.W. Norton, 1992), pp. 78–82; Lionel Jensen, *Manufacturing Confucianism: Chinese Tradition and Universal Civilisation* (Durham: Duke University Press, 1997); Hans van de Ven, "Introduction", in *Warfare in Chinese History*, ed. van de Ven (Leiden: Brill, 2000), pp. 1–32.

[3] The classic study of China's international relations, which is based on the "tribute system", is *The Chinese World Order: Traditional China's Foreign Relations*, ed. John King Fairbank (Cambridge, Mass.: Harvard University Press, 1968). The standard model is described in Fairbank, "A Preliminary Framework", in this volume, pp. 1–19. A seminal work on China's military and security affairs is *Chinese Ways in Warfare*, ed. Frank A. Kierman and John K. Fairbank (Cambridge, Mass.: Harvard University Press, 1974). The standard statement of the Chinese

"disesteem of violence" is Fairbank, "Introduction: Varieties of the Chinese Military Experience", pp. 1–26 in that volume.

4   See Basil H. Liddell Hart, *Strategy: The Indirect Approach* (London: Faber and Faber, 1941); John Keegan, *A History of Warfare* (London: Hutchinson, 1993), pp. 214–5.

5   The seminal essay on the tributary system is John K. Fairbank and Ssu-yü Têng, "On the Ch'ing Tributary System", *Harvard Journal of Asiatic Studies* 6, no. 2 (June 1941): 135–246. See also Fairbank, "Tributary Trade and China's Relations with the West", *Far Eastern Quarterly* 1, no. 2 (Feb. 1942): 129–49. But an earlier source of the concept is T.F. Tsiang, "China and European Expansion", *Politica* 2, no. 5 (March 1936): 1–18.

6   For a discussion of this school and other approaches to Chinese foreign policy, see Bin Yu, "The Study of Chinese Foreign Policy: Problems and Prospect", *World Politics* 46, no. 2 (Jan. 1994): 235–61.

7   This estimation is based on Nicola Di Cosmo, *Ancient China and Its Enemies: The Rise of Nomadic Power in East Asian History* (Cambridge: Cambridge University Press, 2002); Jacques Gernet, *A History of Chinese Civilisation*, trans. by J.R. Foster (Cambridge: Cambridge University Press, 1982); Denis Twitchett, ed., *The Cambridge History of China*, Vol. 3: *Sui and T'ang China, 589–906*, Part I (Cambridge: Cambridge University Press, 1979); Herbert Frank and Denis Twitchett, eds., *The Cambridge History of China*, Vol. 6: *Alien Regimes and Border States* (Cambridge: Cambridge University Press, 1994); Frederick W. Mote, *Imperial China, 900–1800* (Cambridge, Mass.: Harvard University Press, 1999); and Morris Rossabi, ed., *China among Equals: The Middle Kingdom and Its Neighbors, 10th–14th Centuries* (Berkeley: University of California Press, 1983).

8   John King Fairbank, "A Preliminary Framework", in *The Chinese World Order: Traditional China's Foreign Relations*, ed. John King Fairbank (Cambridge, Mass.: Harvard University Press, 1968), pp. 1–19.

9   Ibid., p. 12.

10   Rayne Kruger, *All under Heaven: A Complete History of China* (Chichester, England: Wiley, 2003), p. 27.

11   Sima Qian, *Records of the Grand Historian*, Han Dynasty II, trans. by Burton Watson (Hong Kong: Columbia University Press, 1993), pp. 140, 143.

12   Mori Masao, "The Tu-chüeh Concept of Sovereign", *Acta Asiatica* 41 (Dec. 1981): 47–75.

13   David M. Farquhar, "The Origins of the Manchus' Mongolian Policy", in *The Chinese World Order*, pp. 199–201.

14   Tono Haruyuki, "Japanese Embassies to T'ang China and Their Ships", *Acta Asiatica*, no. 69 (Nov. 1995): 39–62, quote p. 51.

15   Ki-baek Lee, *A New History of Korea* (Seoul: Ilchokak, 1984), p. 105; Roger Tennant, *A History of Korea* (London: Kegan Paul, 1996), p. 80.

16   See a concise summary of foreign relations in ancient China in Jing-shen Tao, *Two Sons of Heaven: Studies in Sung-Liao Relations* (Tucson: University of Arizona Press, 1988), pp. 1–9.

17   Alastair Iain Johnston, *Cultural Realism: Strategic Culture and Grand Strategy in Chinese History* (Princeton: Princeton University Press, 1995), p. 184.

18   Wolfgang Bauer, "Einleitung", in *China und die Fremden: 3000 Jahre Auseinandersetzung in Krieg und Frieden*, ed. Bauer (Munich: Beck, 1980), pp. 7–8.

19   Ian Mabbett, ed., *Patterns of Kingship and Authority in Traditional Asia* (London: Croom Helm, 1985).

20   For the traditional Vietnamese view of Vietnam as a domain of manifest civility, see Liam Kelley, "Vietnam as a 'Domain of Manifest Civility' (Van Hien chi Bang)", *Journal of Southeast Asian Studies* 34, no. 1 (Feb. 2003): 63–76.

21   Alexander Barton Woodside, *Vietnam and the Chinese Model: A Comparative Study of Vietnamese and Chinese Government in the First Half of the Nineteenth Century* (Cambridge, MA: Harvard University Press, 1971), p. 18.

22   There was no monolithic and unified Vietnamese world view. Neither was there a monolithic and unified Chinese view of the world. I use the singular form here to refer to the view of each domain's court. The court's world view might differ from that of some elite circles, particularly the cultural and the local elites.

23   Tao, *Two Sons of Heaven*, p. 2.

24   Alexander L. Vuving, "The References of Vietnamese States and the Mechanisms of World Formation", *Asien* 79 (April 2001): 62–86.

25   Vuving, "References of Vietnamese States".

26   Tran Quoc Vuong, "Dan gian va bac hoc" [Popular and scholarly], in idem., *Trong coi* [Inside the Realm] (Garden Grove, CA: Tram Hoa, 1993), pp. 159–95.

27   Takashi Inoguchi, "China's Intervention in Vietnam and Its Aftermath (1786–1802): A Re-examination of the Historical East Asian World Order", in *Rethinking New International Order in East Asia: U.S. China and Taiwan*, ed. I Yuan (Taipei: Institute of International Relations, 2005), pp. 361–403, internet edition at <http://iir.nccu.edu.tw/chinapolitics/rethinking/12.doc>, p. 4.

28   Quoted in Truong Buu Lam, "Intervention versus Tribute in Sino-Vietnamese Relations, 1788–1790", in *The Chinese World Order*, p. 173.

29   Woodside, *Vietnam and the Chinese Model*.

30   Brantly Womack, *China and Vietnam: The Politics of Asymmetry* (Cambridge: Cambridge University Press, 2006), p. 129.

31   Nguyen The Long, *Chuyen di su, tiep su thoi xua* [Stories of Diplomatic Exchanges in the Past] (Hanoi: Van hoa Thong tin, 2001), pp. 97–113.

32   Lam, "Intervention versus Tribute", pp. 174–6.

33   Long, *Chuyen di su*, p. 190.

34   For a discussion of the role of historians in Vietnamese and Chinese politics, see W.O. Wolters, "Historians and Emperors in Vietnam and China", in *Perceptions of the Past in Southeast Asia*, ed. Anthony Reid and David Marr (Singapore: Heinemann, 1979).

35   I focus my discussion here on relations between the governments that are currently based in Beijing and Hanoi. Thus I do not discuss the foreign relations of the

Republic of China (Nanjing, Chongqing, and Taipei) and the Republic of Vietnam (Saigon).

36   For an explanation of the transition from culturalism to nationalism in China, see Joseph Levenson, *Liang Ch'i-ch'ao and the Mind of Modern China*, 2nd ed. (Berkeley: University of California Press, 1959). For examples of culturalism as the primary form of expression in pre-colonial Vietnamese foreign affairs, see Woodside, *Vietnam and the Chinese Model*.

37   For a discussion of Vietnamese world view in the Cold War era, see Eero Palmujoki, *Vietnam and the World: Marxist-Leninist Doctrine and the Changes in International Relations, 1975–93* (London: Macmillan, 1997).

38   Mark Mancall, *China at the Center: 300 Years of Foreign Policy* (New York: Free Press, 1984), p. 352.

39   Ibid., pp. 354–5, 364, 401.

40   Lin Biao, "Renmin zhanzheng shengli wansui" [Long live the victory of the people's war], *Renmin ribao* [People's Daily], 3 September 1965, p. 3. Quoted from Chen Zhimin, "Nationalism, Internationalism and Chinese Foreign Policy", *Journal of Contemporary China* 14, no. 42 (Feb. 2005): 44. See also Mancall, *China at the Center*, p. 429.

41   Chen, "Nationalism", p. 45; Mancall, *China at the Center*, pp. 434, 471–4.

42   Michael Pillsbury, *China Debates the Future Security Environment* (Washington, D.C.: National Defense University Press, 2000), ch. 1.

43   Alexander L. Vuving, "The Two-Headed Grand Strategy: Vietnamese Foreign Policy since Doi Moi", Paper at the conference "Vietnam Update: Strategic and Foreign Relations", Singapore, 28 November 2004.

44   For a thorough critique of sovereignty, see Stephen D. Krasner, *Sovereignty: Organized Hypocrisy* (Princeton: Princeton University Press, 1999); Stephen D. Krasner, ed., *Problematic Sovereignty: Contested Rules and Political Possibilities* (New York: Columbia University Press, 2000).

PART TWO

New Perspectives in Changing Asia

Chapter 4

Dealing with the Dragon: The China Factor in Myanmar's Foreign Policy

Maung Aung Myoe

Ever since her independence in 1948, Myanmar foreign policy has been preoccupied with China. Myanmar leaders are well aware of their large and powerful neighbour who historically exerted influence or suzerainty over Myanmar in the pre-colonial days. Political elites in Myanmar have long been concerned with the Chinese intention towards Myanmar, and the Myanmar leadership had worried about "Great Han Chauvinism" as they are fully aware of the assertion of Chinese suzerainty over Myanmar in the pre-colonial past. The idea of viewing Myanmar within the Chinese sphere of influence has also imbedded in the minds of the Chinese leadership. Both nationalist and Communist alike, Myanmar was considered as a Chinese vassal or a tributary state and a part of China's historical and natural sphere of influence; that however was not the case as far as Myanmar was concerned. The Myanmar anxiety over the "Chinese imperial mentality" was proved right when Myanmar's first ambassador presented his credentials to the Chinese head of the state in 1949. Despite being the first non-communist nation to recognize the new Communist regime led by Mao Zedong and the People's Republic of China (PRC), when Ambassador U Myint Thein was about to present his credentials to Mao Zedong he was advised that one of Mao's deputies would receive them. The Myanmar ambassador refused to present the credentials on the grounds that he brought credentials from one sovereign nation to another and could not present to one of lesser dignity than the head of state. Yangon instructed the ambassador that unless he could present his credentials to the head of the state he should return home. With this threat of withdrawing diplomatic recognition, Mao himself received the Myanmar ambassador.[1]

Taking all the relevant factors into consideration, the Myanmar government decided that it was in the interests of newly independent Myanmar to adopt a neutralist foreign policy with a high degree of flexibility in deciding international issues. This, it was felt, would guarantee the peace and stability and freedom from foreign interference which was imperative for national development. In this way, while it maintains amicable relations with countries near and far, Myanmar could receive bilateral and multilateral assistance as long as those countries did not violate Myanmar's sovereignty. However, initially, the PRC was not happy with Myanmar's neutralist foreign policy. As an ideologically committed Communist state with a profound interest in championing revolutionary forces around the world, the PRC under Mao Zedong took the militant position that there were only two camps in the world — anti-imperialist democratic and anti-democratic imperialist — and that the countries in the world must be in favour of either imperialism or socialism, and that "neutrality" was merely a camouflage. China considered that a third road simply did not exist. In November 1949 in Beijing, Liu Shaoqi denounced the Myanmar Prime Minister U Nu, along with Nehru and Sukarno, for being a neutralist sitting on the fence.[2]

In such a situation, how to maintain friendly and peaceful relations with China without compromising its neutralist foreign policy was one of the main concerns for the Myanmar decision-makers. In fact, understanding China and rationalising China's place in regional and international politics has been an important continuing exercise for the Myanmar government in the past decades. It was in this context that the Myanmar government formulated her China policy. In the early 1950s, the government coined the term "*Pauk-Phaw*" (kinfolk) to guide and denote her bilateral relations with China.[3] Living on the periphery of the PRC, the Myanmar government has been cautious in her relations with the authorities in Beijing. Myanmar leaders were worried that the PRC would interfere in their internal affairs because of the disparities in power and the geographical proximity of the two countries. With the benefit of hindsight, the events in the late 1960s proved that these fears and worries were well-justified.

Sino-Myanmar relations can be conveniently divided into three historical periods: the Anti Fascist People's Freedom League (AFPFL)/

Union Party (UP) period (1948–62); the Revolutionary Council (RC)/ Burma Socialist Programme Party (BSPP) period (1962–88); and the State Law and Order Restoration Council (SLORC)/State Peace and Development Council (SPDC) period (1988–).

The AFPFL/UP Period (1948–62): The Years of Charting the Waters

At the time of Myanmar independence in January 1948, the Anti-Fascist People's Freedom League (AFPFL) formed a government and established diplomatic relations with China under the Kuomintang (KMT). Then in late 1949, it withdrew its diplomatic recognition from the KMT and recognised the newly-established People's Republic of China (PRC) under the leadership of the Chinese Communist Party (CCP). The AFPFL was in power for ten years and in 1958, it was forced to transfer power to the Caretaker Government led by General Ne Win. After general elections in 1960, the Caretaker Government transferred power to the elected government led by U Nu who formed the Union Party, a splinter of the AFPFL. Rule by the UP lasted for merely two years before General Ne Win seized power in March 1962. Nevertheless, the period between 1948 and 1962 can be considered as the parliamentary regime period.

With some outstanding issues like undemarcated boundaries and the presence of KMT remnants on Myanmar soil, the AFPFL government was worried that the PRC might make excuses to interfere in Myanmar's internal affairs, for it had leverage, such as the overseas Chinese population, communist insurgents, and aboveground leftist political opposition, to pressure the Myanmar government. Despite the Chinese rhetoric of Myanmar being an imperialist stooge, the Chinese government did not act beyond words. Nevertheless, as mentioned earlier, Myanmar was the first non-Communist country to recognise the PRC, and it adopted, and has maintained, the "One-China Policy" up to the present.

One of the first major security issues that the AFPFL government faced in the context of Sino-Myanmar relations was the presence of KMT troops on Myanmar soil, also known as "KMT Aggression". The KMT, having been defeated by the Communist forces, escaped into Myanmar in late 1949 and planned to use it a springboard for attacking the PRC. The People's Liberation Army (PLA) then engaged in mopping up the KMT remnants near the Sino-Myanmar border. Myanmar was worried about being accused by China of harbouring its enemy, the KMT, who were being secretly armed by the US government. Just a month after the Communists came to power in China, Premier Zhou Enlai warned that any government which offered refuge to the KMT forces should bear the responsibility for handling this matter and all its ensuring consequences.[4] Then in early 1950, the PRC warned again that it would not tolerate Myanmar accommodating KMT troops on her side of the border.[5] Myanmar brought this case before the United Nations only to find to her disappointment that the world body would not even name the aggressor, simply stating in the resolution that foreign troops were on Myanmar soil. Nevertheless, through both diplomatic means [primarily the four-party talks among Myanmar, Thailand, the United States, and Taiwan] and military actions, the KMT issue was eventually resolved by the early 1960s; at one stage the Tatmadaw [Myanmar Armed Forces] and the PLA coordinated joint military operations against the KMT. With regard to the KMT issue, the Chinese government had displayed remarkable constraint and understanding towards Myanmar and did not push Myanmar to the extent that the latter felt insecure and looked for assistance from anti-PRC countries. In December 1954, Prime Minister U Nu publicly acknowledged his gratitude to the Chinese government on this matter. However, despite the restraint there was certainly Chinese pressure imposed on the Myanmar government.

The PLA troops on Myanmar soil in the period between 1953 and 1956 represented a major security problem for Myanmar, though this was a well-kept secret of the 1950s. China stationed its troops on land it claimed as its own, as the PRC did not recognise the boundary line it had transgressed which was drawn by the British in 1941. As far as the Chinese government was concerned, it was a disputed territory. The Myanmar government decided not to go public on this issue and just engaged in quiet diplomacy so as not to jeopardise Sino-Myanmar relations, which were ceremoniously based on the so-called five principles of peaceful co-existence. It was also acutely aware of the arcane ineffectiveness of international bodies like the UN, especially after its disappointment with the KMT issue in 1953. The Myanmar government, therefore, was of the opinion that going public and confronting the PRC might just invite the direct involvement of the world powers, turning Myanmar into a battleground; and the issue might have become more complicated if the US had decided to intervene openly on the side of the KMT.

Several reports were made by field commanders to the War Office in Yangon. about PLA incursions into Myanmar territory claimed by the PRC. Moreover, Yangon was aware that some Chinese authorities were involved in fomenting secessionist sentiment among the national minorities in the border region, in hope that they would join autonomous areas established by the PRC state in the 1950s. In order to avoid clashes with the PLA troops, on 25 March 1953, General Ne Win instructed Colonel Chit Myaing, commander of No. 6 Brigade at Lashio, not to send his troops across the Thanlwin River. But on 17 January 1955, with the approval of the War Office in Yangon, Colonel Chit Myaing despatched a 68-day flag march into the Wa sub-state to explore the situation there and nurture a good friendship with the local people. Meanwhile, in October 1954, the Myanmar government assigned a secret mission, headed by Colonel Saw Myint, to find out how many PLA troops were residing in Myanmar territory and to investigate the Sino-Myanmar border stretching from the India-China-Myanmar tri-junction to the Lao-Myanmar border. The report of this "Operation Yein Nwe Par" became a point of reference for the Myanmar delegation in border negotiations. The issue of PLA troops in Myanmar became public when the *Nation* newspaper in Myanmar reported it for the first time in June 1956. U Nu went to China to discuss the issue and finally the PRC agreed to settle it peacefully.

Another outstanding issue in the Sino-Myanmar relationship, as mentioned earlier, was the undemarcated boundary. When the Nationalist Chinese government refused to accept 1,000 rupees as rent for the Namwan Assigned Tract in 1948, the Myanmar government realised that the boundary issue would soon emerge. In the early 1950s, the PRC government published an atlas of China in which a large segment north of Bhamo was claimed as Chinese. In this way, China pursued a policy of "cartographic aggression".

By the mid-1950s, there were three closely linked issues in Sino-Myanmar relations: the undemarcated boundary; the aggression of KMT remnants; and the incursion of PLA troops. While these issues were at the top of its agenda, the Myanmar government was shrewd enough to encourage China, along with India, to inaugurate the so-called Bandung Era. This represented a kind of moral pressure on the Chinese government to resolve the bilateral issues in a peaceful and friendly manner. U Nu duly recognised and accepted China's important role in regional peace and stability. While insisting on Myanmar's strict neutrality in international issues, particularly in the Cold War divide, Prime Minister U Nu cultivated a personal friendship with the Chinese leadership, which was later known in Sino-Myanmar relations as *Pauk-Phaw* [kinfolk] relations.

The year 1954 can be considered a watershed year in Sino-Myanmar relations. First, Zhou Enlai came to Myanmar in June and then, U Nu for the first time paid an official visit to China in December. Both leaders succeeded in nurturing closer relations through frank discussions, and confirmed their commitment to the Five Principles of Peaceful Coexistence.[6] Zhou Enlai came to Myanmar again in April 1955 on his way back from Bandung where he was well-received. The context of the Five Principles of Peaceful Coexistence, the Bandung spirit, and the *Pauk-Phaw* relationship, the Myanmar government tried to resolve the outstanding issues between the two countries. During his visit to Beijing in December 1954, U Nu enquired about the Burma Communist Party (BCP) cadres in China. The PRC simply denied their existence; but the Myanmar government knew by then that over 100 BCP members were taking political courses and military training in China. Nevertheless, in a joint communiqué issued on 12 December 1954, the two governments agreed to settle the boundary issue "in a friendly spirit at an appropriate time through normal diplomatic channels". Yet the progress was rather slow. Several rounds of negotiations and exchanges of letter followed. In the meantime, a Myanmar military delegation led by General Ne Win went to China on 21 September 1955. When the delegation ended the tour in early November 1955, some of the members of the delegation came back to Myanmar overland via Yunnan. Leaving Kunming on 14 November, the Myanmar delegation accompanied by two PLA generals arrived at Lashio on 18 November. While the two PLA generals were still in Lashio, Colonel Chit Myaing received a report of a PLA incursion and ordered his troops to engage the intruders while he filed a complaint with the visiting generals. This incident was kept secret until July 1956 when the *Nation* newspaper revealed details of the PLA troops on Myanmar soil. Therefore, by late 1956, the overlapping territorial claims and the presence of PLA troops became immediate security issues for Myanmar. In order to avoid the clashes between the two armed forces, at the end of July 1956 the PRC proposed that the forces of the two countries should maintain the *status quo* in the disputed areas pending a negotiated settlement. The Myanmar government was also unhappy with alleged PRC support for the left wing political forces in Myanmar, especially in the 1956 election, although no reference to Chinese involvement was made in the press.

Meanwhile, the Sino-Indian boundary issue became increasingly prominent in the later part of 1950s, especially after the first state visit of Chinese Premier Zhou Enlai to New Delhi in 1956. Taking advantage of Chinese interest in settling the Sino-Myanmar border negotiation and demarcation as an example of her "flexibility, generosity, and spirit of compromise" in boundary negotiations,[7] the Myanmar government decided to push ahead with the negotiation for the Sino-Myanmar border demarcation. Initially, the PRC was strongly against the idea of accepting the "1941 Line" drawn by the British as it viewed the line as an indication of unequal treaties. Later, Beijing agreed to incorporate the "1941 Line" with some natural and historical boundary lines. The process was speeded up when the two governments decided to settle the issue through negotiations based on the principles of "give-and-take" and friendship, rather than legalistically. In his capacity as the president of the AFPFL, U Nu went to China in October 1956. There he was assured by the Chinese government that, starting from the end of November 1956, PLA troops would be withdrawn from the area west of the 1941 line while Myanmar troops would also be required to withdraw from Hpimaw, Kangfang and Gawlum, and that the withdrawal was to be completed before the end of 1956.[8] Negotiations on border demarcation continued and finally on 28 January 1960 General Ne Win, as the prime minister of the Caretaker Government, signed a "package deal" with the Chinese government that included an agreement on the question of the boundary between China and Myanmar and a treaty of friendship and mutual non-aggression between the two countries. In accordance with the agreement, both parties worked on the detailed boundary demarcation and finally the boundary agreement was signed on 1 October 1960. For Yangon, the successful settlement of the border issue had removed the anxiety of any future Chinese incursion into Myanmar territory. With an exchange of a few square kilometres (see map), the boundary was peacefully demarcated. Premier Zhou Enlai subsequently held up the Sino-Myanmar boundary agreement to the Indian government as a model, for it was necessary to substantiate China's claim of not having any territorial claims on neighbouring countries, as outlined by Premier Zhou Enlai on 23 April 1955 at the Bandung Conference.

Although the signing of the mutual non-aggression pact, Article Three of which stated that "each contracting party undertakes not to carry out acts of aggression against the other and not to take part in any military alliance directed against the other contracting party", may have formally limited Myanmar's freedom of action in respect of

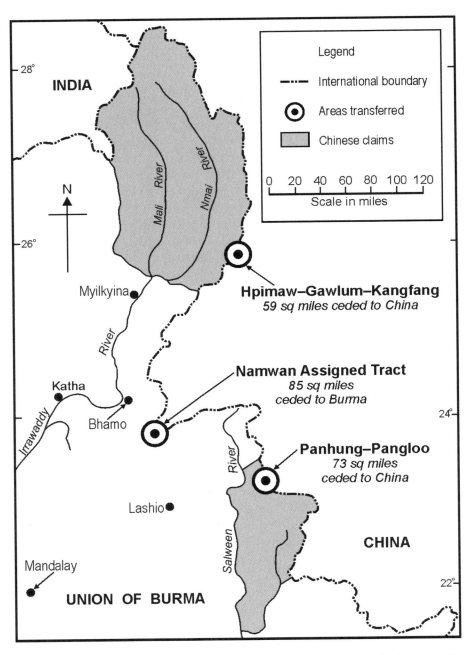

Burma-China border area showing lands originally under dispute and those actually transferred according to the 1960 Sino-Burmese agreement.

its self-defense, for a neutralist country like Myanmar it did not pose any foreign policy problem. In fact it even enhanced her security. The "package deal" was praised in the Chinese press as "a new example for friendship, co-operation and amicable relations among the Asian countries".[9] About the time the border demarcation named "Operation Burma Boundary" was carried out, the Tatmadaw also launched a major military operation against the KMT remnants in the border area. It was believed that some 20,000 PLA troops were also involved in joint operations, codenamed "Operation Mekong", in December 1960. This military pressure finally led to the evacuation of some 4,000 KMT troops in March 1961, and six months later the Myanmar government estimated that not more than 700 KMT troops remained in the area. By late 1961, all the outstanding issues between the two countries had been more or less resolved.

The RC/BSPP Period: Into the Years of Living Dangerously

The Revolutionary Council (RC) came to power through a military coup against the elected government led by U Nu on 2 March 1962. A few months later, the RC declared the Burmese Way to Socialism (BWS) and formed the Burma Socialist Programme Party (BSPP), the only legal party to exist in Myanmar between 1964 and 1988, to carry out a social revolution in Myanmar. The RC transferred its power to the BSPP government in 1974 after nationwide general elections. The BSPP rule came to an end when the military took over the state on 18 September 1988 in the aftermath of the 1988 political upheaval. In the early years of the Revolutionary Council's rule,[10] the Sino-Myanmar relationship was particularly warm as it witnessed an intense exchange of high-level state visits between the two countries: President Liu Shaoqi came to Myanmar in April 1963 and April 1966 and Premier Zhou Enlai and Foreign Minister Chen Yi in February and July 1964, while Ne Win went to China in July 1965. In April 1963, Liu Shaoqi described Sino-Myanmar relations as "a brilliant example of peaceful co-existence between nations with different social system".[11] In July 1964, during Zhou Enlai's visit to Myanmar, both countries reaffirmed their undertaking contained in Article Three of the Treaty of Friendship and Mutual Non-Aggression concluded in 1960. Although Article Three prohibited Myanmar from entering any military alliance targeted against China, it did notprevent Myanmar from procuring weapons from Western or NATO sources. Despite its close relations with China and its knowledge of the Sino-Soviet rift, the RC government displayed its neutralist foreign policy by sending more and more Myanmar scholars to the Eastern Bloc countries which were under Soviet influence, for further studies.

New problems in the Sino-Myanmar relationship began to surface when Ne Win went to China in July 1965. During his meetings with the Chinese leaders, the latter drew attention to developments in Vietnam and tried to enlist Myanmar's support, however nominal. Ne Win solemnly remained indifferent and discreetly stated that a major source of international tension was the disregard of the five principles of peaceful co-existence. Then in April 1966 in Yangon, Liu Shaoqi made a subtle hint that Ne Win should show more anti-imperialist zeal and come out in support of Vietnam. Ne Win was again unmoved, showing nothing more than his deep concern over the escalation of the Vietnam war. The government in Yangon was not prepared to follow China's lead in a so-called anti-imperialist struggle; it maintained a strictly neutral position.

By late 1965, it appeared that China was not really satisfied with Myanmar's foreign policy in respect of several issues on which the Myanmar government's strictly neutral foreign policy clashed with China's position. Meanwhile, in December 1965, General Ne Win received American Senator Mike Mansfield, the first high-ranking American political figure to visit Myanmar since the 1962 coup. Ten months later, Ne Win himself appeared in Washington; not a word about American policy in Vietnam was said. Although Beijing had become increasingly disappointed with Myanmar's neutralist policy, it did not show any displeasure publicly until anti-Chinese riots broke out in Myanmar in mid-1967.

Yet the Chinese government had already begun to pull levers to pressure Yangon to comply with its interests. By mid-1964, Myanmar exiles and communist cadres residing in China, known as the Guizhou group and the Sichuan group, were mobilised for political and military training, in preparation for the eventual opening of a military front in Myanmar in the name of the Burma Communist Party. About the same time, the overseas Chinese community in Myanmar was infiltrated by the Chinese Red Guards, as the PRC had decided to export its revolution to Myanmar. The overseas Chinese community in general and Chinese schools in particular became focal points of tension as the impact of the Cultural Revolution spilled over into Myanmar. By June 1967, Chinese students in Myanmar appeared wearing "Mao badges and armbands" and singing "Mao is the red sun in our heart". In response the Ministry of Education issued a regulation on 19 June 1967 which forbade the wearing of any political insignia except those approved by the ministry. When Chinese students failed to comply with the government regulations, the tension between Chinese students and the authorities escalated; it resulted in the death of a Chinese technician and the deportation of the Xinhua representative in Yangon, believed to be a Red Guard. The government finally declared martial law and issued a dusk-to-dawn curfew.

As overseas Chinese in Myanmar began to dramatise their devotion to the Cultural Revolution in China, confrontation between the two nations intensified and their relations reached a nadir of postwar history. The Sino-Myanmar relationship had become a casualty of the Chinese Cultural Revolution. Now the PRC decided to openly endorse the armed struggle being waged by the BCP. The PRC sent "Chinese Volunteers" to help their Myanmar comrades and attached liaison teams to the Headquarters of the new BCP front. Between 1968 and 1978, according to Myanmar intelligence sources, the PRC provided the BCP with about 30,000 rifles, millions of rounds of ammunition, an unknown quantity of mines and hand grenades, a few hundred heavy artillery pieces, about Yuan 20 million for general military expenditure, over 60 trucks, various other military equipment, and several thousand sets of uniforms. Moreover, the PRC provided intercepted combat intelligence for the BCP troops and sent military advisory teams. Medical facilities as well as military training institutes in China were made available for the BCP troops. The PRC helped the BCP with weapons factories, a telecommunication network and a broadcasting station. It also built roads in the BCP-controlled so-called "Liberated Zone". According to a former Central Committee member of the BCP, the PRC had provided about 60,000 rifles by 1985.[12]

During this period the PRC downplayed state-to-state relations with the Myanmar government in favour of party-to-party relations with the BCP. Chinese use of this two-pronged policy had been part of her political leverage in relations with Myanmar since 1968 and persisted for at least the next 17 years. While Myanmar nationalism was rekindled, at the BSPP seminar held on 6 November 1969, General Ne Win requested the Myanmar public to remain calm. In spite of the imminent Chinese threat, the Myanmar government did not try either to counterbalance it or to bandwagon with it. The government under the leadership of General Ne Win made many overtures to try to normalise relations with China. Despite all the difficulties it faced in the border area, especially with an ever stronger BCP insurgency, the Myanmar government did not make any conspicuous move toward either the Soviet Union or the United States. With all these concerted efforts to convince the PRC of its sincerity, goodwill, and amity, normal diplomatic relations were finally restored in March 1971 with the sending back to Yangon of the Chinese ambassador.

The official visit of General Ne Win to Beijing in August 1971 perhaps signalled the formalisation of this restoration of diplomatic relations. While state-to-state relations were restored, party-to-party relations between the CCP and the BCP continued. Being cognizant of the Chinese interest in championing revolutionary armed struggle in the third world, the Myanmar government learned to live with this dual-track diplomacy. Therefore from 1971, while Beijing could preserve its image as the leader of communist revolutionary warfare, the Myanmar government had to cope with continuing the party-to-party relations between the BCP and the CCP. China appears to have been interested in using the Sino-Myanmar relationship as a model in her relations with other Asian countries from which it had become estranged since the mid-1960s. There seemed to be some tacit understanding on the BCP issue between the Chinese and Myanmar leadership during U Ne Win's 1981 visit. China appeared to hint that it should continue to provide assistance to the BCP, which otherwise would result in the BCP turning to the Soviet bloc for assistance, and to seek Myanmar's understanding for this. This mutual understanding permitted a low level of Chinese assistance to the BCP until around 1985. Throughout the late 1970s and early 1980s, during the exchanges of state visits between the two countries, Chinese leaders usually accused the Soviet Union of hegemonist expansion in Southeast Asia, while Myanmar leaders tried to avoid the issue. However, China had come to realize that Myanmar would not deviate from its stated neutralist foreign policy by supporting Chinese positions on international issues.

By June 1985, China began to embrace a new strategic view that "early, major and nuclear war [was] no longer deemed imminent" and that the Soviet military threat to China had diminished. The PLA was instructed to prepare only for "local war or limited war" scenarios. The rhetoric about Soviet hegemonist expansion began to fade. China now decided to correct its past mistakes and to pursue amicable relations with Asian neighbours. In March 1985, Chinese President Li Xiannian came to Myanmar for a state visit during which the Chinese president publicly admitted the mistakes of the Chinese government in the past. Li Xiannian said: "Sino-Myanmar relations were once affected by the internal problems in China. Yet our Myanmar friends adopted a forward-looking attitude, which deeply touched us."[13] Then in May 1985, U Ne Win was invited as the chairman of the BSPP, on a party-to-party basis. After this 1985 meeting between U Ne Win and the Chinese leadership, relations significantly improved. More and more friendly advice on economic reform in Myanmar came from Chinese leaders. The PRC/CCP also withdrew support from the BCP. Even during the 1988 political upheaval in Myanmar, there was no evidence that China played a role.

The SLORC/SPDC Period: Towards Normalisation and Cooperation

The State Law and Order Restoration Council (SLORC) came to power through a military coup on 18 September 1988. It was renamed the State Peace and Development Council (SPDC) on 15 November 1997. Initial Chinese policy towards Myanmar at the time of the 1988 up-heavals was to adopt a wait-and-see attitude. The Chinese government was particularly concerned with the brief but threatening presence of a US naval flotilla comprising the Aircraft Carrier *Coral Sea* and four other warships in Myanmar territorial waters on 12 September 1988.[14] According to Myanmar intelligence sources, the PLA deployed troops along the Sino-Myanmar border and put them on high alert. By early 1989, the PRC government had made a clear stand of support for the Myanmar government. Since then, Sino-Myanmar relations have been further cemented by the exchange of bilateral visits as well as political relations, military and security co-operation, trade, aid and investment.

To the government in Yangon, Myanmar occupies a strategic posi-tion that deserves attention from Beijing. In September 1991, in the state-owned newspaper (apparently with explicit permission from the leadership), a senior Tatmadaw officer stated: "The two nations have resolutely resolved that whoever governs them and whatever systems they practise, they will continue to uphold the traditional friendship for ever and ever because these two nations, according to geopolitics, are interdependent."[15] In this context, it appears that Myanmar believes that China has always regarded Myanmar as an important factor in her security. Again, a decade later, in the words of an official spokesman of the SLORC/SDPC government, Myanmar is "the weak link in the regional China containment policy", though he never explained in detail how Myanmar fits into this scenario.[16] Nevertheless, by adhering to the Chinese rhetoric about US attempts to contain China, the Myanmar government could create some space for diplomatic manoeuver. Moreover, in the light of the new global distribution of power and geopolitical reality of the post-cold war period, since the early 1990s the Chinese government has been following what it calls a "policy of good neighbourliness". Its hallmarks are accommodation and restraint in her relations with neighbours and the application of political-diplomatic support, military-security cooperation, and development assistance in the forms of trade, aid and investment as foreign policy strategies towards neighbouring countries.

Sino-Myanmar relations since 1988 can be safely described as the period of multi-sectoral linkages and ever closer relations. These have gone beyond the traditional sphere of political-diplomatic relations to military-security and economic cooperation. There are several factors that have allowed the two countries to forge a closer relationship. The most important was probably the Chinese decision to refrain from interfering in Myanmar affairs; China by then knew very well that state-to-state relations would serve Chinese interests better. China took advantage of the West's condemnation and isolation of the Myanmar military regime. Thus China became a major security guarantor for Myanmar. The Tiananmen Square "incident" of May 1989 in China further strengthened bilateral relations since both countries faced similar political pressure from the West. In the post Cold War security environment, China has become a major challenger to the US hegemonic position, which makes China believe that the United States follows a "containment policy" against China. It is thus that Myanmar began to take an important place in China's security calculus in term of both geopolitics and geostrategy. Moreover, China helped the Myanmar government resolve its insurgency by encouraging the armed groups along the Sino-Myanmar border area to enter ceasefire agreements with the Myanmar government, and it helped strengthen the military capability of the Myanmar armed forces; the Myanmar government was grateful for these services and therefore, considered China a friend.

In term of political relations, Sino-Myanmar relations have witnessed ever closer links between the two countries. The Chinese government provides political-diplomatic support that the Myanmar government badly needs. The PRC government has confirmed its commitment to the Five Principles of Peaceful Coexistence with Myanmar and has emphasised the importance of the principle of non-interference in the internal affairs of one country by another. The exchange of state visits between the two leaderships attests the close relationship between the two countries. In 2004, General Khin Nyunt even described the current state of Sino-Myanmar relations as "*Nyi-Ako*" [sibling] relations, a step higher than the usual "*Pauk-Phaw*" [kinsfolk] relations. The Myanmar government stood by China on the Taiwan issue, the bombing of the Chinese embassy in Belgrade, and the spy plane incident with the US air force off Hainan island. Whenever the occasion arises, the Myanmar government does not hesitate to confirm her position on the "One China" policy.

China in turn provides much needed diplomatic support for Myanmar on almost all occasions. When Myanmar's chairmanship of ASEAN became an issue, the Chinese government supported the Myanmar position.[17] Political consultation has also become a part of Sino-Myanmar relations since 1992. It is now clear that both sides cherish the "*Pauk-Phaw*" relationship. In his message to the Myanmar head of the state on 4 January 2007, Chinese president Hu Jintao stated: "China and Myanmar are good-neighbouring countries linked by common mountains and rivers while the two peoples enjoy pro-found *Pauk-Phaw* friendship." In a similar context, Chinese premier Wen Jiabao sent a message to his Myanmar counterpart on 4 January 2007 and said: "The further development of the Sino-Myanmar friendly relations with the deepening of exchanges and cooperation in all fields has brought substantive benefits to both peoples. The Chinese Government treasures the *Pauk-Phaw* friendship between China and Myanmar, and is willing to make joint efforts with the Myanmar side for the consolidation of the traditional friendship, the enhancement of mutually beneficial cooperation, and the continuous promotion of the relations between China and Myanmar."

The most prominent feature in Sino-Myanmar relations since 1988 is the close cooperation between the two armed forces. In October 1989, the then Myanmar commander-in-chief (Army) went to China. This marked the beginning of a new era of closer military ties between the two armed forces. Since 1989, China has become a major supplier of weapons for Myanmar, and is estimated to have supplied over US$1.5 billion worth of weapons in the period 1989–2006. This included over 150 aircraft, 16 warships, an unknown quantity of tanks, armoured personnel carriers, anti-aircraft missiles and guns, signal equipment, small arms and ammunition, and other logistic materials. Weapons procurement was accompanied by training packages. Between 1990 and 1999, the Tatmadaw sent a total of 615 personnel to China: 206 from the army, 79 from the navy and 330 from the air force. According to another set of data, between 1990 and 2005, the Tatmadaw sent a total of 914 personnel for 163 different courses in China, mostly at PLA's institutes: 665 officers and 249 other ranks. Arms proliferation is a Chinese strategy to engage Myanmar. Some speculation about the military cooperation between the two armed forces involves alleged signal intelligence stations along the coastal regions of Myanmar. Moreover, port calls of Chinese warships in Myanmar in early May 2001 caused concern among Myanmar watchers.[18] Exchanges of visits between senior commanders of both countries have been a feature of the bilateral military cooperation.

Security cooperation along the Sino-Myanmar border is another important aspect of the bilateral relations. Both countries are concerned over the security along the porous border between them. The border area is notorious for transnational crimes. The two sides have thus agreed to set up "Border Representative Agencies" headed by local battalion commanders, "Contact Stations", and "Contact Points" along the border.

Another important feature of Sino-Myanmar relations in the SLORC/SPDC period has been the growing cooperation in the areas of development assistance, trade, and investment. Some critics of the Myanmar military regime, following the line of "Modern World System" theory, would call the pattern of trade, aid, and investment relations between China and Myanmar a "Centre-Periphery" relation: the wealth flows from the periphery to the centre and the authority or influence flows from the centre to the periphery. Since 1988, international donors have stopped all developmental assistance to Myanmar. The West led by the United States has also imposed economic sanctions on Myanmar. Thus, China has become a major source of development assistance and trade. China-Myanmar border trade has thrived, and low-price (but poor-quality) consumer goods have literally flooded the Myanmar market. In fact both countries had been planning the expansion of border trade even well before the collapse of the BSPP regime in September 1988.

Sino-Myanmar trade has been growing steadily since 1988. According to Chinese statistics, the total value of bilateral trade in 1989 was just US$313.72 million; with China enjoying a trade surplus of US$61.60 million. By 1995, it had reached the total value of

Military Delegations between Myanmar and China

Sr.	Name	Position	Year
From Myanmar			
1	Gen. Than Shwe	Deputy Commander-in-Chief; C-in-C (Army)	Oct. 1989
2	Maj. Gen. Tin Oo	Chief of Staff (Army)	Dec. 1989
3	Maj. Gen. Thein Win	C-in-C (Air Force)	April 1992
4	Lt. Gen. Tin Oo	Chief of Staff (Army)	Nov. 1994
5	Gen. Maung Aye	Deputy Commander-in-Chief; C-in-C (Army)	Oct. 1996
6	Lt. Gen. Tin Ngwe	C-in-C (Air Force)	Sept. 1997
7	Lt. Gen. Tin Oo	Chief of Staff (Army)	May 2000
8	Maj. Gen. Myint Swe	C-in-C (Air Force)	Sept. 2001
9	Vice Admiral Kyi Min	C-in-C (Navy)	May 2002
10	Lt. Gen. Thura Shwe Mann	Chief of Staff	Dec. 2002
11	Vice Senior Gen. Maung Aye	Deputy Commander-in-Chief; C-in-C (Army)	Aug. 2003
12	Lt. Gen. Soe Win	Chief of Air Defence	July 2004
13	Lt. Gen. Myat Hein	C-in-C (Air Force)	April 2005
14	Vice Senior Gen. Maung Aye	Deputy Commander-in-Chief; C-in-C (Army)	June 2006
From China			
1	Lt. Gen. He Qizong	Deputy Chief of General Staff	Nov. 1991
2	Gen. Chi Haotian	Minister of Defence	July 1995
3	Gen. Zhang Wannian	Vice Chairman (Central Military Commission)	April 1996
4	Lt. Gen. Li Jinai	Political Commissar, General Armament Dept	June 1999
5	Gen. Fu Quanyou	Chief of General Staff	Apr. 2001
6	Gen. Wu Quanxu	Deputy Chief of General Staff	Dec. 2003
7	Lt. Gen. Sun Zhiqiang	Deputy Chief of General Logistic Dept	Dec. 2004
8	Gen. Ge Zhengfeng	Deputy Chief of General Staff	Dec. 2004
9	Gen. Liang Guangli	Chief of General Staff	Oct. 2006

US\$767.40 million with China seeing a surplus of US\$468.30 million. In 2004, China reported that the total value of bilateral trade was US\$1,145.35 million with a Chinese surplus of US\$731.50 million. Between 1989 and 2005, China accumulated a total of US\$6,438.86 million in trade surplus with Myanmar. Myanmar-Yunnan border trade accounts for about 55 per cent of the total Sino-Myanmar trade value; over 80 per cent of Myanmar exports to China and about 40 per cent of Myanmar imports from China come through Yunnan border trade. Myanmar is the largest trading partner of Yunnan and, Myanmar's Yunnan trade constitutes 10 per cent of Myanmar's total trade. While Myanmar exports raw materials, agricultural products, livestock, fishery products, and forest products, China floods Myanmar with its cheap finished products ranging from foodstuffs to electronics. The trade imbalance will continue to grow; while the Myanmar government also needs to address the issue of illegal trade.

Myanmar's Official Trade with China (US\$ million)

Year	Export	Import	Total Value	Balance
1988	137.10	133.61	270.71	+ 3.49
1989	126.06	187.66	313.72	− 61.60
1990	104.08	223.54	327.62	− 119.46
1991	105.92	286.17	392.09	− 180.25
1992	131.27	259.04	390.31	− 127.77
1993	164.83	324.70	489.53	− 159.87
1994	143.34	369.11	512.45	− 225.77
1995	149.55	617.85	767.40	− 468.30
1996	137.41	521.12	658.53	− 383.71
1997	73.41	570.09	643.53	− 496.68
1998	62.04	518.86	580.90	− 456.82
1999	101.68	406.53	508.21	− 304.85
2000	124.82	496.44	621.26	− 371.62
2001	134.19	497.35	631.54	− 363.16
2002	136.89	724.75	861.64	− 587.86
2003	169.52	910.22	1,079.74	− 740.40
2004	206.94	938.44	1,145.38	− 731.50
2005	274.40	934.85	1,209.25	− 660.45

Source: *China Statistical Yearbook* (Various Years).

Yunnan's Share of China's Trade with Myanmar (US$ million)

Year	Export			Import			Value		
	Yunnan	*China*	*%*	*Yunnan*	*China*	*%*	*Yunnan*	*China*	*%*
1999	245.99	406.53	60.51	53.53	101.68	52.65	299.52	508.21	58.94
2000	293.01	496.44	59.02	69.93	124.82	56.02	362.94	621.26	58.42
2001	251.51	497.35	50.57	97.22	134.19	70.21	348.73	631.54	55.22
2002	296.08	724.75	40.85	110.70	136.89	80.87	406.78	861.64	47.21
2003	356.83	910.22	39.20	135.96	169.52	80.20	492.79	1079.74	45.64
2004	386.61	938.44	41.20	164.71	206.94	79.59	551.32	1145.38	48.13

Sources: *China Statistical Yearbook; Yunnan Yearbook.*

China uses development assistance as an instrument in winning friends and influencing people in recipient countries. Chinese development assistance usually comes in the forms of grants, interest free loans, or concessional loans. According to the Myanmar government, between 1989 and 2006, the Chinese government provided over Yuan 2.15 billion and US$400 million in various forms of loan.[19] There was also debt relief of Yuan 10 million and Yuan 200 million grant aid. The Chinese government also helped the Myanmar government secure private financial loans from Chinese banks and business firms. In this way, since 1988, China helped the Myanmar government build eight out of nine new sugar factories [US$158 million], 20 new hydroelectric power plants [US$269 million], 13 out of 45 new factories under the Ministry of Industry-1 [US$198 million], and 12 out of 21 new plants under the Ministry of Industry-2 [US$137 million]. In addition, China also upgraded six factories under the Ministry of Industry-2 [US$346 million], supplied six ocean-going vessels, and built a dry dockyard [US$25 million]. In 2006, Chinese firms were building seven out of 11 new hydro-electric plants in Myanmar [US$350–400 million]. In the same year, the Chinese government also presented 130 train coaches to Myanmar Railways.

In terms of Foreign Direct Investment (FDI), Chinese investment strategy in Myanmar reflects the Chinese version of mercantilism. Official Chinese FDI in Myanmar is rather small. Officially, as of 28 February 2005, China had invested US$130.92 million in 22 projects in Myanmar and it ranked only 13th among investors. In the oil and gas sector, Chinese companies signed production contracts in 11 blocks:

4 off-shore and 7 inland.[20] China also plans to build an oil pipeline from Myanmar to China, and is also interested in the Kyaukphyu-Kunming corridor, which is both politically and economically motivated. Chinese investments are now also in the mining industry, particularly nickel. Recently, China has proceeded to invest in the hydroelectricity generation in Myanmar, and signed a joint venture investment in the Shweli Hydroelectric Plant on 31 December 2006.[21] It is clearly evident that Myanmar offers both energy assets and means of energy transportation for an energy-hungry China.

Conclusion

Since her independence in January 1948, the Myanmar government had tried to find a way to deal with (at one time) ideologically hostile and traditionally chauvinistic China. Neither the Sino-centric world order of tributary relations nor the Westphalian world order of sovereign equality could adequately reflect the nature of Sino-Myanmar relations. Since the 1950s, the Myanmar government has realised that her bilateral relations with China should best be conducted in the context of promoting the Five Principles of Peaceful Coexistence, the Bandung spirit, and the "*Pauk-Phaw*" relationship. Yet, the relationship is asymmetric and it is between unequal kinfolk or siblings.

By bringing China into the Bandung process and allowing her to play an important role in regional security, the Myanmar government believed that China would become a responsible member of the community of nations. Myanmar confirmed that it maintained a "One-China" policy and outstanding bilateral issues were peacefully resolved in a friendly manner. In fact, Sino-Myanmar relations became a model that the PRC government would like to promote with other countries. Sino-Myanmar relations therefore helped to promote China's international image. This fairly stable and correct relationship was also placed on the level of personal diplomacy between the leaders of the two countries in the name of "*Pauk-Phaw*" relations. By signing the treaty of mutual non-aggression and friendship in 1960, the Myanmar government duly recognised the Chinese strategic interest in Myanmar. While Myanmar did not join any military alliance targeting China, it continued to conduct its foreign relations on the basis of a neutralist foreign policy; thus, the Myanmar government made known to the Chinese that Myanmar would not balance against nor band-wagon with China.

This relatively trouble-free relationship was interrupted by the Chinese decision to export revolution abroad. The Sino-Myanmar relationship became a casualty of the Chinese Cultural Revolution. Despite the serious security threat, Myanmar maintained its neutralist foreign policy and tried to restore normal diplomatic relations with China. By the time this was accomplished in the early 1970s, the Myanmar government had already learnt to live with Chinese dual-track diplomacy of state-to-state and party-to-party relations, and this relationship, in a way, recognised Beijing's prominent role in international armed revolutionary struggle by communist parties. By the mid-1980s, as a new geopolitical situation emerged, China decided to correct its past mistakes and Myanmar's strictly neutralist policy began to pay off. The Chinese government offered friendly advice on economic reform in Myanmar and helped with some development aid. At the time of political upheaval in Myanmar in August–September 1988, China appeared to stay clear of Myanmar's internal affairs, though there were serious concerns about possible external military intervention. By then, the PRC had likely realised that correct state-to-state relations with the Myanmar government would serve Chinese [strategic] interests better in Myanmar and beyond.

Sino-Myanmar relations since 1988 have witnessed ever closer cooperation between the two countries in several areas, and the direction in which the relations have developed in recent years has certainly had strategic implications for regional security. In particular, the closer military cooperation between the two countries has caused alarm and concern in some neighbouring countries. However, this is by no means a major shift in the traditional foreign policy of strict neutrality. There is a general misunderstanding about Myanmar's closer relations with China. In reality, the government in Yangon has always been concerned about foreign influence and external interference in Myanmar and has always intended to diversify its foreign relations, thus, it has manoeuvred to keep its foreign policy based on strict neutrality but this has become possible only in the late 1990s. Despite different assessments of the impact of the rise of China, the Myanmar government is certainly aware of the expansion of the Chinese strategic frontier and its sphere of interests, if not influence. By repeating the Chinese rhetoric of the US containment of China, Myanmar highlights its own geopolitical significance to the government in Beijing. As the Chinese government needs to assure all that its rise will be a peaceful one, the Myanmar government has realised that it will have more space for diplomatic manoeuvre; thus, Myanmar has been able to cultivate closer relations with other great powers like Russia and India and regional organisations like ASEAN, without jeopardising her relations with China.

When the Myanmar government decided to modernise its armed forces and build its warfighting capabilities, China offered generous terms to supply relatively modern armaments, but not by any means state-of-the-art weapons. China used the arms proliferation method to extend and sustain its influence in the region. These closer military ties marked a major shift in Myanmar's threat perception of China, from potential threat to a friend. Weapons procurement from China had some problems as the Tatmadaw was used to Western or NATO standard weapons. Chinese weapons were considered inferior in quality. For more reliable and better-quality arms, Myanmar went to Russia and other Eastern European countries. Since the late 1990s, Myanmar's arms procurement pattern has changed and become more diversified, indicating that Myanmar does not rely entirely on China for its force modernisation.

While China is an important source of cheap consumer goods and an export destination for Myanmar, Myanmar is also vital in China's development strategy for its western provinces. Myanmar is the shortest possible outlet to the Indian Ocean for Yunnan Province and it is the best and most cost-effective means or a venue to export Yunnan products to the European markets. Myanmar could also serve as a goods transit trade point for Chinese products, particularly those from the western provinces, to Thailand, Bangladesh, India, and even to other Southeast Asian countries. Sino-Myanmar trade, particularly the Yunnan-Myanmar trade, will continue to grow; Myanmar will certainly benefit not only from the 1.4 billion Chinese market but also from the 1.2 billion Indian market as well. In terms of development assistance, China will continue to support Myanmar's industrialisation efforts and infrastructural development, at least for the foreseeable future, as the West continues its sanctions on Myanmar. In the area of FDI, China will continue its investment in strategic sectors, especially in energy. In this respect, Myanmar can engage in oil and gas diplomacy. Chinese gas and oil pipelines through Myanmar and the Kyaukphyu-Kunming corridor will serve as a key development link for China.

In sum, though the Sino-Myanmar relationship may be asymmetric in favour of China, Myanmar skillfully plays the "China card" and it still enjoys considerable space in her conduct of foreign relations. Myanmar has constantly repositioned her relations with China to its best advantage. As long as it recognises the legitimate strategic interests of China in Myanmar, the Myanmar government will be left to conduct her foreign relations within the context of its non-aligned policy, and China will likely support Myanmar's drive for active participation in international community and regional organisations. In addition, with the growing significance of Myanmar to China in geopolitical and geo-strategic terms as well as its own drive for modernisation and development, China is likely to base its diplomacy on the good neighbourliness policy and the Five Principles of Peaceful Co-existence. It is most likely that Myanmar will position her China policy somewhere between balancing and band-wagoning, but it will continue to conduct her China policy in the context of the traditional *Pauk-Phaw* relations that will allow Myanmar flexibility in her foreign relations.

Notes

Unreferenced information in this chapter are derived from Myanmar government records that are generally not accessible.

1 Tibar Mende, *South-East Asia between Two Worlds* (London: Turnstile Press, 1955), p. 154.

2 Jay Taylor, *China and Southeast Asia: Peking's Relations with Revolutionary Movements* (New York: Praeger Publishers, 1976, second edition), p. 193.

3 Diplomatic letters of pre-colonial Myanmar, especially during the Konebaung period (1752–1885), clearly indicated that Myanmar kings regarded Chinese emperors as equal, addressing them by the term *Akyidaw* [Royal Friend]. Chinese emperors, however, usually referred to themselves as *Naungdaw* [elder brother] and the Myanmar king as *Nyidaw* [younger brother]. The term *Pauk-Phaw* had been commonly used in Myanmar during the colonial period to refer to Chinese men.

4 Evelyn Colbert, *Southeast Asia in International Politics* (Ithaca: Cornell University Press, 1977), p. 133.

5 William C. Johnstone, *A Chronology of Burma's International Relations 1945–1958* (Rangoon: Rangoon University Press, 1959), p. 19.

6 These principles are: Mutual respect for territorial integrity and sovereignty; non-aggression; non-interference in each other's internal affairs; equality and reciprocity; and peaceful coexistence.

7 Chien-peng Chung, *Domestic Politics, International Bargaining and China's Territorial Disputes* (London: RoutledgeCurzon, 2004), p. 104.

8 *A Victory for the Five Principles of Peaceful Co-existence*, p. 6.

9 Ibid., editor's note.

10 General Ne Win came to power on 2 March 1962 through a military coup d'etat and formed the Revolutionary Council (RC) to rule the country. Later, the RC declared the "Burmese Way to Socialism" on 30 April 1962 and formed the Burma

Socialist Programme Party (BSPP) on 7 July 1962, with 22 core members. In March 1964, the RC government passed a law banning all political parties and organisations except the BSPP and its affiliates, thus commencing a period of one-party socialist regime in Myanmar. The RC took control of the state and the direct military rule came to an end in January 1974 when the BSPP formed the government under a new constitution; this BSPP rule collapsed in September 1988.

11 *Peking Review*, 6, 17 (26 April 1963): 7–8.

12 *Directorate of Defence Services Intelligence Reports* (Statements given by U Sai Aung Win on 29 June 1990).

13 *Working People's Daily* (6 March 1985).

14 When the military authorities lodged a complaint and sought explanation from the US embassy, the latter explained that the warships were for the evacuation of US embassy staff in Myanmar. The authorities then pointed out that 276 people, including some US embassy staff, had been evacuated in the evening of 11 September on a chartered flight. Indeed, the US embassy had repeatedly requested permissions from the Myanmar authorities for a C-130 military aircraft to land in Yangon for evacuation. The Myanmar authorities rejected the request by explaining that such an activity might lead to further confusion among the general public and send a wrong signal to regional neighbours. On 13 September, the US embassy issued a statement that the US fleet in the Myanmar territorial water was just a rumour.

15 *Working People's Daily* (3 September 1991).

16 Hla Min, *Political Situation of Myanmar and Its Role in the Region* (Yangon: News and Periodical Enterprises, 2001), p. 36 (internet version).

17 Chinese Foreign Minister Li Zhaoxing arrived in Yangon on 27 July 2005, aiming not only to promote the traditional and friendly ties between China and Myanmar but also to show support for the Myanmar government which decided to relinquish ASEAN Chairmanship in 2006, by skipping the ASEAN Regional Forum (ARF).

18 *FEER* (10 May 2001).

19 Myanmar received Chinese development assistance loans of US$64 million in 1979, US$15 million in 1984 and Yuan 80 million in 1987.

20 The China National Offshore Oil Corporation Myanmar Ltd (CNOOC-Myanmar Ltd) operates in A-4, M-2, M-10, PSC-M, PSC-C1 and PSC-C2. Another China state-owned SINOPEC signed contracts for PSC-D. Again, China's state-owned China National Petroleum Corporation (CNPC) also won contracts to upgrade the old oilfields in central Myanmar: I-3, R-2, N-3, and I-4. It is estimated that Myanmar, both offshore and inshore, has reserves of 2.46 trillion cubic feet of natural gas and 3.2 billion barrels of crude oil. Like Chinese companies, India's ONGC and GAIL are also investing in Myanmar by forms a consortium with Daewoo.

21 *Myanma Alin* (1 January 2007); Yunnan United Power Development Co. Ltd. signed the contract.

Chapter 5

Visions of History, Trajectories of Power: China and India since Decolonisation

Prasenjit Duara

Chinese and Indian leaders of the mid-twentieth century saw it as their destiny to transform not only themselves, but the world. As their anti-imperialist consciousness became intertwined with their self-perception as inheritors of two great world civilisations, decolonisation presented an opportunity for these nations to offer an alternative to the colonial past.

Unlike leaders in Southeast Asian countries, Indian leaders like Jawaharlal Nehru regarded India in the immediate post-war period as equally qualified with China to lead Asia and the decolonising world. Indeed, after 1949, Nehru sought to exercise this leadership precisely by bringing communist China into a realm of engagement with non-communist societies in Asia and the West. This scenario, however, changed rapidly during the 1950s and India soon found itself pre-occupied with issues in South Asia itself. The paper outlines how the Chinese leadership was effective in utilising a Westphalian-type Panchasheela model of international relations to further its interests among its neighbours while confining India to South Asia. Improvement in the relations between the two nation-states in recent years and the concomitant growth in the status of India in South, Southeast and East Asia has led to a re-configuration of the political scenario. Ironically, it is precisely at this present moment when the two giants are developing the capacity to realize some version of the decolonisation ideals that these ideals have dimmed. As such, the re-configuration presents a cauldron of opportunities and risks for the region as a whole.

The Early Period: Ideals and Problems

The transformation of decolonising societies into nation-states, a process that accompanied the idealism of the anti-imperialist movement actually generated inescapable tensions. The Westphalian-Vatellian system of nation-states with its ideal of self-regulating, competitive sovereign units, only partially reflected the entire range of relationship between states even during the twentieth century. Despite the theory of mutual respect, these states were engaged in a competition for resources that entailed not only military conquest and colonisation, but also annexation or domination of each other's territories. Moreover, in a recent reflection, Adam Watson notes that the hegemonic powers within the Westphalian system always aimed to modify the internal behaviour of other states and communities — a distinctly un-Westphalian activity.[1]

Viewed from outside, it seems that the Westphalian-Vatellian system had the unacknowledged function of restricting access differentially to resources in the world, particularly through colonial control. Not only were polities that were not part of, or allowed into, the system regarded as controlled colonial resources, but through both formal agreements and extra-treaty actions and violence, states established their political and economic dominance in the system. Resistance to hegemony by aspiring powers entailed considerable violation of the rules of the system as in the well-known cases of Germany, Japan and others. Indeed, following world-system theorists, I have argued that by the late nineteenth century there developed an intrinsic relationship between imperialism and nationalism. In the competition for resources, mobilising the nation marshaled material and psychological resources for imperialist conquest, while imperialism abroad furthered nationalism and national power. This kind of competitive pressure often led to the breakdown of the system, as during the two world wars. Thus, participation in a system of nation states meant participating in a system which had historically been based upon the integration of imperialism and nationalism.[2]

How then could the new states enter a competitive system without being imperialistic? One could argue that external competition was not necessary to the new iteration of the Westphalian-Vatellian system in the United Nations model. To some extent this is undoubtedly true. China, following the Soviet Union, was avowedly built upon non-capitalist foundations and the onset of the Cold War gave new nations such as India the ideas and space for autarkic development. But competition had deeper discursive roots than capitalist economics in modern society. By the nineteenth century, nations came to be premised upon a progressive vision of history that promised endless growth. Even if this growth was not based on a zero-sum game, it involved competition on the part of the nation for scarce resources and status. Growth entailed expansionism that was not only territorial and economic, but had political and psychological dimensions.

Even though the People's Republic of China denounced the international system as capitalistic, it was invested in the entire narrative of progress and competition. This sanctioned the mobilisation of people to produce and sacrifice for the socialist nation. Note the 1958 Great Leap Forward slogan to overtake steel production in Britain and France in 15 years. The construction of socialism around the nation-state and its discursive commitment to a linear history and progressive future entailed a competitive understanding of the world which would, under particular historical circumstances, enable both unconditional nationalism and capitalism to prevail. Gandhi had a deeper critique of modernity and its assumptions about history, masculinity and progress. But his programme of self-sufficient communities was not a practicable one and it was easily incorporated and marginalised by Nehru's vision of a modern industrial future for India.

Under these circumstances was there much room, if you will, for alternative modernities? How did the structure of a competitive nation-state system constrain the ideological choices of society? What were these alternatives? For China, the goal of its leadership of the anti-imperialist movement was to produce revolutionary socialist societies among the decolonising nations. For India, the goal was to realize the Nehru-Gandhian ideals of peace, non-alignment and constitutionalism. From an outcome-blind 1950s perspective, India's nuclear programme was almost as unexpected as China's turn to capitalism. Both believed that their recent historical achievements as well as their deeper historical greatness entitled them to lead the new nations of the world along alternative paths.

As early as in 1947, India held the First Asian Relations Conference in New Delhi when it put together a series of exhibitions revealing the greatness and influence of Indian culture, religion and trade that had extended from Himalayas to Southeast Asia, Persia and Central Asia. The Buddhist University of Nalanda which collected scholar-monks from East, Central and even West Asia (the idea of which is now being revived) was the best expression of this cosmopolis. Indians were particularly proud of their historic influence in Southeast Asia. They imagined the perfection of Indian civilisation in the past of this greater Sanskritic world, or even empire, which was all the better for it to have been made not by power and wealth, but by ideas and values (Baruah 2005).[3] The struggling KMT regime in China sent a delegation to the conference and was quick to match the Indian claims with still more extensive ones.

The Chinese narrative of greatness derived not only from imperial China having exerted a wide civilising influence across much of Asia, but also having extended through the tribute system, considerable political and economic power over the regions. The most famous expression of its imperial extension was the famous Zheng He expeditions carried out during the Ming dynasty. Although, there are some fantasy accounts of the expeditions having reached the Americas, it is clear that they reached the Cape of Good Hope before the Portugese.

To be sure, the earlier Republican narratives of tributary sovereignty and heroic Chinese pioneers settling and civilising the Southeast Asian regions were not fore-grounded by the Communists. Indeed, both the Indians and Chinese quickly learnt that these civilising narratives could only be perceived by Southeast Asians as reproducing familiar patterns of imperialist behaviour. However, during the early PRC, since China's geopolitical influence was hampered in the east by Japan, and in the north and west by the Soviet Union, as Stuart-Fox points out, its best chance to establish itself as a regional power was Southeast Asia.[4] I would add that the Himalayan region also represented another, though lesser, geopolitical zone of potential influence.

Thus both societies had what we might call civilisational narratives which justified the leadership of each to the decolonising world. Between the late 1940s until the Bandung Conference of 1955, both states conducted a flurry of diplomatic exchanges and events to build the organisational bases to achieve their goals. The Government of India continued to conduct conferences of Asian societies whereas the People's Republic of China held the World Federation of Trade Unions, an effort to bring trade unions across the world into a single international organisation not unlike the UN, in Beijing, as early as November 1949. Burmese socialists also took the lead in organising the Asian Socialist Conferences which brought together Asian socialist parties and sought to more actively include Africa in the decolonising movement as well as create the basis for China's participation in the Bandung conference.[5]

By the time of the landmark Bandung Conference of 1955, civilisational chauvinism was kept in check and the leaders of the two nations unfolded their approaches and messages to the decolonizing world.

As is well-known, contrary to expectations, it was Zhou Enlai who succeeded in achieving the moral high ground, while Nehru was unable
to extricate the Indian side from the arguments with the Pakistanis.
Indeed, I think it is fair to say, that from that time, India's status in
Southeast Asia never did rise much higher until recent times.

From the end of the Bandung conference, immersed in its problems within South Asia and the Himalayan region, India developed no
coherent policy towards Southeast Asia, much less a sphere of influence,
and declined in importance in that region. In part, the close relationship that developed between China and Pakistan succeeded in keeping
Indian strategic concerns within South Asia for most of the post-
independence period.

In the next part of the chapter, I will argue that after this period,
it is less fruitful to compare the two countries than to explore their
relationships. China became involved in the effort to engage Indian
concerns within South Asia, and India found it difficult to exercise its
hegemony even within that region. For over 30 years, India was unable
to extricate itself or exercise sufficient leadership to break through this
containment.

Territorial Consolidation

The alternative civilisational goals towards which the leadership of
India and China aspired to guide the new nations remained in uneasy
tension with the tasks of nation and state-building. The first of these
tasks was the definition and consolidation of the national territory. The
PRC had the advantage of drawing upon a half century of thinking
on this question during the Republic and under the KMT. The KMT,
which controlled a small part of the Chinese territory, nonetheless,
claimed not only the Qing empire, but regions that were part of the
Qing and pre-Qing tribute system and beyond, including what they
called the "lost territories".[6] The PRC claims tended to stick to the
extent of the Qing empire.

However, the Qing empire was not a nation-state and there en-
sued the problem of "incommensurable sovereignty". For decolonising
nations emerging from old empires, such as the Qing or the British, the
territorial problem was among the most enduring. Nationalists of the
dominant ethnicity or group made claims upon regions or territories of
the old empire — the principle of *uti possidetis*. But it was practically
difficult for Indian and Chinese nationalists to extend or sustain the

principle of nationality in several parts of the old empires. The peripheral regions of the Qing empire whether in Tibet, Mongolia or Xinjiang had multiple and flexible political affiliations and incorporation into the empire was often based on patronage of common religious or other cultural symbols, rather than the modern conception of absolute belonging to a territorial nation.[7]

Similarly, the British Indian Empire incorporated regions and communities along lines of differentiation that enabled the Muslims of the empire to deny any obligation to the successor Indian state. The northern, Himalayan states of Kashmir, Nepal, Sikkim and Bhutan remained nominally sovereign, but were dependencies of the British Government in India. Strategically, this vast region and Tibet served as a buffer for the British imperial government which was focused on protecting India from other, especially Russian, imperial powers.[8]

In other words, the principle of belonging to a national territory was incommensurate with the historical practice of loose affiliations and flexible incorporation into empire. Moreover, dominant nationalists were often making their claims on these regions precisely at a time when elites of these regions or communities — such as the Mongols or British Indian Muslims — were also developing a national consciousness. This was the basis, for instance, of the rejection by Muslims of the British Indian Empire to join with the Republic of India, the Tibetan and Mongol refusal to participate in a Chinese nation, and so on. The contestation over claimed territories is also a reminder of the difficulty of separating or containing the differences between nationalism and imperialism.[9]

Between real independence of the periphery and its full incorporation, there were, of course, other modalities of dealing with the incommensurability problem, but they were often unsatisfactory. The Republic of India was forced to relinquish territories to Pakistan; seized much of Kashmir (and several other princely states); and entered into treaties with Nepal, Bhutan and Sikkim that essentially restored their status as buffer states that the British had created to the north (in 1973, India incorporated Sikkim into the Indian Union). As with India, China too developed border differences with most of its contiguous states, but the most publicised and dramatic problem was, of course the Tibetan one. The history of the Chinese incorporation of Tibet is a well-known one that I need not rehearse here. It is, however, instructive to follow how China sought to contain or limit the effects of its forceful integration of the periphery on its relations with its neighbours and sustain its anti-imperialist rhetoric.

The doctrine used by the Chinese leadership to produce this effect was the doctrine of the Five Principles of Peaceful Coexistence or Panchasheela. The five principles include mutual respect among nations, peaceful co-existence, equality, mutual non-aggression and non-interference in the internal affairs of others. It originated in a treaty known as the Agreement between the Republic of India and the People's Republic of China on the Trade and Intercourse between the Tibet Region of China and India signed on 29 April 1954. Later Nehru would publicise it widely and make it the core of new India's civilisational message in Bandung and elsewhere as the guiding philosophy of the non-aligned movement. As we know, it was also of great significance to the political philosophy of the Indonesian state.

Panchasheela was a kind of Westphalian doctrine for the era of decolonisation. The goal was to enable states to engage in relationships by setting aside troublesome or insoluble issues. In contrast to Westphalian-Vatellian era when most of the world was prey to the few nation-states, this time around, what seemed fairer about it was the fact that most of the world was becoming divided up into nation-states. Nonetheless, it could still be used instrumentally by forcibly incorporating a contested region and declaring it to be part of the national territory, as both China and India were to do. Despite India's flaunting of the rhetoric, the Chinese government utilised the Five Principles more effectively.

The clarity of the Chinese approach to the Five Principles emerged from its recent historical experience. Dong Wang has shown that as the Unequal Treaties in China took centre stage in the rise of Chinese nationalist consciousness, a school of legal practitioners, including such figures as Wellington Koo, W.W. Yen, Alfred Sze, and C.T. Wang among others, emerged with a strong belief in the capacity of international law to rectify the inequality among sovereign states. From the Republic through the revolution, the KMT regime did succeed in gaining international recognition through legal processes. Of course, respect for international law was hardly seen as the only means to attain recognition and respect for the political values that China stood for.[10] Communist revolution and nationalist resistance represented another means to achieve these international goals and the Cultural Revolution represented the period when they were in full ascendance, overwhelming law. But the 1950s was more circumspect; or to put it another way, if world Maoist revolution represented the civilisational goals of the PRC, Panchasheela represented its state-building goals and the Maoist regime utilised both instruments with considerable success until the Cultural Revolution.

I believe the idea of Panchasheela is continuous with this conviction in the demonstrated value of law as a means of securing state sovereignty. In the view of the communists, pre-WWII international law
was imperialistic and could not fully secure China's sovereignty. Panchasheela was better in that regard: it was anti-imperialist but gave the
state full autonomy within its claimed sovereign territory. Thus, once
the Chinese government obtained recognition by India of its claim to
Tibet in the 1954 treaty, it proceeded entirely on the supposition that
China acted within Panchasheela principles, whereas it could claim
that India, by asserting rights over the Himalayan states, was engaging
in hegemonism. In staking this high ground, the PRC regime ignored
two historical realities, neither of which was fully commensurable with
modern principles. The first was that for most of the past century, the
entire Himalayan region had become a vast buffer zone between the
British, the Russian and the Qing empires. From the Indian perspective, the Chinese had acquired the largest of these buffers in Tibet; why
should they deny the right to Indians to regard the Himalayan kingdoms as their buffer? Second and more profoundly, there was an asymmetry in the Chinese perception of the two empires: the British Empire
was regarded by the PRC as imperialist, whereas the Qing Empire was
seen as proto-nationalist. We know well, however, that the republican
revolution of 1911 saw the Manchus as barbarian alien conquerors.

Looking back at the 1950s, it would seem that Nehru, who appeared to determine foreign policy (like Mao and Zhou in China), had
little sense of statecraft. From Sardar Patel, the "iron man of India",
whose tough-minded advice on China Nehru never took in the 1950s,
to Foreign Minister Jaswant Singh at the end of the century, the early
foreign policy of the Republic of India has been criticised for having
been overly influenced by the unrealistic Gandhian notions of pacifism
and idealism. The main charge has been that Nehru naively trusted
the PRC leadership beginning with his concession of China's central
demand on recognition of Tibet. Once this became a *fait accompli*,
India had little basis on which to negotiate the border issues that became the cause of the flare-up in 1962. To be sure, the Indian leadership's inexperience with foreign policy matters certainly had much to do
with Nehru's "naïve" China policy, if that is what it was. At the same
time, however, bringing the PRC into the international arena dominated by the US and the Western powers by promoting China's cause
in the UN, the Korean War and participation in Bandung etc. — the
period known in India as "Hindi-Cheeni bhai-bhai" — was a crucial part

of Nehru's strategy of exercising leadership in the new bloc of decolonised nations. It is fairer to say that Nehru's strategy backfired.[11]

The Sino-Indian conflict of 1962 caused a reversal in Indian attitudes toward China and put Indian policy towards its neighbours firmly on a realpolitik track. The policy of militarily absorbing its small neighbours Goa and Sikkim, of helping bisect Pakistan through military intervention, the military intervention in Sri Lanka in 1987, the economic sanctions that crippled Nepal when that country sought to develop independent military ties with China in 1987 and the nuclear tests of 1998 leave no doubt about a much tougher attitude towards the South Asian area which India sought forcibly to establish as its sphere of influence. From another angle, Indian realpolitik may be seen to have represented its containment in South Asia and one might even see India as being mired in an area much smaller than that envisioned by Nehru and other founders.

Two factors need to be considered in the shrinking of India's Asian role to South Asia. The first seems to be a failure to imagine its role in the wider region, especially after the disappointments of the non-aligned movement. India made no effort to join any regional organisations in Southeast Asia after Bandung. Even with respect to people of Indian origins in the region, and in marked contrast to the Chinese efforts to protect and woo the overseas Chinese population in Southeast Asia since the early twentieth century, the government of the Republic of India was decidedly uninterested in ethnic Indians in the region.

To be sure, compared to the Chinese presence in Southeast Asia which is at about 20 million today, the Indian presence was numerically smaller and less influential. The large Chinese influx into Southeast Asia took place between 1850 and the early twentieth century. Between 1801–50, the outflow of people from China was about 200,000; this outflow into Southeast Asia increased to well over a million between 1876–1925. Moreover, although most Chinese emigrated as coolies, many of them were successful merchants and entrepreneurs who played an important role politically and financially in the nationalist movement in China.[12] With the exception of Burma, the numbers and influence of Indian population in Southeast Asia was much smaller.[13] The activism of the Indian National Army of Subhash Chandra Bose which rallied many South Asian soldiers during the Pacific War was of a shorter duration and had a more limited impact on Indian nationalism.

Sir Badruddin Tyabji, a career diplomat wrote, "I realised how superficial, how ill-informed, almost callous, that view had been; and above all, how far we had failed in utilising this enormous reservoir of Indian capital (men, money, skills, energy and know-how) overseas for building up the new India of our Five-Year Plans, our foreign policy, and our conception of inter-national affairs." Indeed, the Indian Overseas Department established by the British Indian government was dismantled and replaced with consular institutions which tended to see these people as mere liabilities.[14] Compare this to the attitude of Liang Qichao and other nationalists who as early as 1906, spoke of the Chinese in Southeast Asia as the great pioneer colonists who civilised China's "new America".[15]

The second factor has been the alliance between China and Pakistan which has kept India busy in South Asia. John Garver has stated that the Sino-Pakistani relationship has probably been the most durable of all of China's foreign relationships. Pakistan has been the recipient of covert nuclear technology from China and is the largest recipient of Chinese military aid. Moreover, China has supported insurrectionary movements in India through the Cultural Revolution. India's intransigence on China's proposal to conduct an East West swap on the Himalayan border issue and China's refusal to recognise, until recently, India's claims of special relations with the Himalayan kingdoms, has kept India focused on its vast northern border.[16]

To be sure, the PRC strategy towards Asia during the Maoist period was scarcely consistently successful, but it demonstrated considerable vision and initiative to keep itself in Asia as a major player while containing the role of its competitors in the region, namely India and the Soviet Union. We have already considered its role in South Asia. In Southeast Asia, China had sought to lead one or another group of nations that has given it some leverage in the super-power game. In the early 1950s, China intervened in the Vietnam War, took a leading role in the 1954 Geneva peace negotiations, and built a successful relationship with Indonesia, Burma and revolutionary movements in the area. Although its status reached a nadir in the Cultural Revolution, it has recovered since the early 1970s. It built a relationship with the US and gained recognition from Thailand and Philippines in its rivalry against the Soviet Union and Vietnam. It conducted what we might call a foreign policy of "walking on two legs" — Panchasheela in state to state relations and revolutionary support in party to party relations.[17] By the selective application of the two legs of revolutionary support and regime support, for instance, of pariah regimes in Cambodia or Myanmar, it succeeded in becoming a major world player even before the Deng Xiaoping era.

Asia after Deng Xiaoping

As is well-known, the ascendancy of Deng Xiaoping in Chinese politics led to a sea change in Chinese foreign relations as well. Over the 1980s, the support of revolutionary movements in other countries was given up, a series of bilateral negotiations were initiated to ease border and political tensions, and the focus turned to trade and investment. This has not only led to significant reduction of fears about the Chinese threat over most of Asia, it inspired the Indians to respond and learn from the Chinese experience, and like the rest of Asia, India too has now become economically invested in the peaceful rise of China. There are two dimensions of this new chapter that appear to be historically significant to me.

The first refers to the manner in which China has sought to resolve political friction. The watchword seems to be: de-link. Set aside presently insoluble issues and work on fronts that promote trade and other exchanges. While China has used this approach towards several countries, it has been particularly dramatic in the Indian case. Although China had made overtures to improve relations with India, it was not until after the Tiananmen Incident of 1989, that Beijing intensified its efforts to reduce its international isolation by courting countries like India. The rapprochement entailed, first of all, de-linking the Sino-Pakistan from Sino-Indian relationship. India gained a small victory in the 1990s when China refused to back Pakistan in internationalising the Kashmir problem by insisting on the UN Declaration of Kashmiri plebiscite as the starting point of negotiations. The Himalayan border issues were also de-linked from other matters, and in 1990, China and India co-operated in the London conference on the depletion of the ozone layer, jointly pressing the developed countries to transfer the necessary technology to the developing ones.[18]

To be sure, de-linking has meant just that and has not necessarily led to reduction in China's support — including military and nuclear support — for Pakistan. Nonetheless, it is unquestionable that Chinese and Indian relations have improved to a degree unimaginable ten years ago, and have even weathered the Indian nuclear tests in 1998. China has since recognised Sikkim as Indian territory, the two countries have opened the Nathu-la pass, made great progress on the border problems, and most of all have escalated trade between the two countries. Trade between the two which was $3 billion in 2000, has risen to $20 billion, and at last year's rate of 38 per cent, China's trade with India is growing far more rapidly than its global trade growth of 23 per cent in 2005. According to Zhibin Gu it is expected to touch $200 billion in a decade or so.[19]

Moreover, investments have also been growing rapidly in each others' economies. Over 150 Indian companies have set up more than 1,000 projects in China, and since 2005, India has become one of the most important overseas markets of project contracts for Chinese enterprises. Indian Minister of State for Commerce, Jairam Ramesh has popularised the notion of "Chindia", a formation that combines the relative strengths of India and China in the world economy.[20] Whether or not such a formation can emerge, there is no shortage of essays touting the unbeatable strength of companies capable of combining their respective strengths. As Subir Roy has put it, Indians are good at the soft stuff (this goes well beyond software) and Chinese are good at the hard stuff (this goes beyond plants and infrastructure into hard policy decisions facilitated by one-party rule). China's labor efficiency is said to be 55 per cent higher than that of India, and India's capital efficiency estimated to be around 45 per cent higher than that in China. Large Chinese firms have size and technology; Indians have managerial skills, R and D, and free market institutions and practices. Whether or not it is a harbinger of business synergy, on 21 December 2005, Indian Oil and Natural Gas Corp and China National Petroleum Corp (CNPC) jointly won a bid for Petro-Canada's 38 per cent stake in the Al Furat oil and gas fields in Syria.[21]

In Southeast Asia as well, China has succeeded in isolating contentious issues such as the Spratly Islands and other border problems and has long given up its support for radical challenges to the Southeast Asian states. Moreover, the creation of the new Nationality Law of 1980 clarified the status of ethnic Chinese born in another sovereign state as citizens of that state and not of China. Except for a few places like Indonesia, this has helped to smooth the relationship between China and these states and enabled these ethnic Chinese to take the lead in developing this relationship without undue suspicions about their loyalty. The booming economic relationships of these nations with China have produced a web of interdependence that ought to make it hard for any one state to act unilaterally.[22]

Needless to say, China's warm embrace of global capitalism and indeed of the neo-liberal order in the world has not steered it towards support of more liberal regimes that are often associated with the spread of global capitalism. This brings me to the second point of historical

significance. China's own example has shown that there is little relationship between liberal institutions and growth, and its historical
critique of Indian development and "soft state" led it, rather, to arrive
at the opposite conclusion. Indeed, given that there is a strong corre-
lation between domestic institutions and foreign policy, it is not surprising that the PRC supports monarchical and militarist polities in
South Asia. This is also consistent with its emphasis on pursuing state
to state relations on the basis of the Five Principles. Nowhere is this
policy more evident than in Myanmar.

Myanmar was historically a tributary kingdom of the Qing empire,
and even in the 1920s, Sun Yat-sen regarded Myanmar as part of
China's "lost territories" (shidi).[23] From 1949 until the 1980s, Burma
maintained a policy of neutrality between India and China, while China
followed its policy of "walking on two legs" of cordial state to state
relations and support, though mostly rhetorical, for the insurrectionary
Burmese Communist Party. When the Burmese junta suppressed the
democracy movement in 1988, India condemned its actions and soon
after, broadcast All India Radio programmes from the border expressing solidarity and information to the democratic resistance. It even
sponsored a UN resolution condemning the junta in 1992. The Indian
stance had the effect of tilting the junta — called SLORC — towards
China which was also drawn to the Burmese regime by the common
fate of having been condemned by the international community for
the June 1989 massacre. The intensification of relations between the
two states led to a veritable boom in military and economic ties; China
provided the military with large amounts of aid, equipment and training.[24]
China also sought to construct highways and shipping routes along the
"Irrawady Corridor" and planned a couple of new ports in the Bay of
Bengal. Indians believe that Myanmar has leased its Coco Islands to
China which enables the latter to monitor India's naval activity and its
missile testing site at Sriharikota.[25]

Until recently, Indian realpolitik was justified by its democratic
values. In the case of Bangladesh, Sri Lanka, Myanmar and even
Nepal and Sikkim, Indian officials claimed to be responding to calls by
democratic groups in those countries to aid them to resist authoritarian
or military suppression. India's claim has not necessarily enhanced its role
as champion for democracy, nor has it gained many friends in the area.
But perhaps the most striking about-face in recent Indian foreign policy
may be seen in the case of Myanmar. In response to the growing Chinese
presence in Myanmar, the Indian position has changed dramatically

and at the present time when the US is planning an unprecedented Security Council resolution against the continued detention of Aung San Suu Kyi, Indian officials are actively wooing the generals. Moreover, India's equally warm embrace of global capitalism in recent years has also induced its leadership to make all kinds of deals with the junta in the area of security, energy, trade and infrastructure projects.[26] Whether we judge this development to be an exercise in *de-linking* politics from economics and state rights, or as the abandonment of the democracy movement, depends, of course, upon one's point of view.

Writing before 2001, John Garver who has written arguably the most exhaustive and useful book on India and China relations, laid out several possible scenarios for the future of that relationship. Arguing against what was becoming the common view that recent trends in Chinese foreign policy suggest that China would permit India to develop South Asia as its sphere of influence because of its greater interests in trade and economic relations, Garver opts for what he regards as the more consistent historical view that the gap between Chinese and Indian interests and their relative power in the world would lead to the diminishment of Indian autonomy even within South Asia and India would probably become a junior partner to China in the region.

The impact of 11 September and the train of conflicts that erupted in its wake, as well as the robust Indian economic development in the last few years would seem to make that proposition rather more dubious at this time. After decades of isolating India and engaging in what the Rudolphs call "off-shore balancing" in South Asia, the US administration has now selected India to become a strategic partner and the two are on the verge of contracting a civilian nuclear deal of gigantic proportions. It also seems clear that, among other goals, the US seeks to develop India as a counter-weight to China. I believe and hope that Indian strategic thinking has matured sufficiently for it not to put all its eggs in one basket. Never in the history of the Republic has India had more propitious international circumstances. In the long run, China will probably be much more important to India's economic and regional interests than any other nation. I am also in agreement with Michael Vatikiotis that the Sino-Indian relationship will in the near future be much more important to Southeast Asia. A healthy relationship between the two will benefit Southeast Asia which lies in the natural path of these two societies by, according to Vatikiotis, reviving the "historical synergies" that were generated before the era of Western colonialism.[27]

Finally, what about the ideals of the decolonisation movement with which I began this essay? With China and India having joined the neo-liberal world order, we appear to be back in the Westphalian system which creates a competitive pecking order, but no alternative vision or route for the dispossessed and the politically oppressed. Is the emancipatory moment of decolonisation finally over?

The world may now be absorbed into the encompassing system of competitive nation-states — a self-enclosed legal and epistemological system, akin to but different from Hardt and Negri's "Empire".[28] But challenges appear from the crevices of the system, from the many open wounds within it, and from the very technological and information circulations that generated the nation-state and which the latter was designed to control to the nation's advantage. In historical fact, these challenges are linked to the decolonisation moment. The emancipatory vision of the decolonisation movement had integrated alternative historical traditions with socialistic justice. Frantz Fanon and Jalal Ali Ahmed are reminders that Islamism stems from roots that are as radical as religious. I came across a confidential report from *The Economist* of 3 November 1955 entitled "Mao and the Moslem World" which expressed fears that the Chinese Communists were banding together and creating a common agenda with Muslim anti-colonial movements across the Middle East. Who could have predicted which one would survive?

But as historians recognise, no system is so closed that it cannot present opportunities for change and therein lies hope; perhaps in the sense of Lu Xun, hoping against hope. The push of the multitudes against borders of all kinds in search of opportunity and justice, new types of cross border alliances supervening state-to-state relations, the disaggregation of state functions and regulatory regimes, and new kinds of trans-national cultural and political allegiances will provide these opportunities just as much as they create problems. Will not the very participation of these populous societies with capacious traditions make a difference? If deterritorialised nations do emerge, might it not be useful to have older models of allegiance such as the Chinese tribute system or other complex arrangements to draw upon?

China not only developed a stable arrangement of power in the tribute system, but also pioneered the multi-national state in the modern era with the Republic of Five Nationalities (*wuzugonghe*) in 1912. It appears to be exhibiting a similar flexibility with regard not only to minority nationalities but also different communities of Chinese like those in Hong Kong and Macao. Perhaps it might be able to stretch this conception to also incorporate the new types of cross-border communities that are emerging with the rampant globalisation of our times. Similarly, new modes of public-private partnerships, grass-roots innovations in micro-finance and local governance, diasporic development, transnational social capitalism and other sprouts of international civil society are developing across democratic Asia and Africa. Might these eventuate into a credible legacy of decolonisation?

Notes

[1]   Adam Watson, *The Evolution of International Society* (London: Routledge, 1992).

[2]   Prasenjit Duara, *Sovereignty and Authenticity: Manchukuo and the East Asian Modern* (Lanham: Rowman and Littlefield, 2003), chapter 1.

[3]   Sanjib Baruah, "The Strange Career of Southeast Asian Studies in India". Paper presented at the International Convention of Asia Scholars (ICAS), Shanghai, China, 22 August 2005, pp. 14–5.

[4]   Martin Stuart-Fox, *A Short History of China and Southeast Asia: Tribute, Trade and Influence* (Australia, NSW: Allen and Unwin, 2003), p. 225.

[5]   Kyaw Zaw Win, "The Asian Socialist Conference in 1953 as precursor to the Bandung Conference in 1955". Paper presented at the 15th Biennial conference of the Asian Studies Association of Australia, Canberra, 29 June–2 July 2004.

[6]   See the maps in Xie Bin, *Zhongguo Sangdishi* (China's Lost Territories). Shanghai: Zhonghua shuju 1936 which include significant sections of Kazakhstan and North India. See also Kataoka, Kazutada, "Shingai kakumei jiki no gozoku kowaron o megutte" (Regarding the theory of five races in the 1911 revolutionary period), in *Chugoku Kindaishi no shomondai*, ed. Tanaka Masayoshi sensei taikan kinen ronji (Tokyo: Kokusho Kankoku, 1984).

[7]   See for instance, Joseph W. Esherick, "How the Qing became China", in *Empire to Nation: Historical Perspectives on the Making of the Modern World*, ed. Joseph W. Esherick, Hasan Kayali and Eric Van Young (Lanham: Rowman and Littlefield, 2006), pp. 229–60.

[8]   Sneh Mahajan, *British Foreign Policy, 1874–1914: The Role of India* (London: Routledge, 2002), p. 22.

[9]   See for instance, Nakami Katsuo, "A Protest against the Concept of the 'Middle Kingdom': The Mongols and the 1911 Revolution", in *The 1911 Revolution in China*, ed. Eto Shinkichi *et al.* (Tokyo: Tokyo University Press, 1984), pp. 129–49.

[10] Dong Wang, *China's Unequal Treaties: Narrating National History*, Lexington Books, (Boulder, Co.: Rowman and Littlefield Publishers, 2005). Cf. 126 and passim.

[11] John W. Garver, *Protracted Contest: Sino-Indian Rivalry in the Twentieth Century* (Seattle: University of Washington Press, 2001), p. 117.

[12] See Lynn Pan, ed., *The Encyclopedia of the Overseas Chinese* (Cambridge, MA: Harvard University Press, 1999), p. 62. See also Prasenjit Duara, "Nationalists

among Transnationals: Overseas Chinese and the Idea of China", in *Crossing the Edges of Empires: Culture, Capitalism and Identities in the Asia-Pacific*, ed. Aihwa Ong and Donald Nonnini (London: Routledge, 1997).

[13] Amarjit Kaur, "Indian Labour, Labour Standards, and Workers' Health in Burma and Malaya 1900–1940", *Modern Asian Studies* 40, 2: (425–475), 425, 432.

[14] Badruddin Tyabji, *Indian Policies and Practice* (New Delhi: Oriental Publishers, 1972), pp. 66–7.

[15] Lu Hun, "Xu" (Preface to Xihuang Zhengyin), *Minbao* 25 (1910): 3977–82, Xihuang Zhengyin, "Nanyang huaqiao shilue" (A brief history of overseas Chinese in Southeast Asia), *Minbao* 25 (1910): 3977–4011, 26: 4087–126. Liang Qichao, "Zhongguo zhimin ba da weiren zhuan" (Eight great Chinese colonists), *Xinmin Congbao* 15 (1906): 81–8.

[16] Garver, *Protracted Contest*, p. 238.

[17] Martin Stuart-Fox, *A Short History of China and Southeast Asia: Tribute, Trade and Influence* (Australia, NSW: Allen and Unwin, 2003), pp. 158, 171, 199.

[18] Garver, *Protracted Contest*, pp. 226–31.

[19] George Zhibin Gu, "It Takes Two to Tango", *Asia Times Online*, 17 Feb. 2005. See also "India, China to achieve $20-b trade target ahead of schedule", *Hindu Businessline*, 10 July 2006 and <http://www.domain-b.com/economy/trade/20060214_growth.html>.

[20] Jairam Ramesh, *Making Sense of Chindia: Reflections on China and India* (New Delhi: India Research Press, 2005).

[21] "India, China to achieve $20-b trade target ahead of schedule", *Hindu Businessline*, 10 July 2006, Jairam Ramesh, *Making Sense of Chindia: Reflections on China and India* (New Delhi: India Research Press, 2005). "ONGC-CNPC wins bid for 38 per cent in Syrian oil fields", *Times of India*, New Delhi, Wednesday, 21 December 2005; Subir Roy, "How to sustain 8 percent growth", *The Economic Times*, New Delhi, 30 November 2005.

[22] Stuart-Fox, *A Short History of China and Southeast Asia*, pp. 212–20.

[23] Garver, *Protracted Contest*, pp. 246–7.

[24] Stuart-Fox, *A Short History of China and Southeast Asia*, p. 212.

[25] Garver, *Protracted Contest*, pp. 258–70. See also Sudha Ramachandran, "India Embraces Myanmar on its Own Terms", *Asia Times Online*, 28 June 2006.

[26] Ibid.

[27] Michael Vatikiotis, "China, India and the Land Between", *Asia Times Online*, 4 March 2006.

[28] Michael Hardt and Antonio Negri, *Empire* (Cambridge, Mass: Harvard University Press, 2000).

PART THREE

The Long March from Empire to Nation

Chapter 6

China's Re-interpretation of the Chinese "World Order", 1900–40s

Kawashima Shin

Introduction

In the view epitomised by John K. Fairbank and Masataka Banno, diplomatic relations between China and surrounding countries took the form of the tributary system until the late nineteenth century. This went into decline with the introduction of the Westphalia system, and China herself eventually accepted the new international order.[1] This approach is typical of those that consider the international political history of East Asia as a conflict between tradition and modernity. However, Takeshi Hamashita has criticised this approach, arguing that the tributary system was a kind of device for trade in this area, so that Britain also sometimes took advantage of the tributary trade system of East Asia.[2] Britain requested a change of trade system at Canton in the 1830s and 1840s, but in the 1880s it did not deny Qing suzerainty over the Korean Peninsula. Moreover, as Toshio Motegi has demonstrated, in the 1870s and 1880s the Qing Dynasty started to re-organise the tribual system and build new provinces in its periphery by adopting modern elements.[3] On the other hand, Takashi Okamoto has demonstrated the double standard by examining in detail the saying that "Korea is a tributary state of Qing, [but is] an independent state."[4] This was used frequently when the Qing court explained its relations with Korea in the 1880s.

Taking off from the numerous empirical studies by Japanese scholars on the tributary system and its transformation, a new stream of research has emerged in recent years. On the one hand, this has challenged Hamashita's argument interpreting the tributary system as a form of trade. These new studies claim that that it was not necessary to conduct tribute in order to trade with Qing China, and that in practice the core of China's trade was not based on the "tributary system" but on *Hu-shi* (互市) or "mutual market trade".[5] This line of argument emphasises once again the political and diplomatic significance of the tributary system. Shigeki Iwai and Minshu Liao advanced a new interpretation that re-positions the Canton System, established in 1757 by the Qing with Western countries including Britain, not as a tributary system but as an institutionalisation of the norms for the mutual market trade system. They also claim that the conflicts over opium and the management of trade in the 1830s and 1840s were not conflicts between the Westphalia system and tribute system, but conflicts around the mutual market trade system.[6] This argument demonstrates a certain distance between the Opium War and the tributary system; and it suggests that the Qing's defeat in the Opium War and the expansion of trade were not directly related to the collapse of the tributary system. A corollary is that the more important cause of this collapse was that Britain, France and Japan had colonised the tributary states of the Qing.

Problems multiplied for the Qing tributary system from the mid-1870s. They included changing modes of trade, as well as the establishment of legations and the etiquette of diplomats. Qing relations with Korea in the 1880s operated on two contradictory tracks, the tributary aspect being under the Ministry of Rites' jurisdiction, and the Westphalian aspect under the Tsungli Yamen's jurisdiction. What made this double standard possible and necessary was the Sino-Japanese War (1894–95). There are other indications that external relations based on the tributary system did not completely disappear with the Sino-Japanese War. These included the supremacy of China in relations with Korea as seen from the content of the 1897 treaty between the Qing and the Korean Empire; the existence of the Chinese settlement and Chinese privilege of consul jurisdiction in the Korean peninsula; the tribute of the Gurkhas to the Qing until the 1911 Revolution; and "tributary" elements in relations with Mongolia and Tibet even after the establishment of the Republic of China in 1912. Nevertheless, the establishment of the Foreign Office in 1901 and China's external relations in the post-Boxer Rebellion era indicated a gradual shift from the double standard to adapting to the Westphalia system.[7] On the one hand China tried to improve its international status, maintain its territorial unity and revise the unequal treaties, while on the other hand promoting movements grounded on nationalism and aimed towards recovering its lost national rights.

As these studies of the traditional international order of China have developed, history is being told differently than the simple conflict between tradition and modernity. Progress in understanding the mutual trade system have made it apparent that China's defeat in a series of wars, including the Opium War, led to the transformation of the trade system which took several decades, rather than the collapse of the traditional international order. It can be said that China's traditional international order was in crisis due to the loss of the tributary states that supported it.

I will in this chapter examine how memories of the tributary system and mutual trade, formed in the period that saw the loss of the "tributary" states and the de facto collapse of the Chinese world order, were manifested and depicted between the years 1900 and 1940, when China was seeking for a Westphalian diplomacy while making efforts to recover its national rights. I will consider how the "lost" territories were perceived by the nationalist-like movement to recover national rights, and how China perceived its "true self", and constructed a new memory of its past. It is also important to consider how Chinese diplomats educated in Western countries perceived China's past relations with its neighbours, especially Japan, while conducting diplomacy under the Westphalia system. This chapter will examine this issue by using articles from magazines, textbooks and maps.

Formation of the Historical Concept of "China" and Its Relations with Surrounding Countries

It is difficult to deny that China is comprised of one historical world; but the use of the name Zhongguo (中国) or "China" as national name, and the formation of a national identity, are not old tales.[8] Traditional history in China comprised a series of dynastic histories, not a national narrative. The construction of a "China" identity gained much attention from the 1900s in the context of Chinese nationalism. Let us refer to Liang Qi Chao's "Introduction to Chinese History" (中国史叙論) concerning the identity formation or consciousness of "China" or "Chinese" that accompanied the Anti-Russian movement (拒俄運動), the anti-American movement, and the anti-Japanese movement reflected in the Tatsumaru Incident (辰丸事件):

What I feel most shameful of is that our country does not have a name. The name of Han (漢) or people of Tang (唐) are only names of Dynasties, and the name "Zhina (Chine/Sina 支那)" that foreign countries use is not a name that we call ourselves. To refer to our history by the name of the Dynasties goes against the idea of respecting our people. Referring to our history by the name China goes against the principle that a name follows the master. The name Zhongguo (中国) or Zhonghua (中華) does seem egotistical and arrogant and may invite criticisms from other countries. All three (name of Dynasty, name by foreign countries, and Zhongguo or Zhonghua) has its own fault, therefore I would like to choose to the name "History of Zhongguo (中国史)", following the oral practice. It is within reason that the people respect their own country, and it is one way to arouse the spirit of compatriots.[9]

Although the histories of the Han, Tang, Ming and Qing Dynasties were already compiled, the history of China as a nation was only discussed in the early twentieth century. It is also during this period that history books included the "modern" element. Let us look at some of the information given in these historical textbooks. The following is the Table of Contents from a history book section introducing the second half of the nineteenth century. This *Elementary School History Textbook* was first published in Shanghai in 1910 and re-printed many times during the ROC period.[10]

Elementary School History Textbook Vol. 4 (高等小学歴史課本 第四冊)

As can be seen from the table, two main themes dominated the period between the late Qing and the early ROC years. The first was the invasion of the great powers, and the second the movements against, and eventual downfall of, the Qing Dynasty. Chapters 66 and 67 explain the loss of tributary states. "After the Opium War and the Franco-British War (Arrow War), the Qing Dynasty's national rights (国权) diminished day by day, and it lost its power to preserve its tributary states. As a result, Myanmar and Vietnam were claimed by someone else."[11]

The Qing had helped Korea and Vietnam against Japanese and French aggression to no avail; they reluctantly recognised the separation of Korea and Vietnam apparently unaware that these countries had already acted as independent states in signing treaties with other foreign countries. Textbooks and history books of this period also discussed how China lost its national rights as suzerain over surrounding "tributary" countries. In this context, the process of loss as suzerain was not "foreign history", but a part of its own national history.

This depiction of history is reinforced through public historical documents and chronologies such as *Diplomatic Documents of Qing* (清季外交史料) and *Manuscript of the History of the Qing Dynasty* (清史稿), which have become reference materials for anyone doing studies on China. In *Diplomatic Documents of Qing*, the emphasis was placed on how China had experienced aggression by Western countires and Japan, and what China should do to recover from such aggression. This material was edited by Wang Yan Wei (王彦威) and Wang Liang (王亮), a father and son team, and published between 1931 and 1932. This is not merely a presentation of the documents, since there are explanations and commentaries in some sections that indicate the editor's intention clearly.[12]

The same emphasis can be seen in the above-mentioned textbooks. Historical recording with an emphasis on the process of loss is significant as it has the potential to encourage movements aimed at recovering national rights. Yet there is also the intriguing admission in the overview of the *Diplomatic Documents of Qing*:

> When looking at the official historiographies of each dynasty, we easily found that these adopted the style of Category (*ji zhuan* 紀伝), and the records of relations with foreign countries were edited only at the volume of 'four barbarians' (四夷) and introduction of foreign countries. Now that the *Manuscript of the History of the Qing Dynasty* is completed, there appears for the first time the heading called 'diplomatic relations (邦交志)' which complements the deficiency of prior official historiographies.[13]

When we look at Volume 153 (No. 128) of this *Manuscript*, the heading is "diplomatic relations", which cannot be found anywhere in earlier historical documents. The text reads: "This section is concerned with the ways to protect our nation from the aggression and invasion from foreign countries." It has been compiled "in order to alert our descendents" and is a record of the absurdity of the invasions by countries that used to be "inferior to China and used to pay tribute to our nation". The "diplomatic relations" of the *Manuscript of the History of the Qing Dynasty* became a standard text for publications related to Chinese diplomatic history and international relations. The authors of the section were Li Jia Ju (李家駒), Wu Guang Pei (呉広霈) and Liu Shu Ping (劉樹屏).

The book also has a heading called "tributary states (屬國)". The nations listed here include Korea, the Ryukyu Islands, Vietnam, Burma, Siam, Laos, the Philippines, Gurkha, Kokand, and Kanjut.[14] *The Manuscript of the History of the Qing Dynasty* was most likely the first document ever to separate the countries of the world into "countries with diplomatic relations" and "tributary states". Tributary states were basically countries that had paid tribute to China, and countries such as Japan were included as one of the countries with diplomatic relations since Japan did not pay tribute during the Qing. However, the world view which separated neighbouring countries (excluding Japan) from other countries was shaped during the late Qing and the early ROC years when "Chinese" history was being constructed.

The Mutual Perception of Japan and China and the Controversy Over History Textbooks

As Japan entered into the international community dominated by Western countries, it perceived itself to be a "civilised" country in the Western sense, fully understanding international standards and abiding by international law. It perceived Qing to be a representative of tradition or the old way, while at the same time seeing it as a threat. As illustrated by Eric Hobsbawm,[15] it is necessary to create tradition in order for "modern" to exist. Japan had begun this process during the Edo period, emphasising its autonomy from Qing China from the late eighteenth century. This was further emphasised when the negotiation for the revision of treaties took place during the Meiji era. Japan's victory in the Sino-Japanese War was perceived as a victory for the civilised world against the uncivilised, or of the modern against tradition. Japan must have found it difficult to accept the new identity of "China" and the formation of "Chinese" history in the beginning of the twentieth century. The widespread idea in Japan that China could not save itself, or that China would disintegrate, was a refusal to accept this identity formation, and led to Japan's refusal to acknowledge China as "Zhongguo (中国)", but rather as "China (支那)".[16] It is evident that this kind of interaction between Japan and China was significant in terms of identity formation.[17]

From China's perspective, Japan was an aggressor, especially after 1900. During the period of the formation of the consciousness of China and the rise of Chinese nationalism, Japan came to be regarded as the most aggressive Asian power. Many of the great powers, other than Japan, based their policy on that of preserving China. Their emphasis on the use of military force against China was also less than that of Japan. Most Chinese diplomats who had studied international law and politics in US and Western countries, like V.K.Wellington Koo, considered Japan as the most dangerous actor toward the status-quo of balance and stability in international politics regarding China.

Both China and Japan regarded the other as an uncivilised country and a negative example. This kind of difference can be seen in the two countries' history education. The controversy over history textbooks arose for the first time in the 1910s when Japan criticised Chinese textbooks for being anti-Japanese. Controversy between China and Japan over textbooks cropped up intermittently from the 1910s through the 1930s. It began with some fiercely anti-Japanese uprisings in China targeted at both the Japanese people and their goods. The Japanese government recognised that these anti-Japanese movements were linked to education in the new schools.

One incident in 1915 was a reaction to Japan's harsh "secret ultimatum" to China, known as the Twenty-one Demands.[18] Japanese newspapers, such as the Osaka *Mainichi Shimbun* and Tokyo *Nichinichi Shimbun*, first reported about anti-Japanese textbooks. Soon after, the Japanese government demanded that the Chinese government prohibit the use and publication of such textbooks. However, Hua Long Tang (湯化龍), China's Minister of Educational Affairs, replied to Japan that these textbooks were just side readers, and were not given official approval, so the government could not prohibit the use and publication of them under the policy of freedom of publication in ROC.[19]

Another incident erupted in Beijing in 1919 during the violent student demonstration against the Versailles Conference, which later came to be known as the May Fourth Movement. The Japanese government hurled back accusations that the outbursts were prompted by "anti-Japanese education", which in turn was fed by "anti-Japanese textbooks". This process was described in an article "New-style textbooks and Japan" in the *Chinese Educational Circle* (中華教育界).[20] The book claimed by Japan to be anti-Japanese was a *Textbook of Chinese Language for Elementary School* published by the Chinese Bookstore (中華書局). In it, Japan was described as follows:

> Japan is an island nation developed after the Meiji Restoration. It placed Okinawa prefecture on <u>our</u> Ryukyu (琉球), forced us to cede our Taiwan, leased our Luda (旅大), annexed Korea, colonised our Manchuria (奉天吉林). It intends to expand its power of transportation and commerce … Japan is a country like a bullet, managed by both domestic and foreign governments. Japan has aimed to target China, and has used any opportunities to invade China as a weak country. Unless we in China come to be a strong country, we cannot remove the shame of our country and enhance our national prestige (Chapter on 'Japan'). Our diplomacy was the most tragic failure of the Qing Dynasty … Japan deprived Ryukyu, annexed Korea; it invaded and has violated our sovereignty continuously (Chapter on 'national shame').[21]

This description was not surprising given the feelings at the time, but Japan could not accept it. The publisher accused by Japan replied that the patriotic sentiments in the textbook were widespread, and the national shame it expressed was not fiction. Therefore Japan's protest was unacceptable.

By beginning its list with Japanese control of "our" Ryukyu, previously interpreted as part of the tributary system, rather than with Japanese aggression against China's territory Taiwan, the textbook emphasised the collapse of the traditional order of China. That is to say, China's loss of a "tributary" state was considered as a loss of China's national rights, reinforcing Chinese nationalism. China's traditional order was regarded as something that was "invaded upon and destroyed". Japan however could not accept this Chinese historical construction. Hence Japan itself set the first spark to the textbook controversy, which has smouldered in East Asia ever since. China's response in 1914 was that the texts in question were not among those approved by the Ministry of Education, claiming that "biased content is not accepted in textbooks approved by the Ministry"; while in 1919, the publisher saw no reason to evade the issue. The controversy over textbooks flared again in 1920 at the League of Nations, when China for the first time criticised Japan for its negative depiction of China.

The Perception of Asia in Japan and China

The conflict between Japan and China over history extended to the history of relations with surrounding countries. The idea of "Asianism (アジア主義)", which emphasised Japan's strong commitment to Asia and its leadership in the independence and liberation of Asia from Western Powers, appeared in Japan in the 1880s.[22] This idea was not only popular in Japan before World War II, but remained so in the post-war era. As this idea of Pan-Asianism was developed, the history of Japan's relations with other Asian countries was re-worked to emphasise the strong relationship between Japan and Asia, and the fact that its relations were built between equals rather than on the basis of superiority as in China's tributary system. Japan's Asianism regarded unfavourably the traditional international order with China at the centre, not least because it sought its own leadership of Asia.

Japan's Pan-Asianism ideas affected China because they were the foundation for Japanese aggression. During the initial stage of Asianism, Japan had requested cooperation from China, and there were Chinese among the symbolic leaders of Pan-Asianism. However, the idea of Pan-Asianism was rarely discussed inside China in the 1910s. In 1919, Li Da Zhao (李大釗) criticised the idea as proclaimed by Japan. He saw Japan's idea of Pan-Asianism as a different name for "Japanism" and its purpose as to "annex China". Moreover, he claimed that what Japan was ultimately aiming for was to make Asia its own; it was "an idea to justify their aggression", "imperialism to annex all the weak people", and "proclaims Japan's militarism and not democracy in Asia". The following is an excerpt from Li's criticism, where he proposed an alternative idea of "New Pan-Asianism", eliminating Japan's leadership and emphasising the self-determination of all Asians: "All people of Asia should be liberated from annexation by others, and must realize self-determination. In order to do so, we must form one big coalition, stand independently from other Western coalitions but cooperate and work together to complete a world federation to promote the happiness for all mankind."[23]

Needless to say, this kind of criticism was grounded in the Japanese invasion of China and the ideas of Woodrow Wilson. From the perspective of modern Japanese political thought, we might ask why the idea of Pan-Asianism that proclaimed Asian solidarity became the foundation of Japan's aggression and invasion. Li Da Zhao's reaction to Japan's Asianism was closely linked to the interpretation of China's traditional international order. On the one hand, Wilsonism was proposed as a set of measures against the new challenge of imperialism by Western Powers, while Japan preferred Asianism. China continued to understand its relations with Asian countries in terms of modernising its traditional international order, and several attempts were in this vein.

One such attempt was made by Sun Yat Sen (孫文) in his *Principle of Nationalism* (2 March 1924). This discussed the relations between China and other Asian countries, especially the positive relations between the Imperial Dynasties and neighbouring people. If there was anything China could learn from Japan in the contemporary world, it was how Japan became one of the ten great powers, so that "when China learns from Japan, China can recover its first-class status". Not only did Sun Yat Sen hereby assert China's historical status as first-class; he also claimed that this status would be secure in the future because it was founded on the idea that, unlike the other great powers, "China will save the weak and assist them when in danger (「濟弱扶傾」)". In his view, "because China had such a peaceful principle toward tributary countries, these countries like Vietnam, Burma and Siam were able to be independent for thousands of years". It was the absence of any such principle in the other great powers that led to the destruction of these small countries. He concluded that, "if China becomes a strong power by the same way as western powers in invading other countries, China would also have no good result just as they have not. So China has to adopt a kind policy toward weak and small countries, and to resist western powers." It seems that Sun Yat Sen ultimately recognised that China must become a great power that was different from other great powers, still central to the neighbouring countries but in a positive and amicable way.

A similar trend can be seen in Sun Yat Sen's famous speech on Pan-Asianism delivered in Kobe, Japan on 28 November 1924. He compared the difference between the rule of right and the rule of might, and requested Japan to move in the direction of the former. The relations between the Chinese Dynasties and surrounding countries were examples of the rule of right. Sun emphasised that China's status was equal to that of Britain and the United States, stating that "between 500 and 2000 years ago, China was supreme in the world". In answer to the question, "What was the situation of the weaker nations toward China then?", he evinced the tributary system. "These weaker countries respected China as their superior and sent annual tributary envoys to China by their own will and with their honor."

In Sun's view China maintained her prestige among smaller and weaker nations not through the use of force such as the sending of an army or navy.

> These weaker nations surrounding China were influenced by Chinese values and virtue without military menace from China. These nations felt its superiority and were willing to absorb them from China and to send tributary envoys to China. Once they were influenced by Chinese values and virtue, they did not send tributary envoys only once or twice, but so many times from generation to generation.[24]

China's relation with surrounding countries, which had been negatively portrayed in Japan's Pan-Asianism, was positively restated by Sun Yat Sen in this anti-imperialist discourse.[25] To a certain degree, although under false pretences, Japan's Pan-Asianism was an opposition to Western imperialism.[26] Sun Yat Sen played a significant role in developing an alternative Chinese Pan-Asianism.

Diversion and Development of Pan-Asianism in China

So-called Pan-Asianism was not a major topic in Chinese intellectual and political circles, whereas Japanese intellectuals loved to discuss it. But some Chinese politicians and intellectuals also raised the issue under some specific context. Sun Yat Sen understood the traditional international order as superior to imperialism. His "Speech on Great Asianism" compared Japan's Asianism to the rule of might in Western imperialism and encouraged Japan to adopt the Chinese way. He sought a synthesis or balance of West and East. There were those in China who stressed the traditional international order, similar to Sun, but at the same time linked it to Chinese nationalism. This led to the belief that the surrounding countries should become a part of China. Another group also emphasised the traditional international order, but in a different sense which both presupposed China's supremacy and asserted its solidarity as the non-aggressor. This position was that of the "Three Principles of the People" stressing both opposition to imperialism and equality and solidarity with other Asian countries.

This dichotomy is evident in the exchange between Ceng Qi (曾琦) and Ma He Tian (馬鶴天) in Shanghai's *Jiu Kuo Daily* (『救国日報』) in 1918. Ceng wrote "when China was a great power, Korea and Annam were her tributary states, but China's status was threatened when she lost her national rights during the late Qing". He therefore emphasised the idea of Greater Pan-Asianism, claiming "China must struggle and make all efforts to become a great power and become supreme in East Asia, and will not only restore Korea, Annam, Siam and Burma but make these into Chinese territory. Japan as well as the countries of the South Seas all received benefits from China. Therefore they are all territories of China." Ma, chief editor of the journal at that time, revised this article and replaced "Great Pan-Asianism" with "New Pan-Asianism". He also revised the content so that it declared that "after China becomes a great power, she will assist in the independence of Korea, Annam, and India, and unite with other nations to oppose other great powers". Ceng was furious after he found out that Ma had altered his article, and the relationship between Ceng and Ma worsened.[27] Ma's opinion implied the fear that a "Greater Pan-Asianism" with China at the centre corresponded to the "Great Pan-Asianism" of Japan. The idea that all tributary states should become territories of China was very provocative.[28] It is noteworthy that a survey of the conflict between Ceng and Ma appeared in a magazine called *New Asia* (『新亜細亜』) which was published during the era of the Nanking Kuomintang Government (see below).

Ceng advanced similar arguments in a speech in Shanghai in 1925, on "The Mission of the Chinese People". He argued that after China had conquered surrounding nations during the Han and Tang Dynasty, "all of these nations were tributary states of China during the Qing Dynasty. However, China never occupied their lands, nor made slaves of their people, nor stole their goods, and never thought of the destruction of these people." China respected their culture and demonstrated the supremacy of the "great Chinese nation" without the use of force.[29] The Chinese nation that sought for peace and practiced cooperation should cooperate with surrounding countries to build a "Greater Asian Republic" and "enjoy the peace, never allow the oppression of great powers and never accept the interference of our evolution by tyrannical empires".

Arguments like Ceng's took root in society to a certain degree. Many followed in his footsteps even though such arguments were not publicly sanctioned. During the process in which the 'Three Principles of the People' transformed into the ideology of government, it also affected interpretations of Sun Yat Sen's speech on Pan-Asianism. Nationalist views such as Ceng's began to be seen in a negative light. This is the context in which Ma's criticism of Ceng appeared in the aforementioned *New Asia*. In the speech on Pan-Asianism, Sun had mentioned China's relations with Gurkha and talked positively about the tributary relations with surrounding nations. However, in the new interpretations of his Pan-Asianism, these traditional relations with the surrounding nations were not emphasised. Hu Han Min (胡漢民) played a significant role in the process of re-definition of Sun's thought.[30] In articles such as "Greater Pan-Asianism and International Technical Cooperation", "Greater Pan-Asianism Revisited" and "Concerning the Greater Pan-Asianism" in the *Three Principles of the People Monthly* (1933–36),[31] Hu criticised Japanese Pan-Asianism as "merely a form of Japanese nationalism". He argued that Sun Yat Sen's Pan-Asianism comprised only a small part of the nationalism of the "Three Principles of the People". Pan-Asianism was in a sense a civic-nationalism, which emphasised the cooperation with surrounding ethnicities as equals and did not touch upon the tributary relations of the past.

In the period before the Manchurian Incident, new definition of Sun Yat Sen's Pan-Asianism could be seen in journals such as *New Asia*. This magazine was published by New Asia Publishing in Nanking in 1930, and involved a group of Kuomintang members including. Zhang Zhen Zhi (張振之), Yu You Ren (于右任), Hu Han Min, Dai Ji Tao (戴季陶) and Ma He Tien, a famous writer in the Northwestern region of China. The aim of the magazine was to claim an "Asia grounded Three Principles of the People" and to criticise "Pan-Asianism" in the Japanese sense. Moreover, Zhang Shen Zhi and Dai Ji Tao had also established a New Asia Academic Society (新亜細亜学会) in Nanking on March 1931, for which *New Asia* also served as the journal.[32] These writers presented a new image of China's relations with its neighbours without any mention of the Imperial precedent. One article read: "The aim is to research the issue of liberation of the Asian nations, founded on the Three Principles of the People. China strives for their independence, and supports all movements toward the liberation of the Asian nations, working together to attain free and equal status."[33]

The magazine also made reference to the history, geography and politics of those under the rule of the great powers, the origin of their colonisation, the movements for liberation, and the future after independence of countries such as India, the Philippines, Annam, Korea, Taiwan/Ryukyu, the East Indies, and Turkey. The article "The Future of Asia-Declaration" stated that the "the President is the saviour of China, and at the same time a saviour of the people in Asia. After the birth of the President, as if life was given to China, the peoples of Asia have slowly awakened and world affairs have started to take a new turn."[34]

Sun's Pan-Asianism was regarded as "Pan-Asianism grounded on the Three Principles of the People"; it was founded on salvation, completely different from that of Japan. Moreover, Sun Yat Sen himself re-defined his Pan Asianism "since the Three Principles of the People will save the Asian people, it is without question that the Three Principles of the People are Pan-Asianism itself. From the perspective of restoring China, Chinese people believe in and devote themselves to the Three Principles of the People. However, from the perspective of people of colour in Asia, people of Asia also believe in and devote themselves to the Three Principles of the People." There is no mention of the tributary relations.[35] In an article on "Pan-Asianism and New Asia", Ma He Tien warned against the misinterpretation of Sun Yat Sen's speech: "There are actually two different interpretations of 'Pan-Asianism'. We have named this magazine *New Asia* based on the Three Principles of the People declared by the President, to prevent people's misinterpretation of the Three Principles, as well as to clarify the general public's understanding of them."[36]

This trend was also seen in a magazine called *New East* (新東方) in the 1930s. The opening pages of the first issue mentioned Sun Yat Sen's Pan-Asianism and the Mission statement of the Magazine declared that "the future of the East is a liberated world where all ethnicities will stand together as equals". That is not to say that the Chinese "Pan-Asianism" criticised by Hu Han Min and Ma He Tien had disappeared from the propaganda activities of the Kuomintang. In magazines such as *New Asia* or *New East* there were articles declaring the supremacy of the Chinese people over the surrounding ethnicities. This idea can also be detected in textbooks.[37] In the maps for educational purposes made by the Ministry of Internal Affairs (内政部) in 1938 and 1939, there were territories marked as "tributary states" that China must recover as its own territory. The territories that China lost included not only Taiwan, but also Siam, Myanmar, Korea and Ryukyu (see map). The ideology of "Pan-Asianism" remained in China even after its transformation into a Japan-centred idea in Japan. The Japanese Asianism calling for solidarity metamorphosed into an ideology of Asian conquest in the late 1930s. It is unclear whether there is a connection between this trend and the publication of a book called *Sinocentrism* by Toshisada Nawa of Kyoto University in 1936.[38] This was probably the first book in Japanese academic circles to criticise the idea of Sinocentrism under that name.

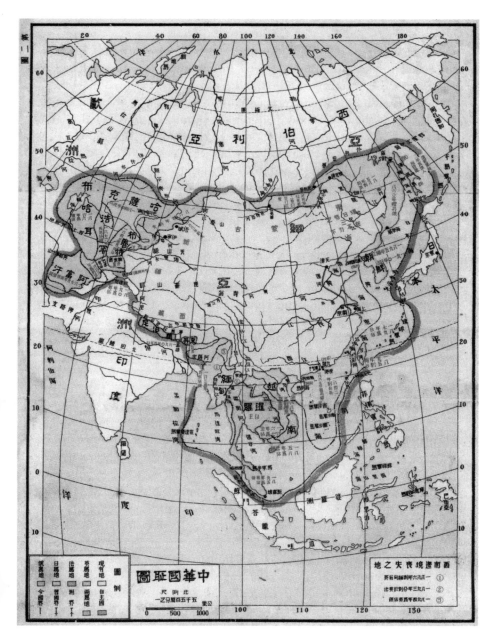

Figure 1 Map of National Shame [Hong Maoxi (洪懋熙), eds., *The New Chinese Map*, authorised by Ministry of Interior for Elementary School (内政部審定小学適用最新中国 地図), Chongqing, Dongfang Yudi Xueshe (東方輿地学社, 1938)].

Conclusion

Recent research on the Chinese traditional international order has indicated that diverse and multi-layered international relations existed in East Asia. Both in terms of ideas and institutions, this may have been a set of individual relations rather than one functioning system. In the debate about whether Chinese diplomacy should be considered from a Westphalian or traditional point of view, the issue of how China perceived herself in the twentieth century has not been sufficiently studied. This chapter has made a contribution to argue some cases about this topic, using Chinese textbooks and magazines from 1900 to 1940.

The concept of "China" and the notion of national history were formulated in the beginning of the twentieth century. Textbooks emphasised the interplay of aggression and resistance, depicting the surrounding tributary states being "taken away" by the invasion of the great powers. The tributary states were, in other words, something China had lost which should be recovered in due course. This view became the grounds for criticising the Japan that "invaded" Ryukyu, clashing with Japan's historical view on the annexation of Ryukyu and the Sino-Japanese War. The textbook issue between China and Japan had already started in the 1910s.

When Wilsonism was being discussed widely after the First World War, Japan's Asianism was presented as an alternative idea. This revived the debate on China's traditional international order. The arguments can be divided into three different groups. The first is the argument represented by Sun Yat Sen that praised the traditional international order as the "kingly way" while criticising imperialism as the rule of might. The second was accompanied by nationalism, whereby all tributary states were regarded as subject states that should become Chinese territory in the future. The third attacked the traditional order stressing China's supremacy, and favoured equality and solidarity among Asian countries. The third became the official viewpoint, without however eliminating arguments in favour of China's traditional order.

The conceptualisation of relations with neighbours was certainly affected by opposition to the discourse about Pan-Asianism in Japan. This can be seen in two different trends: the positive recollection of traditional relations, as against equality and solidarity with the surrounding countries. While both trends opposed imperialism, the former differed in presuming the supremacy of China. Officially the Kuomintang emphasised the latter, though not without some contrary indications. There was an increasing emphasis on equality during the Sino-Japanese War, to oppose Japan's Pan-Asianism.[39] To continue the research on China's perception of world order, it remains necessary to look at the development of the perception of Asia in socialist China and Taiwan in the second half of the twentieth century.

Notes

1   Banno Masataka, *China and the West 1858–1861: The Origins of the Tsungli Yamen* (Cambridge [MA]: Harvard University Press, 1964); John King Fairbank, ed., *The Chinese World Order: Traditional China's Foreign Relations* (Cambridge [MA]: Harvard University Press, 1968).

2   Takeshi Hamashita, "近代中国の国際的契機:: 朝貢貿易システムと近代アジア" [*International Opportunities of Modern China: Tributary Trade System and Modern Asia*] (Tokyo: Tokyo University Press, 1990).

3   Toshio Motegi, "変容する近代東アジアの国際秩序" [*Transition of the International Order in Modern East Asia*] (Yamakawa Publishing, 1997).

4   Takashi Okamoto, "属国と自主のあいだ" [*Between Tributary State and Autonomy*] (Nagoya: Nagoya University Press, 2004).

5   The tributary system (冊封) in Qing dynasty refers to the exchange of envoys between China and neighbouring polities, or the sending of envoys by neighbouring countries to China for recognition and legitimacy as tributary kings. The Ministry of Rites (礼部) and local generals were responsible for the system in China. In Ryukyu's case, tributary envoys (冊封使) from China were given letters of authorisation for their kings, as well as a Chinese calendar which they were requested to use when visiting China. The envoys from neighbouring polities brought ordered gifts to the Chinese Emperor as a symbol of gratitude. The envoys were given in China the same symbolic rank as their kings, both being treated as servants of the Chinese emperor. China did not interfere with the domestic affairs of the tributary states, nor their relations with other countries. An army was sent only following a request for military assistance. Besides the political aspect, the tributary system has another aspect as official trade: (1) exchanging gifts between emperor and king, (2) trade at the market at Beijing, (3) trade at regulated ports and periphery markets, and so on (朝貢). This trade was conducted by Chinese (overseas Chinese and Chinese merchants).

6   Min Shu Liao, "互市から見た清朝の通商秩序" [*Trade Order during the Qing Dynasty Seen from the Mutual Market Trade System*], unpublished PhD dissertation, School of Law and Politics, Hokkaido University, 2006.

7   Shin Kawashima, "中国近代外交の形成" [*Formation of Modern Chinese Diplomacy*] (Nagoya: Nagoya University Press, 2004).

8   Ibid.

9   Liang Qichao, "飲冰室合集" [*Collected Works of Yinbingshi*] (Vol. 6). The original text appeared in 『清議報』 (*Qing Bulletin*) in 1901.

10 "高等小学歴史課本 第四冊" [*Elementary School History Textbook* No. 4] (First edition. Shanghai: Chinese Publishing, 1910 [distributed from 1911] and Revised Sixth edition, 1913).

11 Ibid., pp. 32–4.

12 E.g. *Diplomatic Documents of Qing* (Overview, Vol. 1) (『清季外交史料』術略、一), where there is a heavy emphasis on the Sino-Franco War and Sino-Japanese War.

13 *Diplomatic Documents of Qing*, Overview, Vol. 2.

14 *The Manuscript of the History of the Qing Dynasty* Vol. 526–29, "Biographies and Tributary States".

15 *Nations and Nationalism since 1780: Programme, Myth, Reality* (Cambridge: Cambridge University Press, 1990).

16 Shin Kawashima, "'支那', '支那国', '支那共和国'—日本外務省の対中呼称政策" ["'China', 'State of China', 'Republic of China' — Japanese Ministry of Foreign Affairs Policy toward the Name of China], 中国研究月報 [*Monthly Bulletin on Chinese Studies*] 571 (September 1995).

17 This mutual effect is not intended in a negative context, but rather following the lead of Jian Hui Liu "日本でつくられた中国の自画像" [Self Portrait of China that was Created in Japan], 中国 21 [*China 21*], 22 (June 2005). He showed that the the self definition of "China" in China was deeply related to the arguments concerning China that took place in Japan, including the division between North and South China.

18 "排日教科書ニ関スル件" [About Anti-Japanese Textbooks], 7 November 1914, in Diplomatic Archives of the Japanese Government (B-1-1-2-089).

19 教育雑誌 [*Journal of Education*] 6, 8 (1914): 72–3 and 69.

20 "新式教科書与日本" [New-style Textbooks and Japan], in 中華教育界 [*Educational Society in China*] 8, First Term (1919).

21 国民学校用新式国文教科書, as cited in "中華書局反論" [Opposition of the Chinese Bookstore], in *Educational Society in China* 8 (1919).

22 Naoki Hazama, "序章 アジア主義とはなにか" ["Introduction: What is Pan-Asianism?"], 『東亜』 (*East Asia*) (No. 410, August 2001).

23 Li Da Zhao, "大亜細亜主義与新亜細亜主義" [Great Pan-Asianism and New Pan-Asianism], 国民雑誌 [*People's Magazine*] 1, 2 (1919) collected in 李大釗全集 [Complete Works of Li Da Zhao] (Beijing: Renmin chuban she, 1959), p. 127.

24 Sun Yat Sen, "大亜洲主義" [Pan-Asianism], in 国父全集 [*Founding Father's Complete Works*] (Taipei: Central Books Publishing, 1957), pp. 507–19. Many newspapers published this speech, however, the content of the speech differ among the newspapers, and many critical works have been published.

25 Etuko Mori, "孫文と朝鮮問題" [Sun Yat Sen and the Issue over Korea], in 孫文研究会会報 [*Journal for Research on Sun Yat Sen*], 13 (1991).

26 Yoshitaro Hirano, "大アジア主義の歴史的基礎" [Historical Foundation of Pan-Asianism] (Kawade Publishing, June 1945), pp. 117 and 132. Kou Takeuchi, "解説 アジア主義の展望" [Commentary on the Development of Pan-Asianism],

in アジア主義 [*Pan-Asianism*], ed. Kou Takeuchi (Chikuma, 1963), pp. 15–8. Shouzo Fujii, "孫文の'大アジア講演'と日本" [Sun Yat Sen and His Speech on Pan-Asianism and Japan], in 海外事情 [*Foreign Affairs*], 26–8 (August 1978).

27 Ma He Tian, "関於'大亜細亜'与'新亜細亜'題名的廻憶" [Consideration on 'Pan-Asianism' and 'New Asia'], in 新亜細亜 [*New Asia*], First Issue, First Term (October 1930): 139–40.

28 It is difficult to confirm Ma He Tian's explanation through the materials from Ceng Qi. See Shen Yulong, ed., "曽慕韓 (琦) 先生日記選" [Ceng Mu Han (Qi)'s Diary] (Taipei: Wenhai Publishing, 1971). One can confirm that Ceng visited Ma He Tien at the publisher in Shanghai on 17 August1918. An article titled "中国之青年與共和之前途" [*China's Youth and Republic*] was submitted to 国体與青年 [*State and Youth*] but there is no confirmation on whether there was a conflict with Ma. In the first pages of Cheng Zheng Mao, "曽琦先生文集" [Works of Ceng Qi] (Academia Sinica, 1993), we can see that the article was published on 国体與青年 [State and Youth]; there is no mention of any interactions with Ma.

29 "The Mission of the Chinese people and the Responsibility of Chinese Youths" (Shanghai Academic Society on Sun Yat Sen), 中華民族之使命與中国青年之責任－答上海孫文主義学会, as cited in Ceng Mu Han Memorial Editing Committee, 曽慕韓先生遺著 [*Memorial Works of Ceng Mu Han*] (Beijing: Chinese Youth Party Central Committee, 1954), pp. 27–9.

30 Akio Ito, "'大アジア主義'と'三民主義'－傀儡政権下の諸問題について" ["'Pan-Asianism' and 'Three Principles of the People' — Problems under the Wang Jin Wei Administration"], in 横浜市立大学論叢人文科学系列 [*Yokohama University Journal Humanities*] (March 1989): 40–1; Shozo Fujii, "孫文の'大アジア講演'と日本" ["Sun Yat Sen and His Speech on Pan-Asianism and Japan"], in 海外事情 [*Foreign Affairs*], 26-8 (August 1978).

31 This appears not only in the 三民主義月刊 [*Three Principles of the People Monthly*], but also in Wang Yang Chong, ed., "胡漢民先生政論選輯: 遠東問題与大亜細亜主義" [*Collected Works of Hu Han Min: Far East Issues and Pan-Asianism*] (Guangzhou: Minzhi Publishing, 1935).

32 Juntaro Kubo, "雑誌'新亜細亜'論説記事目録" ["Records of Articles in the Magazine 'New Asia'"], in 神戸大学史学年報 [*Annual Journal of History Kobe University*], 17 (2002).

33 "本刊徴稿内容" ["Content of Articles in This Magazine"], in 新亜細亜 [*New Asia*] First Issue, First Term (October 1930).

34 "亜細亜之将来－創刊宣言" ["Asia's Future-Declaration"], in 新亜細亜 [*New Asia*], First Issue, First Term (October 1930): 9.

35 Ibid., pp. 12–3.

36 Ma He Tian, "関於'大亜細亜'与'新亜細亜'題名的廻憶" [Consideration on "Pan-Asianism" and "New Asia"], in 新亜細亜 [*New Asia*], First Issue, First Term (October 1930): 139–40.

37   Huang Song Lan, "清末・民国期地理教科書の空間表象―領土・疆域・国恥"
      [Expression of Space in Late Qing and ROC Geography Textbooks], 中国研究
      月報 [*Monthly Chinese Studies*], 59–3 (March 2005).

38   Toshisada Nawa, *Sinocentrism* [中華思想] (Tokyo: Iwanami, 1936). Prof. Nawa
      recognised that *Sinocentrism* (中華思想) disappeared after late Qing, while
      China kept it for a few thousand years.

39   In China's foreign relations with Siam (one of the few independent countries in
      Asia) and the provisional government of Korea, one cannot confirm the tendency
      toward restoring the old type of relations under the Qing, as Ceng argued. See
      Shin Kawashima, *Formation of Modern Chinese Diplomacy*, pp. 355–99.

Chapter 7

The "Peaceful Rise of China" after the "Century of Unequal Treaties": Will History Matter?

Zheng Yangwen

The "peaceful rise of China" has grabbed international headlines, fascinated world leaders, and galvanised academic debate. How peaceful China's rise will be, I shall argue in this chapter, depends on how she reconciles with the "century of unequal treaties". The rising tide of Chinese nationalism makes this problematic. This chapter focuses on two important issues — What are the "unequal treaties"? How are they perceived/debated in history and taught in schools? A reading of the "unequal treaties" is essential first in order to comprehend the gravity of their terms and conditions. Then the chapter turns to some of the late Qing — early Republican political writings and contemporary textbooks to see why the "unequal treaties" might matter in the coming decades.

The Qing court and the Republic of China (ROC) regime signed more than two hundred treaties with a long list of countries that begins with Britain and includes many European countries, the United States, Japan and Russia in the period from the end of the First Opium War in 1842 to the end of the Second World War in 1945. They were labelled 不平等條約 *bu ping deng tiao yue* or "unequal treaties" because they included terms and conditions forced upon China rather than desired by the Chinese regimes in question. The ROC regime (driven to Taiwan in 1949) displayed the Chinese copy of the Treaty of Nanking in June 1997 and suggested that Britain hand Hong Kong back to Taiwan, not China, since at least it owned the Treaty. The handover of Hong Kong and Macao in 1999 have inspired historians; but systematic studies of the 不平等條約 or "unequal treaties" would require global and cross-disciplinary collaboration.[1] This is imperative as China rises with renewed confidence and economic power.

The "Unequal Treaties"

The "unequal treaties" were terms and conditions that a long list of foreign countries forced upon the late Qing court and the Republic of China regime. Many ordinary Chinese can name the major treaties:

> The Treaty of Nanking 南京條約 (1842)
> The Treaty of Aigun 璦琿條約 (1858)
> The Treaty of Tianjin 天津條約 (1858)
> The Convention of Peking 北京條約 (1860)
> The Treaty of Shimonoseki 馬関條約 (1895)
> The 2nd Convention of Peking 北京條約 (1898)
> The Boxer Protocol 辛丑條約 (1901)
> The Twenty-one Demands 二十一條款 (1919)

These major treaties were often, but not always, followed by satellite treaties. The Treaty of Nanking is a good example. Signed between Britain and the Qing court due to the Qing's loss of the First Opium War in 1842, it was followed by:

> The *Wanxia* Treaty between China and the United States in July 1844
> The *Huangpu* Treaty between China and France in October 1844

In other words, when China lost the First Opium War to Britain, the two other great powers of the time also benefited as they managed to extract similar concessions from the Qing even though they were not involved in the war at all. France and America were watching and learning from the British; they were developing their own designs for China as the British Empire expanded to other parts of the world. The fierce competition among European powers had extended to China, an old empire herself now under the whip of new empires.

Another situation was that of multiple treaties. This was the case with the Treaty of Tianjin and the Convention of Peking, as the Qing lost the Second Opium War to a coalition of British, French, Russian and American troops. The Qing court had to sign a treaty with each one of them in June 1858, namely:

The Sino-Russia Treaty of Tianjin on the 13th
The Sino-US Treaty of Tianjin on the 18th
The Sino-British Treaty of Tianjin on the 26th
The Sino-French Treaty of Tianjin on the 27th

Russia, not just France and America, was eager to join the race for empire. China's long-time neighbour in fact had extracted the Treaty of Aigun a month earlier in May 1858, which ceded the left bank of the Amur River to Russia; in other words, it re-drew the borders of Russia's Far East. The Russians were closing in, followed immediately by Japan, Germany and other European countries.

The Chinese originals of these treaties were taken to Taiwan by the Republic of China regime in 1949. The Imperial Maritime Customs kept copies of these treaties as they executed treaty terms and conditions; its great Inspector General Robert Hart had ordered at least three compilations in 1875, 1887 and 1908. There were also individual efforts. Samuel Couling compiled a list of the Qing treaties in 1907. His research yielded 32 treaties between Britain and China, 68 between other powers and China, and 22 relating to China made between foreign powers. This was followed by Huang Yuebo in the 1930s and Wang Tieya in the 1950s. Two comprehensive compilations appeared in 2004 and 2005. They were compiled by the Chinese Bureau of Maritime Customs, using the copies they have, and Helongjiang People's Publisher; I have found the latter (see Appendix at the end of this chapter) helpful as it contains both English and Chinese entries, albeit only up to 1902.[2]

The sheer number of the treaties and the foreign countries they involved indicates the enormous impact they had on Chinese polity, economy and society. The first 15 treaties are generally not considered "unequal" since they were peace or boundary agreements between the Qing and Russia. However, their inclusion in the long list of "unequal treaties" serves to demonstrate the compiler or the publisher's stance, constrained by their education and government control, towards the so-called "unequal treaties".

To understand the basic component of these treaties, we start from the mother of all "unequal treaties" — The Treaty of Nanking, which marked the end of the First Opium War, 1839 to 1842, between Britain and the Qing Empire. It was signed on board the British battleship HMS *Cornwallis* in Nanking on 29 August 1842. This was the first of many wars and unwanted treaties to come. Major terms of the Treaty are:

1. China to cede Hong Kong and nearby small islands to the UK
2. China to open five port cities: Guangzhou (Canton), Xiamen (Amoy), Fuzhou (Foochow), Ningbo and Shanghai to British trade
3. China to pay 15 million taels of silver as reparation for the British naval expedition and 6 million for the destruction of British merchant-owned opium
4. China to accept fixed tariffs for British goods
5. China to grant extraterritoriality to British subjects

First-time readers of the Treaty of Nanking might find it puzzling that opium is scarcely mentioned in the treaty that brought the war in its name. This explains the politics of treaty-making on the one hand and the origin of the war on the other. To understand these British demands on China, we must examine the origin of the war. Opium was brought to China as tribute from Southeast Asia since the early mid-Ming period. Its transformation from a medicinal herb to a recreational drug in the seventeenth century changed the nature of consumption. The eighteenth century saw the explosion of a consumer revolution as the middle classes took up smoking. The demand for opium grew and this coincided with the rise of the British East India Company in the intra-Asia trade. The British had been competing with the Dutch in the region and they were desperate for something the Chinese would buy with silver so that they could use the silver to buy tea from China. China had absorbed the world's silver supply, as she only accepted silver for foreign trade since the Ming era, if not earlier. The increase of opium imports, along with domestic cultivation fuelled by the popularity of opium, made it possible for the ordinary urban consumer to smoke opium by the early nineteenth century. This led to addiction and social destruction of various kinds on the one hand, and the outflow of silver or the bankruptcy of local governments on the other.

The Daoguang Emperor's response was prohibition; he despatched Commissioner Lin Zexu to Canton to solve the problem in March 1839. Commissioner Lin, known as an uncorrupted official, took a hard line. He surrounded the so-called 13 factories where the foreign trading community lived and worked within two weeks of his arrival. He ordered the Chinese servants to leave, and cut off their provisions in the hope that opium merchants, mostly British, would surrender their stock. He also asked these merchants to sign a bond and promise not to bring opium to China if/when they came back to do business. British merchants and others managed to hold on for nearly two months until late May 1839, when they surrendered approximately

20,283 chests of opium and left China. This opium was burned in public witnessed by a handful of missionaries.

News of the "confinement of the Queen's subjects" and "confiscation of British properties" reached London quickly and became the pretext for retaliation in the name of protecting the Queen's subjects and British commercial interest. British grievances were far more than just that. The Qing court had limited all foreign trade to Canton where corruption was rampant. The inconvenience of being confined to the waterfront of Canton and rigid bureaucratic procedures had long annoyed those who traded with China. They had longed for change; opium now seemed to have provided the perfect opportunity. The debate on the origin of the war has generated controversies, and not only among historians. Would it have been a Rice War had the commodity been rice? Tan Chung's *China and the Brave New World*, written 30 years ago, remains one of the very few studies devoted to the origin of the conflict. Tan pointed out that even John Quincy Adams, then American President, had something to say about the conflict:

> The cause of war is the *Kotow*: the arrogant and insupportable pretensions of China, that she will hold commercial intercourse with the rest of mankind, not upon terms of equal reciprocity, but upon the insulting and degrading forms of relation between lord and vassal.[3]

Adams might have read or been briefed about the famous kowtow episode of Lord Macartney when he visited China in 1793. The rhetoric and practice of lord and vassal had been applied by the Middle Kingdom towards her neighbours in Asia, and this did not change when the Europeans entered the China theatre. These enterprising Europeans did not know that commerce and profit-making stood at the bottom of the hierarchy of Confucian philosophy. The court benefited from the revenues maritime trade generated, and believed it could best maintain a tight control over it through only one port — Canton. The idea that trade was vital to the survival of a country was foreign to the Ming-Qing Chinese authorities; they did not recognise that China could be the largest market for the products of the Industrial Revolution. It seems this was a conflict of cultures. This is why historians like Li Chien-nung, echoed by Tan Chung, Chang Hsin-pao, John L. Cranmer-Byng and Victor Purcell, called it a "culture war". As Li put it: "The war between China and England, caused superficially by the problem of opium prohibition, may actually be viewed as a conflict of Western and Eastern cultures."[4]

While many subscribed to the culture war theory, they also believed that British commercial expansion was "the vital force that brought on the cultural conflict". Trade was the agency, and it convinced economic historians like Michael Greenberg that it was a "trade war":

> To the Chinese the war was fought over the Opium question; but for the British merchants the issues were wider. 'The grand cardinal point of the expedition' was to Matheson 'the future mode of conducting the foreign trade with China'.[5]

Capitalist expansion would lead to war and colonialism, as Karl Marx predicted. To follow this line of thought, there would have been a Rice War if the disputed commodity was rice. On yet another level, some scholars, W.W. Willoughby and W.A.P. Martin among them, believed that the war was exactly what it was called, an "Opium War". Martin concluded: "This war, which bears a malodorous name, was waged for the purpose of compelling China to submit to the continuance of an immoral traffic."[6] Historians returned to the topic of opium in the late 1990s after the debate disappeared in 1978; *Opium Regimes: China, Britain and Japan, 1839–1952* and *The Social Life of Opium in China* among others have already shed new light on the origins of this conflict.[7]

The debate helps us comprehend the origin of the war; it leads us to the "unequal" nature of the treaties — extraterritoriality, trading privileges, compensation for war expenses and opium destroyed. Few would deny that these demands were forced upon the Qing court; but scholars disagree on their consequences in China. Economic historians have argued about the effect of Western capitalism on China's own socio-economic transformation nicknamed Chinese capitalist sprouts, which had started during the *Ming* period if not earlier. Albert Feuerwerker believed that imperialism had aborted "the promising capitalist sprouts in handicraft industry and commerce".[8] Others, however, have taken the view that foreign trade and investment contributed to China's modernisation. Hao Yen-p'ing has emphasised that: "China's trade with the West during the nineteenth century gave impetus to a full-fledged mercantile capitalism that constituted a commercial revolution"; while Gregory Blue has argued that "the opium trade was instrumental in integrating China into the world market".[9]

Both arguments have substance. Western capitalism did destroy and weaken some indigenous industry and commerce, but it also helped create and nurture new ones. With the help of post-Mao hindsight, one can see that however humiliating to governments, some of the terms benefited China in the long run. How can we associate humiliation with benefit? Timothy Weston and Yeh Wen-hsin have recently demonstrated the importance of separating politics from economics as they charted China's march from empire to nation and modernity, which manifested in different places with various trajectories.[10] This alternative can be applied to the study of the "unequal treaties". We can separate the political from the economic, the short-term from the long-term consequences.

Politically, the "unequal treaties" were most humiliating to the Qing court, the Republic of China and the Chinese political public. The sense of injustice and victimhood lives in national memory today; it has been and will continue to be used and abused by politicians, diplomats, journalists and ordinary people. Like a knife, it can be sharpened at troubled times when political regimes need a common enemy and when China sees an opportunity for revenge, even if it is just rhetoric. One obvious "unequal" provision was the clause in the Treaty of Nanking requiring China to pay for war expenses and opium destroyed. This kind of interest-bearing indemnity would increase and eventually bankrupt not just local governments but the Qing Empire itself, as it amounted to a colossal amount of money that could never be repaid. This burden was born by ordinary Chinese rather than the rich and powerful. It fuelled anti-Qing rebellions and revolutionary parties, which de-legitimised and ultimately overthrew the Qing dynasty. A particularly weighty condition was extraterritoriality, through which foreign influences would gradually transform Chinese politics, culture and society. The sudden and overwhelming Western intrusion, ranging from political thought and artistic form to social institutions and cultures of consumption, began to work on the population. The outbreak of the Taiping Rebellion had much to do with the spread of Christianity, just as the emergence of new consumer cultures was linked to the influx of Western commodities and lifestyles, not to mention the impact of Western technology. From government and art genres to educational institutions and economic models, today's China bears witness to what started after the Treaty of Nanking.

The "unequal treaties" favoured foreigners, but they also opened China up for international trade and economic penetration which ultimately modernised the country. They threw China into a larger economic system and began a long process of economic integration. Would the post-Mao reform have succeeded so spectacularly without the foundation laid by the "unequal treaties"? Chinese capitalist sprouts may ultimately have come to full bloom on their own (if isolation can be imagined), but it would have taken a longer time to integrate native capitalism into the world system had it not been for forceful Western intrusion. Opium itself is a good example. The trade in opium, along with other foreign imports, had begun during the Ming epoch; and it became part of a large commercial and financial system by the eighteenth century. The Treaty of Nanking officially plunged it into the global system, as international banks were established to facilitate its transaction, as Southeast Asian countries began opium tax farming for the China market, and as new opium tax schemes inside China helped the Qing court raise fund to fight rebellions and finance modernisation. The emergence of these practices helped to create a sophisticated banking system, the Hong Kong Shanghai Banking Corporation for example; it gave birth to new companies and more importantly churned out a class of professionals who benefited from Westernisation, and who in turn helped to advance China's course of modernisation. The economic development that resulted from the "unequal treaties" in the late Qing and Republican era, although interrupted by the Communist Revolution until the post-Mao era, had ultimately laid a solid foundation, ironically or not, for the "peaceful rise of China".

The long-term economic consequences of the "unequal treaties" seem to have begun to unfold only recently. This might have materialised earlier had the Republic of China won the battle in 1949, or had a less radical faction of the CCP controlled the helm after 1949. But the political consequences are much more complex. The "unequal treaties" seemed crushing in the late nineteenth and early twentieth centuries when the Qing disintegrated, but they also provided the Nationalists and Communists with a political platform and helped them to assert their legitimacy. Judging from recent waves of anti-American and anti-Japanese riots, patriotism has become a smoking gun of the Communist regime. To understand how the Communists may use their last powerful weapon, we must see what have been made of the "unequal treaties".

Debating and Teaching the "Unequal Treaties"

The Qing political and intellectual elite woke up to the defeat of the Opium War; in fact, they woke up to the reality of the "unequal treaties". This section looks at the debates around them from the late Qing to the Republican era by sampling the political writings that first called for 修約 *xiu yue* or "revise the treaties" and then 廢約 *fei yue* or "annul the treaties", and then how the "unequal treaties" are taught in schools today.

Imperial China labelled itself *The Middle Kingdom* and subjected its smaller neighbours to the rhetoric and system of tribute relations analysed in several of the chapters in this book. This was on the one hand a monopolised form of trade, and on the other hand diplomacy, keeping the "barbarians" under control. This system was applied to Europeans, "barbarians" from afar, ever since their ships reached the Chinese coast in the sixteenth century. Early Europeans tried to work around the system, like the Portuguese sending a lion to the Kangxi emperor having heard that he liked lions. But in contrast with Asian "barbarians", the European trade and presence in China expanded rapidly, to the point where it could not be accommodated by the traditional tribute system. Neither could the city of Canton, the only foreign trade port designated by the Qing court, cope with the changes. It was left to the British to challenge the system and change the game in their own favour.

The British challenge, soon to be followed by others, including China's former vassals, threw China's political and intellectual elite into a long journey of searching and understanding the world beyond China. Many of them, like the Chinese people in general, have never reconciled with the British challenge, which led to the "century of unequal treaties". This explains why nationalism is alive and well in China today; the national narrative or collective memory has not forgotten about the "unequal treaties", while the West might have moved on and away from The Age of Empire. The British challenge made the Qing court and elite realize that they faced much stronger powers in the world; it also made some see the need for change. How could a small island country humble a mighty empire? What was it that enabled them? How could Chinese civilisation, which had managed to survive conquest by Mongols and Manchus, be threatened by something new and mysterious? The quest to understand the West originated from here; this was political awakening. This was the beginning of what became a long process, as China learned or was taught how to deal with the West, and it in many ways is still ongoing. One response was that they felt victimised and looked for an explanation in the wrongdoing of the British and others. This is normal, as Chinese pride felt hurt and wronged; many other proud empires had similar reactions. The Chinese blamed first the British, then the Westerners in general and later the Japanese in particular for China's downfall. Anti-Qing and later anti-imperialist patriotic literature and movements emerged ever since the Opium Wars (1839–42 and 1856–60).

It is hard to pinpoint who first raised the cry of 修約 *xiu yue* or "revise the treaties"; but we can hear such voices in the works of many late Qing and early Republican era writers. They included He Qu 何啓 (1858–1914), Hu Litan 胡禮坦 (1847–1916), Zheng Guanying 鄭觀應 (1842–1922), Wang Tao 王韜 (1828–97), Chen Zhi 陳熾 (1855–1900), Ma Jianzhong 馬建忠 (1844–1900) and many more. Dong Wang believes that the term "unequal treaties" first appeared in 1908, but I would argue that it was implicit earlier than that, given the fact the above-mentioned scholars had already debated revising the treaties in the late nineteenth century and annulling the treaties immediately after the First Sino-Japanese War in 1898, as I will discuss later.[11] How could they argue for revision if the treaties were not considered "unequal"? Post-Opium War reform-minded scholars, political thinkers and social figures discussed many aspects of the treaties, especially extraterritoriality and the privileges foreigners enjoyed; they called for revision to treaty terms and conditions. Wang Tao thought and wrote much about this after his tour of Europe:

> Extraterritoriality is not practised in Europe but only in Turkey, Japan and China. If Western merchants, missionaries and officials who operate and live in China make trouble or commit any crimes, we have no right to punish them.[12]

Britain agitated for extraterritoriality before the Opium War; it led to the War; and remained the sour point in Sino-British and Sino-European diplomatic relations. Although the various dynasties since at least the Han had received and accommodated foreigners, these had been treated patronisingly as vassals and "barbarians" needing access to the land of civilisation and plenty. Even rule by alien Manchus did not undermine the rhetoric of civilisation and barbarism, of "master" and "guest", as fundamentally as the Opium War and the extraterritoriality that followed.

When some were more concerned with extraterritoriality and what it brought to China, others such as Chen Zhi were indignant about tax and trade privileges: "Taxation is the right and sovereignty of a country; it is not something that another country can dictate, control or take over."[13] Commercial and financial gains were the bottom line for the British and many others; they were also harsh realities that the government had to deal with, even though China would ultimately benefit from this economic intercourse with the West. The concern over the burden of the unequal financial terms was not unfounded, as this would ultimately bring the Qing dynasty to an end. Most of the terms were in the form of war reparations and trade privileges. The Imperial Maritime Customs was established to collect taxes to help repay these foreign debts. Although many of the urban professionals and the new middle class benefited from the Western intrusion, the same elites harboured distrust and even hatred of the foreigners. Some, like Wang Tao and Chen Zhi who themselves benefited from the Western presence, would become vocal, while others would become early-generation nationalists. The commercial terms that privileged Western nations and Japan made many, not just scholars and officials, see the difference between peace agreements and commercial exploitation. They put forward the call 不背和約只修改商約, or "not to betray the peace treaty but only to revise the commercial terms", to address the unequal aspect in commerce and profit-sharing. Believing that China was bound by the treaties no matter how unfair they seemed, they called for treaty revision. This shows their limited understanding of international law and world affairs, and how far they could push to revise or annul treaties. It would not take too long for them to realise that China did not need to abide by the treaties at all.

The call to 廢約 *fei yue* or "annul the treaties" was first raised after the First Sino-Japanese war in 1895, when China was shaken to its core by the defeat at Japanese hands. It became a permanent call ever since the "Hundred-day reform" of 1898. The advocates of change included Tan Sitong 譚嗣同 (1865–98), Tang Chaichang 唐才常 (1867–1900), Liang Qichao 梁啓超 (1873–1929), Kang Youwei 康有爲 (1855–1927), Wang Kangnian 汪康年 (1860–1911) and many more. They were reformers, some radical and others moderate. They believed that China was 瓜分 or "sliced like a melon" by the different empire-building Western nations, Russia and Japan. If the First Opium War woke up the Qing elite, the First Sino-Japanese War was an emergency call that demanded action. It made many see the urgency of radical reform; it speeded up the slow pace of change and modernisation. If defeat at powerful Western hands was humiliating, defeat at Japanese hands, a smaller country that China had always considered inferior, was not acceptable. This can be seen from Kang Youwei's writings:

> With a piece of paper, the Japanese took tens of thousands of miles from southern Manchuria, Mongolia, Shandong and Fujian (Taiwan). They

control the pulse of our country with financial and military advisors. They tell us that we are their Protectorate as they police our key cities and run our factories.... Protectorate is just another name for losing our country.[14]

The achievements of a traditionally disparaged people through rapid modernisation, Westernisation to a large extent, shook the whole nation, not just the political and intellectual elite. Yet more shocking news was to follow. The war reparation package for the Japanese was 200,000,000 taels of silver.[15] This was added to the indemnities, with interest, from earlier treaties, soon to be topped up by the Boxer Rebellion compensation of 450,000,000 taels, increasing through an annual interest of 4 per cent. China's population was about 450 million at that time, in other words each Chinese would pay one tael of the Boxer indemnity. Frank King's recent article characterised as "Nothing but Bad", the disastrous Boxer indemnities and how they were paid.[16]

As Britain and America were becoming more enlightened in their China policy in the early twentieth century, their earlier policies were rallying and inspiring Chinese reformers. The combination of political domination and economic exploitation served to strengthen the determination to free China from the grip of imperialists and the "unequal treaties". The nationalists turned humiliation into strength; as Jing Tsu has argued.[17] The tragic failure of the "Hundred-day reform" in 1898 turned many reformers into revolutionaries; the call to annul the "unequal treaties" became a fundamental part of their platform in the following decade. What made the revolutionaries different from the reformers was that they called for the overthrow of the Qing dynasty. Only by getting rid of the political regime that signed them could China get rid of the "unequal treaties". They did not foresee that their new revolutionary regime would also be subjected to "unequal treaties".

Many of the Nationalist Revolution leaders, Yang Yulin 楊疏麟 (1872–1911), Song Jiaoren 宋教仁 (1882–1913), Dai Jitao 戴季陶 (1890–1949) and Sun Zhongshan (Sun Yatsen) 孫中山 (1866–1925) in particular, were adamant in their call. More so would be early generation Communists. If the protests of previous generations were directed toward treaty terms, these revolutionaries aimed at the fundamental problem of China's sovereignty in the modern system of nation-states. Yang Yulin wrote: "The existence of a country lies in its independence and sovereignty. They can not be intervened and violated by others."[18] Students would play a major role in both Nationalist and Communist Revolutions. Li Shucheng wrote "Military, Law, rivers and oceans, finance, transportation and communication, they are all in the hands of foreigners? Where is our sovereignty?"[19] This generation of Chinese nationalists saw the bottom line as full membership in the club of sovereign states. If Imperial China had been the principal obstacle to a "Westphalian" system of sovereign equality, the nationalists sought precisely that for their newly-imagined nation-state. Nevertheless the Republic of China regime was too divided and dependent on western support to achieve the abolition of the "unequal treaties". Anti-imperialism was a key political platform which the CCP used to rally support before 1949; and it became a political weapon which the CCP could use anytime after 1949. While the West and Japan have largely forgotten the hard lessons they taught China, the shame and pain of history have been kept alive in China by the CCP's use of that weapon. One important example is the 愛國主義教育 or "patriotic education programme".

Not enough scholars have questioned how the post-Mao Communist regime and its intellectual elite have developed the sense of victimhood and used it to garner support. The rise of new powers, regional or global, has seldom been peaceful, as we can see from both Chinese and world histories. When some worry that China's rise may not be peaceful, others have brushed aside the China Threat theory. Without taking sides in the debate about how peaceful China's rise may be, I will analyse current middle-school history textbooks to show how the "unequal treaties" are being taught and why this might matter as China rises.

Picture 1 is the cover of a history textbook for eighth grade, the second year in Chinese middle school with pupils aged about 14 years old. Three images occupy the front page. They are Commissioner Lin Zexu or the symbol of Chinese resistance, the signing of the Treaty of Nanking on board the *Cornwallis* or the badge of British imperialism, and the ruins of 圓明園 or Garden of Perfect Brightness burned by British and French troops during the Second Opium War in 1860, the symbol of Western hegemony. These images sit against the background of newspaper reports on the May Fourth Movement or the rise of the CCP and its leadership in the battle against imperialists. The goal of teaching an eighth grader or a 14-year-old history is obvious on the front page — humiliation and patriotism. This story of victimhood takes precedence over the colossal changes, triumphs and disasters, some far more important than shame and pain, of modern China.

Lesson One shown in Pictures 2 and 3 is titled "The Invasion of the Hegemonic Powers and the Resistance of the Chinese People". It is

Picture 1

[**Source of Pictures 1–6**: 岳麓书
社义务教育课程标准实验教科
书之《中国历史》(八年级上册).
Reproduce with permission].

obvious that the CCP emphasised the Opium War, which they believe
raises the curtain of modern China. In doing so, they highlighted
external factors rather than the internal problems of modern China.
Lesson One sets the tone for the lessons to come. The hero of the War
or symbols of patriotism, General Guan Tianpei, was present; so were
the badge of British hegemony — the Treaty signing scene. Humiliation and imperialism darkened the sky of modern China while the
CCP emerged to lead resistance and revolution. As homework shown
in Picture 4, students are asked to think about "How did the Treaty
of Nanking violate China's sovereignty?" They are also asked to discuss
the following question: "During the Opium War, China was defeated
by the British who only had a dozen battle ships and several thousand
soldiers. What are the reasons for China's defeat?" The first question
is designed so that students understand how the Treaty of Nanking
violated China's sovereignty in great detail, that is, the political and
economic concessions that China had to accept. It will help students
see the "unequal" part of this treaty and others to come. The second
question is meant for students to see China's weakness. When one is

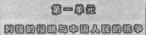

第一单元
列强的侵略与中国人民的抗争

第 1 课 鸦片战争

🦋 林则徐虎门销烟

19 世纪前期，英国为了扩大国外市场，推销工业品，掠夺原料，把中国作为主要的侵略目标。但在正常的中英贸易中，中国的瓷器、茶叶等在英国畅销，英国的呢绒、布匹等工业品在中国销路不好。英国为了改变这种局面，采取不正当手段进行可耻的鸦片走私，牟取暴利。

> 英国为什么要选用鸦片向中国走私？鸦片是一种毒品，人一旦吸食，就会上瘾，很难戒除。长期吸食，会使人身体衰弱，精神萎靡，丧失劳动能力，甚至危及生命。中国人口众多，如果吸食成风，就会成为鸦片的广大市场，给英国带来巨额利润。英国把鸦片从它的殖民地印度贩运到中国，售价比成本要高出 4～6 倍。

鸦片不断输入，白银大量外流，威胁到清朝的财政，也加重了人民的负担。由于吸食鸦片的人越来越多，人们身心健康受到严重摧残，官吏更加腐败，军队战斗力削弱。

1767 年以前，英国每年向中国输出的鸦片不过 200 箱（每箱 50～60 千克），1839 年则达到 4 万多箱。美国也从土耳其贩运鸦片到中国。1821—1840 年间，中国白银外流至少在 1 亿元以上，平均每年流出 500 万两白银，相当于清政府每年总收入的 1/10。

1

1841 年 2 月，英军大举进攻虎门。广东水师提督、61 岁的关天培亲临前线指挥，他带领官兵宣誓："人在炮台在，不离炮台半步！"当英兵拥上炮台时，他挥出腰刀与敌人肉搏，受伤数十处，仍大呼杀敌，壮烈牺牲。

1841 年 5 月 29 日，一股英军窜到三元里抢劫，被愤怒的群众打死 8 人。群众预料英军一定会前来报复，便联络附近 103 乡共同抗击英国侵略者。第二天，数千群众包围了英军占领的四方炮台，英军反扑，群众且战且退，把敌人引到牛栏冈。早已埋伏在这里的群众，手持大刀长矛，一齐冲杀过来，打死打伤英军 50 余人。

关天培(1781—1841)

🦋 中英《南京条约》

1842 年 8 月，英国强迫清政府签订了《南京条约》。这是中国近代第一个不平等条约。

《南京条约》签订时的情景

《南京条约》的主要内容有：中国割让香港岛给英国；赔款 2100 万元[1]；开放广州、厦门、福州、宁波、上海五处为通商口岸；

① 这里的"元"是指银元，每枚编量为 7 钱 2 分至 3 分。

第一单元 列强的侵略与中国人民的抗争

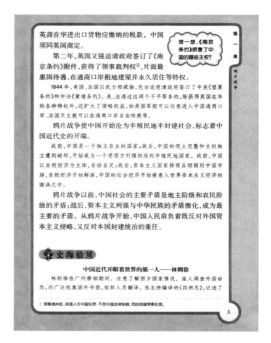

Picture 4

weak, one becomes a sitting duck. These questions are designed to expose the ugliness of imperialism and emphasise the need to strengthen China by defending and fighting for one's motherland.

Remembering the humiliations China suffered is one way to stir up patriotism because it brings out the sense of outrage and victimhood, and it lays bare the need for justice, if not revenge. This is best seen through the homework in Pictures 5 and 6. As a review of the lessons, students are asked: "Which of all the unequal treaties since the Opium War demanded indemnity from the Qing government? Which treaties demanded the most?" The answer is simple and straightforward. All the treaties that resulted from armed conflicts demanded indemnities, headed by the Boxer Protocol that demanded 450 million silver taels, followed by the Treaty of Shimonoseki that demanded 200 million silver taels. Four hundred and fifty million was the population of China at that time, as students would have been told. What a well-calculated indemnity — virtually one tael per Chinese head.

The heavy emphasis on the Japanese explains why Japan can be used as a button to activate the nationalist atomic bomb. The Chinese and Japanese ways of remembering history are quite striking. While

第4课 八国联军侵华

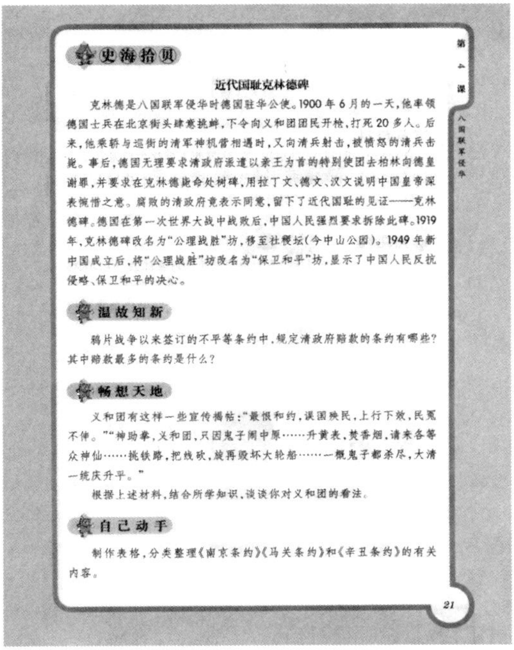

史海拾贝

近代国耻克林德碑

克林德是八国联军侵华时德国驻华公使。1900年6月的一天，他率领德国士兵在北京街头肆意挑衅，下令向义和团团民开枪，打死20多人。后来，他乘轿与巡街的清军神机营相遇时，又向清兵射击，被愤怒的清兵击毙。事后，德国无理要求清政府派遣以亲王为首的特别使团去柏林向德皇谢罪，并要求在克林德毙命处树碑，用拉丁文、德文、汉文说明中国皇帝深表惋惜之意。腐败的清政府竟表示同意，留下了近代国耻的见证——克林德碑。德国在第一次世界大战中战败后，中国人民强烈要求拆除此碑。1919年，克林德碑改名为“公理战胜”坊，移至社稷坛(今中山公园)。1949年新中国成立后，将“公理战胜”坊改名为“保卫和平”坊，显示了中国人民反抗侵略、保卫和平的决心。

温故知新

鸦片战争以来签订的不平等条约中，规定清政府赔款的条约有哪些？其中赔款最多的条约是什么？

畅想天地

义和团有这样一些宣传揭帖：“最恨和约，误国殃民，上行下效，民冤不伸。”“神助拳，义和团，只因鬼子闹中原……升黄表，焚香烟，请来各等众神仙……挑铁路，把线砍，旋再毁坏大轮船……一概鬼子都杀尽，大清一统庆升平。”

根据上述材料，结合所学知识，谈谈你对义和团的看法。

自己动手

制作表格，分类整理《南京条约》《马关条约》和《辛丑条约》的有关内容。

21

Picture 5

22

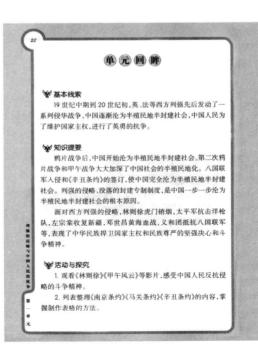

单元回眸

基本线索

19世纪中期到20世纪初，英、法等西方列强先后发动了一系列侵华战争，中国逐渐沦为半殖民地半封建社会，中国人民为了维护国家主权，进行了英勇的抗争。

知识提要

鸦片战争后，中国开始沦为半殖民地半封建社会。第二次鸦片战争和甲午战争大大加深了中国社会的半殖民地化。八国联军入侵和《辛丑条约》的签订，使中国完全沦为半殖民地半封建社会。列强的侵略、没落的封建专制制度，是中国一步一步沦为半殖民地半封建社会的根本原因。

面对西方列强的侵略，林则徐虎门销烟，太平军抗击洋枪队，左宗棠收复新疆，邓世昌黄海血战，义和团抵抗八国联军等，表现了中华民族捍卫国家主权和民族尊严的坚强决心和斗争精神。

活动与探究

1. 观看《林则徐》《甲午风云》等影片，感受中国人民反抗侵略的斗争精神。

2. 列表整理《南京条约》《马关条约》《辛丑条约》的内容，掌握制作表格的方法。

列强的侵略与中国人民的抗争 第一单元

Picture 6

Japanese textbooks seldom teach their students about Japanese atrocities during the Second World War; the Chinese ones seek to perpetuate them in memory. Neither is constructive to better relations now and in the future. For homework, students are asked to watch two films: Lin Zexu and Sino-Japanese War. The CCP and its fleet of artists have used imported art genres and media like ballet and film, hence imperialist in nature, to maintain and strengthen their political platform. To finish the lesson, students are asked "Make a spreadsheet on the content of the Treaty of Nanking, the Treaty of Shimonoseki and the Boxer Protocol. Learn the method to make a spreadsheet." Teaching about the "unequal treaties" was not enough; the CCP is instilling a deep and long memory of Western and Japanese imperialism in the young and innocent. This may have consequences.

Instead of looking at the positive changes and monumental achievement since the Opium War, the CCP now focuses on the negative side. In doing so, it refreshes memories of humiliation, rouses a sense of injustice, and reinforces patriotism as the source of their own legitimacy and rule. The sense of victimhood, compounded with China's rising economic power and renewed political confidence, presents a potent combination. The bomb of patriotism was activated during the Belgrade bombing, when Chinese students waged war on the American embassy in Beijing. Even should it wish to, the Chinese government may not be allowed by its aroused people to forgive and move on. What will it take a rising China to move on from this sense of outraged victimhood? Will China expect apologies from the West as she has demanded from Japan? How can historians and educators help shorten the distance between history or the "century of unequal treaties" and the future to help make China's rise "peaceful"?

Appendix

No. 编号	Title (Languages) 名称（语种）	Date 日期
1	Treaty of Nipchu, or Nerchinsk 尼步楚界约（法、英、中文本）	1689年9月7日 中俄签订
2	Treaty of Nipchu, or Nerchinsk 尼步楚界约（俄、拉丁文本）	1689年9月7日 中俄签订
3	Bur Treaty 布连斯奇界约（俄、拉丁文本）	1727年9月1日 中俄签订
4	Bur Treaty 布连斯奇界约（中文本） 中俄签订	1727年9月1日
5	Bur Treaty: Boundary Protocol 阿巴哈依图界约（俄文本）	1727年9月1日' 中俄签订
6	Bur Treaty: Boundary Protocol 阿巴哈依图界约（中文本）	1727年10月12日 中俄签订
7	Kiakhta Boundary Treaty 恰克图界约（法、中文本）	1727年10月12日 中俄签订
8	Kiakhta Boundary Treaty 恰克图界约（俄、拉丁文本）	1727年10月12日 中俄签订
9	Bur Treaty: Boundary Protocol 色楞额界约（俄文本）	1727年11月8日 中俄签订
10	Bur Treaty: Boundary Protocol 色楞额界约（中文本）	1727年11月8日 中俄签订
11	(Supplementary) Treaty of Kiakhta 恰克图界约第十条（修改）（法文本）	1768年10月30日 中俄签订
12	(Supplementary) Treaty of Kiakhta 恰克图界约第十条（修改）（俄文本）	1768年10月30日 中俄签订
13	(Supplementary) Treaty of Kiakhta 恰克图界约第十条（修改）（中文本）	1768年10月30日 中俄签订
14	International Protocol 国际议定书（史称恰克图市约）（俄文本）	1792年2月20日 中俄签订
15	International Protocol 国际议定书（史称恰克图市约）（中文本）	1792年2月20日 中俄签订
16	Treaty of Nanking 南京条约（又称江宁条约）（英、中文本）	1842年8月29日 中英签订
17	Declaration Respecting Transit Duties 内地税声明（英、中文本）	1843年6月26日 中英签订

No. 编号	Title (Languages) 名称（语种）	Date 日期
18	General Regulations Under Which The British Trade is to be Conducted At the Five Ports of Canton, Amoy, Foochow, Ningpo, and Shanghai 五口通商章程（英、中文本）	1843年10月8日 中英签订
19	Supplementary Treaty of Hoomun Chai (The Bogue) 善后事宜清册附粘和约（又称五口通商附粘善后条约或虎门条约）（英、中文本）	1843年10月8日 中英签订
20	Chinese Re-arrangement of the Preceding Tariff, Under Classes of Goods 附粘和约附海关出进口货物税则分类（英文本）	1843年10月8日 中英签订
21	Tariff of duties on the foreign trade With China 五口通商章程附海关出进口货物税则（按英文字母排列）	1843年10月8日 中英签订
22	Chinese Version of the Tariff of Duties on the Foreign Trade with China 附粘和约附海关出进口货物税则分类（中文本）	1843年10月8日 中英签订
23	Treaty of Wang-Hea 望厦条约（又称五口贸易章程）（中文本）	1844年7月3日 中英签订
24	The Tariff of Duties to be Levied on Imported and Exported Merchandise At the Five ports 五口贸易章程附海关出进口货物税则分类（英文本）	1844年7月3日 中美签订
25	Chinese Version of the Tariff of Duties On the Trade of the United States with China 五口贸易章程附海关出进口货物税则分类（中文本）	1844年7月3日 中美签订
26	Treaty of Whampoa 黄埔条约（五口贸易章程）（法、中文本）	1844年10月24日 中法签订
27	Tariff of Duties Fixed by the Treaty of Whampoa 五口贸易章程附海关出进口货物税则分类（法文本）	1844年10月24日 中法签订
28	Tariff of Duties Fixed by the Treaty of Whampoa 五口贸易章程附海关出进口货物税则分类（中文本）	1844年10月24日 中法签订
29	Convention of Bocca Tigris 英军退还舟山条约（英、中文本）	1846年4月4日 中英签订

No. 编号	Title (Languages) 名称（语种）	Date 日期
30	Treaty of Canton, 1847 广州条约（1847年）又称五口通商章程 （瑞、英、中文本）	1847年3月20日 中、挪、瑞签订
31	Tariff annexed to the Treaty of Canton 广州条约附海关出进口货物税则（瑞典文本）	1847年3月20日 中、挪、瑞签订
32	Tariff annexed to the Treaty of Canton 广州条约附海关出进口货物税则（英文本）	1847年3月20日 中、挪、瑞签订
33	Tariff annexed to the Treaty of Canton 广州条约附海关出进口货物税则（中文本）	1847年3月20日 中、挪、瑞签订
34	Treaty of Kuldja 伊犁塔尔巴哈台通商章程（法、中文本）	1851年8月6日 中俄签订
35	Treaty of Kuldja 伊犁塔尔巴哈台通商章程（俄文本）	1851年8月6日 中俄签订
36	Treaty of Aigun 瑷珲城和约（法、中文本）	1858年5月28日 中俄签订
37	Treaty of Aigun 瑷珲城和约（俄文本）	1858年5月28日 中俄签订
38	Treaty of Tien Tsin, 1858 天津条约（1858年）（法、中文本）	1858年6月13日 中俄签订
39	Treaty of Tien Tsin, 1858 天津条约（1858年）（俄、法文本）	1858年6月13日 中俄签订
40	Treaty of Tien Tsin, 1858 天津条约（1858年）（英、中文本）	1858年6月18日 中美签订
41	Treaty of Tien Tsin, 1858 天津条约（1858年）（英、中文本）	1858年6月26日 中英签订
42	Treaty of Tien Tsin, 1858 天津条约（1858年）（法、中文本）	1858年6月27日 中法签订
43	Treaty Addendum 和约章程遗补（法、中文本）	1858年6月27日 中法签订
44	Agreement annexed to the Treaty of Tientsin (1858) Concerning the new Tariff and the Commercial Regulations 天津条约附新定税则和通行章程的协定 （法、中文本）	1858年6月27日 中法签订
45	New Tariff annexed to the Treaty of Tientsin 天津条约附新定税则（法文本）	1858年6月27日 中法签订

No. 编号	Title (Languages) 名称（语种）	Date 日期
46	New Tariff annexed to the Treaty of Tientsin 天津条约附新定税则（中文本）	1858年6月27日 中法签订
47	Trade Regulations appended to the Tariff 通商章程善后条约（英、中文本）	1858年11月8日 中英签订
48	English Text of Tariff Annexed to British Treaty of Tien Tsin 天津条约附海关进出口货物税则（英文本）	1858年11月8日 中英签订
49	Chinese Text of Tariff Annexed to British Treaty of Tien Tsin 天津条约附海关进出口货物税则（中文本）	1858年11月8日 中英签订
50	Commercial Regulations appended To the Tariff 通商章程善后条约（法、中文本）	1858年11月24日 中法签订
51	Convention of Peking, 1860 北京条约（1860年）（又称续增条约） （英、中文本）	1860年10月24日 中英签订
52	Convention of Peking, 1860 北京条约（1860年）（又称续增条约） （法、中文本）	1860年10月25日 中法签订
53	Ratification by His Majesty the Emperor of China of the British and French Treaties of Tien Tsin (1858) And of the conventions of Peking (1860) 中、英、法互换条约批准书（英、中文本）	1860年10月28日 中、英、法签订
54	Additional Treaty of Peking, 1860 北京续增条约（1860年）（法、中文本）	1860年11月14日 中俄签订
55	Additional Treaty of Peking, 1860 北京续增条约（1860年）（俄文本）	1860年11月14日 中俄签订
56	Additional Article to the Treaty of Peking 北京条约另款（又称勘分东界约记） （俄、法文本）	1861年6月28日 中俄签订
57	Additional Article to the Treaty of Peking 北京条约另款（又称勘分东界约记）（中文本）	1861年6月28日 中俄签订
58	Treaty of Tien Tsin, 1861 天津条约（1861年）（又称和好、贸易、船只事宜和约章程）（德、法、中文本）	1861年9月2日 中德签订
59	Tariff annexed to the Treaty of Tientsin 天津条约附海关进出口货物税则（德文本）	1861年9月2日 中德签订

No. 编号	Title (Languages) 名称（语种）	Date 日期
60	Tariff annexed to the Treaty of Tientsin 天津条约附海关进出口货物税则（法文本）	1861年9月2日 中德签订
61	Tariff annexed to the Treaty of Tientsin 天津条约附海关进出口货物税则（中文本）	1861年9月2日 中德签订
62	Commercial Regulations annexed to The Tariff of 1861 通商章程善后条约（德、法、中文本）	1861年9月2日 中德签订
63	Convention of Peking for the Land Trade Between Russia and China 陆路通商章程（中文本）	1862年3月4日 中俄签订
64	Convention of Peking for the Land Trade Between Russia and China 陆路通商章程（俄文本）	1862年3月4日 中俄签订
65	Tariff of Duties Appended to the Convention of 1862, for the Land Trade Between Russia and China 陆路通商章程附海关进口货物税则（中文本）	1862年3月11日 中俄签订
66	Tariff of Duties Appended to the Convention of 1862, for the Land Trade Between Russia and China 陆路通商章程附海关进口货物税则（俄文本）	1862年3月11日 中俄签订
67	Treaty of Tientsin, 1862 天津条约（1862年）（又称西洋国议定通商章程条款）（葡、英、中文本）	1862年8月13日 中葡签订
68	Treaty of Tientsin, 1863 天津条约（1863年）（英、中文本）	1863年7月13日 中丹签订
69	Tariff and Rules of Trade annexed to the Treaty of Tientsin 天交条约附通商章程（英、中文本）	1863年7月13日 中丹签订
70	Tariff of Dutie annexed to the Treaty of Tientsin 天津条约附进出口货物税则（中文本）	1863年7月13日 中丹签订
71	Treaty of Tientsin, 1863 天津条约（1863年）（英、荷、中文本）	1863年10月6日 中荷签订
72	Protocol of Chuguchak 勘分西北界约记（英、中文本）	1864年10月7日 中俄签订
73	Treaty of Tientsin, 1864 天津条约（1864年），又称和好贸易条约（西班牙、中文本）	1864年10月10日 中西签订

No. 编号	Title (Languages) 名称（语种）	Date 日期
74	Treaty of Tientsin, 1864 天津条约（1864年），又称和好贸易条约 （英文本）	1864年10月10日 中西签订
75	Note on Tonnage Dues 完纳船钞注释（法、中文本）	1865年9月 中法签订
76	Treaty of Peking, 1865 北京条约（1865年），又称通商条约 （法、中文本）	1865年11月2日 中比签订
77	Commercial Regulations annexed to The Tariff of 1865 北京条约附通商章程（法、中文本）	1865年11月2日 中比签订
78	Tariff annexed to the Treaty of Peking 北京条约附海关进出口税则（法文本）	1865年11月2日 中比签订
79	Tariff annexed to the Treaty of Peking 北京条约附海关进出口税则（中文本）	1865年11月2日 中比签订
80	Convention to regulate the Engagement of Chinese Emigrants By British and French Subjects 续定招工章程条约（英、中、法文本）	1866年3月5日 中、英、法签订
81	Treaty of Peking, 1866 北京条约（1866年），又称和约通商章程 （意、中文本）	1866年10月26日 中意签订
82	Treaty of Peking, 1866 北京条约（1866年），又称和约通商章程 （英文本）	1866年10月26日 中意签订
83	Commercial Regulations annexed to The Treaty of Peking 北京条约附通商章程（意、中文本）	1866年10月26日 中意签订
84	Commercial Regulations annexed to The Treaty of Peking 北京条约附通商章程（英文本）	1866年10月26日 中意签订
85	Tariff annexed to the Treaty of Peking 北京条约附海关进出口货物税则（意文本）	1866年10月26日 中意签订
86	Additional articles to the treaty Between The United States of America and the Ta-Tsing Empire of The 18th June 1858 天津条约续增条款（英、中文本）	1868年7月28日 中美签订

No. 编号	Title (Languages) 名称（语种）	Date 日期
87	Article Concerning False Manifests Annexed to the Treaty of Tientsin (1861) 天津条约附漏报捏报罚办声明（德、法、中文本）	1868年9月2日 中德签订
88	Revised Convention of Peking for The Land Trade between Russia and China 改订陆路通商章程（英、中文本）	1869年4月27日 中俄签订
89	Revised Convention of Peking for The Land Trade between Russia and China 改订陆路通商章程（俄文本）	1869年4月27日 中俄签订
90	Treaty of Peking, 1869 北京条约（1869年）（又称通商和约章程）（德、中文本）	1869年9月2日 中奥签订
91	Treaty of Peking, 1869 北京条约（1869年）（又称通商和约章程）（英文本）	1869年9月2日 中奥签订
92	Commercial Regulations annexed to The Treaty of Peking 北京条约附通商章程（德、中文本）	1869年9月2日 中奥签订
93	Tariff annexed to the Treaty of Peking 北京条约附海关进出口货物税则（德文本）	1869年9月2日 中奥签订
94	Tariff annexed to the Treaty of Peking 北京条约附海关进出口货物税则（中文本）	1869年9月2日 中奥签订
95	Supplementary Convention to the Treaty of Tientsin (1858) 天津条约附约（英、中文本）	1869年10月23日 中英签订
96	Supplementary Rules and Tariff 附约善后章程及海关进出口税则（英、中文本）	1869年10月23日 中英签订
97	Treaty of Tientsin, 1871 天津条约（1871年）（又称中日搞好关系条规）（英、中文本）	1871年9月13日 中日签订
98	Treaty of Tientsin, 1871 天津条约（1871年）（又称中日搞好关系条规）（英文本）	1871年9月13日 中日签订
99	Treaty of Tientsin, 1871 天津条约（1871年）（又称中日搞好关系条规）（日文本）	1871年9月13日 中日签订

No. 编号	Title (Languages) 名称（语种）	Date 日期
100	Note showing differences between the Chinese and Japanese Versions of the Treaty of Tientsin 天津条约中、日文本差异注释（英、中文本）	1871年9月13日 中日签订
101	Regulations of Trade annexed to the Treaty of Tientsin 天津条约附通商章程（英、中文本）	1871年9月13日 中日签订
102	Regulations of Trade annexed to the Treaty of Tientsin 天津条约附通商章程（英文本）	1871年9月13日 中日签订
103	Regulations of Trade annexed to the Treaty of Tientsin 天津条约附通商章程（日文本）	1871年9月13日 中日签订
104	Note showing differences between the Chinese and Japanese Versions of the Regulations of Trade 通商章程中、日文本差异注释（英、中文本）	1871年9月13日 中日签订
105	Japanese Tariff annexed to the Treaty of Tientsin, 1871 天津条约附日本海关进出口货物税则（中文本）	1871年9月13日 中日签订
106	Japanese Tariff annexed to the Treaty of Tientsin, 1871 天津条约附日本海关进出口货物税则（日文本）	1871年9月13日 中日签订
107	Chinese Tariff annexed to the Treaty of Tientsin, 1871 天津条约附中国海关进出口货物税则（中文本）	1871年9月13日 中日签订
108	Chinese Tariff annexed to the Treaty of Tientsin, 1871 天津条约附中国海关进出口货物税则（日文本）	1871年9月13日 中日签订
109	Convention of Tientsin (1874) 天津协约（1874年）（又称秘鲁华工专条） （西、英、中文本）	1874年6月26日 中秘签订
110	Treaty of Tientsin 1874年天津条约（又称「通商条约」） （西、英、中文本）	1874年6月26日 中秘签订
111	Agreement of Peking and appended Guarantee 北京协定附加会议凭单（英、中文本）	1874年10月31日 中日签订
112	Agreement of Peking and appended Guarantee 北京协定附加会议凭单（日文本）	1874年10月31日 中日签订
113	Certificate of Exchange of Convention and Treaty of Tientsin 天津条约和专条互换批准证书（西、英、中文本）	1875年8月7日 中秘签订
114	Agreement Between the Ministers Plenipotentiary of the Governments of Great British and China 英中两国政府全权大臣之协定，又称「烟台条约」 （英、中文本）	1876年9月13日 中英签订

No. 编号	Title (Languages) 名称（语种）	Date 日期
115	Convention of Peking Respecting Chinese Emigration to Cuba 会订古巴华工条款（西、英、中文本）	1877年11月17日 中西签订
116	Supplementary Convention, 1880 续修条约（1880年）（德、中、英文本）	1880年3月31日 中德签订
117	Special Stipulations annexed to the Supplementary Convention 续修条约附善后章程（德、中、英文本）	1880年3月31日 中德签订
118	Protocol Prolonging term for the Exchange of Ratifications of the Supplementary Convention (1880) 续修条约附互换批准延长期议定书 （又称「续修条约附照录凭单」）（英、中文本）	1880年8月21日 中德签订
119	Supplemental Treaty Between the United States and China Concerning Commercial Intercourse and Judicial Procedure 中美通商往来和司法程序增补条约 （又称「续约附款」）（英、中文本）	1880年11月17日 中美签订
120	Treaty of St. Petersburg 圣彼得堡条约（又称「改订条约」） （法、中文本）	1881年4月24日 中俄签订
121	Treaty of St. Petersburg 圣彼得堡条约（又称「改订条约」）（俄文本）	1881年4月24日 中俄签订
122	Regulations for the Land Trade Between Russia and Chin 改订陆路通商章程（法、中文本）	1881年4月24日 中俄签订
123	Regulations for the Land Trade Between Russia and China 改订陆路通商章程（俄文本）	1881年4月24日 中俄签订
124	Treaty of Tientsin, 1881 天津条约（1881年）（又称「和好通商条约」） （葡、法、中文本）	1881年10月3日 中巴签订
125	Maritime and Overland Trade Regulations 商民水陆贸易章程（英、中文本）	1882年10月1日 中朝签订
126	The Rules for the Traffic on the Frontier between Liaotung and Corea 边民交易章程（英、中文本）	1883年3月 中朝签订

No. 编号	Title (Languages) 名称（语种）	Date 日期
127	Convention of Tientsin, 1884 天津协定（1884年）（又称「永敦和好简明条款」） （法、中文本）	1885年5月11日 中法签订
128	Protocol of Paris 巴黎议定书（又称「停战条款」）（英、法文本）	1885年4月4日 中法签订
129	Protocol of Paris 巴黎议定书（又称「停战条款」）（中文本）	1885年4月4日 中法签订
130	Imperial Decree Ordering the Execution of the Convention of Tientsin 大清帝国颁布实施天津条约之命令（法、中文本）	1885年4月13日 中法签订
131	Convention of Tientsin 天津会议专条（英、中文本）	1885年4月18日 中日签订
132	Convention of Tientsin 天津会议专条（日文本）	1885年4月18日 中日签订
133	Treaty of Tientsin, 1885 天津条约（1885年）（又称「中法条约」） （法、中文本）	1885年6月9日 中法签订
134	Additional Article to the Agreement of Chefoo, 1876 烟台条约续增专条（英、中文本）	1885年7月18日 中英签订
135	Convention of Tientsin, 1886 天津协定（1886年）（又称「滇粤陆路通商章程」） （法、中文本）	1886年4月25日 中法签订
136	Convention Relating to Burma and Tibet 通商交涉条款（英、中文本）	1886年7月24日 中英签订
137	Memorandum of discrepancies in The Two texts of the Treaty of Tientsin 天津条约所附两国税则差异之备忘录（英、中文本）	1886年 中日签订
138	Memorandum of discrepancies in The Two texts of the Treaty of Tientsin 天津条约所附两国税则差异之备忘录（中文本）	1886年 中日签订
139	Protocol of Lisbon 里斯本议定书（又称中葡会议草约）（葡、英文本）	1887年3月26日 中葡签订
140	Protocol of Lisbon 里斯本议定书（又称中葡会议草约）（中文本）	1887年3月26日 中葡签订
141	Protocol of Exchange of Retifications 互换条约文凭（葡、英、中文本）	1887年4月28日 中葡签订

No. 编号	Title (Languages) 名称（语种）	Date 日期
142	Additional Commercial Convention, 1887 续议商务专条（1887年）（法、中文本）	1887年6月26日 中法签订
143	Additional Commercial Convention 续议界务专条（法、中文本）	1887年6月26日 中法签订
144	Treaty of Peking 北京条约（又称「通商和好条约」） （葡、英、中文本）	1887年12月1日 中葡签订
145	Appended to the Treaty of Amity and Commerce 会议专约（葡、英、中文本）	1887年12月1日 中葡签订
146	Agreement respecting the Collection of dues on opium at Macao 《会订洋药如何徵收税厘之善后田款》 (葡、英、中文本)	1887年12月1日 中葡签订
147	Sikkim-Tibet Convention 藏印条约（英、中文本）	1890年3月17日 中英签订
148	Chungking Agreement: Additional Article to the Agreement of Chefoo 烟台条约续增专条（英、中文本）	1890年3月31日 中英签订
149	Regulations Regarding Trade, Communication, and pasturage, to be Appended to the Sikkim-Tibet Convention 哲、藏条约附属通商、交涉、游牧章程 （英、中文本）	1893年12月5日 中英签订
150	Convention giving effect to Article III of the Convention relating to Burma And Tibet 续议滇缅界、商务条款（英、中文本）	1894年3月1日 中英签订
151	Emigration Treaty between the United States of America and China 限禁来美华工保护寓美华人条约（英、中文本）	1894年3月17日 中英签订
152	Armistice 停战条款（英、中文本）	1895年3月20日 中日签订
153	Armistice 停战条款（日文本）	1895年3月20日 中日签订
154	Treaty of Shimonoseki 马关条约（又称「讲和条约」）（英、中文本）	1895年4月17日 中日签订
155	Treaty of Shimonoseki 马关条约（又称「讲和条约」）（日文本）	1895年4月17日 中日签订

No. 编号	Title (Languages) 名称（语种）	Date 日期
156	Prolongation of Armistice 停战展期专条（英、中文本）	1895年4月17日 中日签订
157	Prolongation of Armistice 停战展期专条（日文本）	1895年4月17日 中日签订
158	Convention Complementary to the Additional Commercial Convention 续议商务专条附章（法、中文本）	1896年6月20日 中法签订
159	Convention Complementary to the Delimitation Convention 续议界务专条附章（法、中文本）	1896年6月20日 中法签订
160	Treaty of Commerce and Navigation 通商行船条约（英、中文本）	1896年7月21日 中日签订
161	Treaty of Commerce and Navigation 通商行船条约（日文本）	1896年7月21日 中日签订
162	Contract for the Construction and Working of the Chinese Eastern Railway 东省铁路公司合同（法文本）	1896年9月8日 中俄签订
163	Contract for the Construction and Working of the Chinese Eastern Railway 东省铁路公司合同（中文本）	1896年9月8日 中俄签订
164	Protocol in Regard to Japanese settlements at the open ports of China 公立文凭（英、中文本）	1896年10月19日 中日签订
165	Protocol in Regard to Japanese settlements at the open ports of China 公立文凭（日文本）	1896年10月19日 中日签订
166	Agreement Modifying the Burma Frontier and Trade Convention 续议缅甸条约附款（又称「中缅条约附款」） （英、中文本）	1897年2月4日 中英签订
167	Convention for the Lease of Kiaochow 德租胶澳专条（德、中文本）	1898年3月6日 中德签订
168	Convention of Peking, 1898 北京条约（1898年）（又称「中俄会订条约」） （俄文本）	1898年3月27日 中俄签订

No. 编号	Title (Languages) 名称（语种）	Date 日期
169	Convention of Peking, 1898 北京条约（1898年）（又称「中俄会订条约」） （中文本）	1898年3月27日 中俄签订
170	Additional Articles to Convention of Peking, 1898 北京条约增订条款（1898年）（又称「租地条款」） （俄文本）	1898年5月7日 中俄签订
171	Additional Articles to Convention of Peking, 1898 北京条约增订条款（1898年）（又称「租地条款」） （中文本）	1898年5月7日 中俄签订
172	Convention for the Extension of Hongkong 展拓香港边界地址专条（英、中文本）	1898年6月9日 中英签订
173	Convention for the Lease of Weihaiwei 租威海卫专条（英、中文本）	1898年7月1日 中英签订
174	Manchurian Railway Convention 东省铁路公司续订合同（中文本）	1898年7月6日 中俄签订
175	Manchurian Railway Convention 东省铁路公司续订合同（英文本）	1898年7月6日 中俄签订
176	Treaty Between China and the Congo Free State 中国与刚果国专章（法、中文本）	1898年7月10日 中刚签订
177	Agreement about the Establishment of a Maritime Customs Office at Tsing Tau 会订青岛设关徵税办法（英、中文本）	1899年4月17日 中德签订
178	Treaty of Seoul 汉城条约（英、中文本）	1899年9月11日 中韩签订
179	Convention relative to the concession of Kwang Chouwan 广州湾租界条约（又称租给广州湾户订条款章程） （法、中文本）	1899年11月16日 中法签订
180	Treaty of Washington 华盛顿条约（西、中、英文本）	1899年12月14日 中墨签订
181	International Protocol 国际议定书（又称辛丑条约）（法、中文本）	9/7/1901 中国与各国签订
182	Agreement Relative to Manchuria 交收东三省条约（俄、法文本）	4/8/1902 中俄签订
183	Agreement Relative to Manchuria 交收东三省条约（中文本）	4/8/1902 中俄签订

No. 编号	Title (Languages) 名称（语种）	Date 日期
184	Revised Import Tariff 续修增改各国通商进口税则（中文本）	8/29/1902 中国与各国签订
185	Revised Import Tariff 续修增改各国通商进口税则（英文本）	8/29/1902 中国与各国签订
186	Commercial Treaty 续议通商行船条约（英、中文本）	9/5/1902 中英签订
187	Additional Articles to Convention of Peking 北京条约增改条款（葡、英、中文本）	10/17/1902 中葡签订

Notes

[1] Wang Dong, *China's Unequal Treaties: Narrating National History* (Lanham [MD]: Lexington Books, 2005); Li Yumin, *Zhongguo Fei Yue Shi* (Beijing: Zhonghua shuju, 2005); Tian, Tao (chief editor), *Qingchao Tiaoyue Quanji* (Ha'erbin: Helongjiang renmin chubanshe, 1999) and Chinese Bureau of Maritime Custom (compiler)., *Zhong Wai Jiu Yue Zhang Da Quan* (Beijing: Chinese Maritime Customs Publishing House, 2004).

[2] Samuel Couling, *The Encyclopaedia Sinica*. (Shanghai: Kelly and Walsh, 1917), pp. 570–1. I thank Victor Pak Ho Leung, a student intern from the Chinese University of Hong Kong at the Asia Research Institute, National University of Singapore and Xu Jialiang, Research Assistant to Dr. Jennifer Ning Chang at the Institute of Modern History, Academia Sinica, who helped to compile and type the list of "unequal treaties" in the summers of 2006 and 2007. See also Perkins, Dorothy, *Encyclopedia of China: The Essential Reference to China, its History and Culture* (New York: Facts on File, 1999).

[3] Tan Chung, *China and the Brave New World* (Bombay: Allied Publishers, 1978), p. 1.

[4] Li Chien-nung, *The Political History of China, 1840–1928* (Princeton: Princeton University Press, 1956), p. 43.

[5] Michael Greenberg, *British Trade and the Opening of China 1800–42* (Cambridge: Cambridge University Press, 1951), p. 212.

[6] W.A.P. Martin, *The Awakening of China* (New York: Doubleday, 1907), p. 155.

[7] Zheng Yangwen, *The Social Life of Opium in China* (Cambridge: Cambridge University Press, 2005); Timothy Brook and Bob Tadashi Wakabayashi, eds., *Opium Regimes: China, Britain, and Japan, 1839–1952* (Berkeley: University of California Press, 2000).

[8] Albert Feuerwerker, "Presidential Address: Questions about China's Early Modern Economic History that I Wish I Could Answer", *Journal of Asian Studies* 51, 4 (1992): 757–69.

9   Hao Yen-ping, *The Commercial Revolution in Nineteenth-Century China: The Rise of Sino-Western Mercantile Capitalism* (Berkeley [CA]: University of California Press, 1986), preface; Gregory Blue, "Opium for China: the British Connection", in *Opium Regimes: China, Britain, and Japan, 1839–1952*, ed. Timothy Brook and Bob Tadashi Wakabayashi (Berkeley [CA]: University of California Press, 2000), pp. 31–54.

10   Joseph W. Esherick, Wen-hsin Yeh and Madeleine Zelin, eds., *Empire, Nation, and Beyond: Chinese History in Late Imperial and Modern Times — A Festschrift in Honor of Frederic Wakeman* (Berkeley: University of California Press, 2006), pp. 275–308.

11   Wang Dong, *China's Unequal Treaties: Narrating National History* (Lanham [MD]: Lexington Books, 2005).

12   Wang Tao, *Taoyuan Wenlu Waibian* (Shanghai: Shanghai shudian, 2002), p. 74.

13   Chen Chi (Ciliang), *Yong Shu* (8 vols., Shenji shuzhuang, 1898), vol 5, p. 13A.

14   Kang Youwei, *Kang Youwei Quanji* (Shanghai: Shanghai guji, 1987), p. 166.

15   From UCLA Center for East Asian Studies website <http://www.international.ucla.edu/eas/documents/1895shimonoseki-treaty.htm> [accessed 9 February 2008].

16   Frank King, "The Boxer indemnity — 'Nothing but Bad'", *Modern Asian Studies* 40, 3 (2006): 663–89. America used the funds to help lay the foundation for today's Qinghua University while Britain has dispensed the Boxer Fund in the form of scholarships and research grants.

17   Jing Tsu, *Failure, Nationalism, and Literature: The Making of Modern Chinese Identity, 1895–1937* (Stanford: Stanford University Press, 2005).

18   Rao Huaimin, ed., *Yang Yuling Ji* (Changsha: Yuelu shushe, 2001), p. 274.

19   Li Shucheng, "Xuesheng zhi Jinzheng", in *Xinhai Gemin Qian Shinianjian Shilun Xuanji*, ed., Zhang Dan and Wang Renzhi (2 vols., Hong Kong: Sanlian shudian, 1964), vol. 1, pp. 452–9.

Chapter 8

Mediating Chinese-ness: Identity Politics and Media Culture in Contemporary China

Anbin Shi

The mass media is perhaps the most accurate barometer of the on-going socio-political transformation in contemporary China. CCTV (China Central Television) aired a 12-episode documentary, *The Rise of the Superpowers* (*Daguo de Jueqi*), chronicling the ebb and flow of the nine major global powerhouses since the fifteenth century, namely, Portugal, Spain, Netherlands, Britain, France, Germany, Russia, Japan and the United States in November 2006. Many China watchers would immediately read it as an implicit manifesto for the supreme leadership's ongoing agenda of "peaceful rise" (*heping jueqi*), aiming at China's entry into the West-dominated "superpower club". The heated debate around this documentary also reminds us of another similar media campaign for political liberalisation and Westernisation in 1988, which was initiated by a CCTV-made documentary, *The River Elegy* (*He Shang*), but which ended abruptly in the 1989 Tian'anmen Incident.

Interestingly, both documentaries and the media campaigns that followed occurred at historical junctures of China's quasi-capitalist reform since 1978. By revitalising the persisting "anxiety of influence" between China and the West, both reflect the urgency of repositioning China in the topography of world geopolitics. Such repositioning would inevitably bring pose a challenge to identity politics in contemporary China. Such categories as class, and socio-cultural, gender and ethnic identities, have all become new battlegrounds for the ongoing global/

local conflicts and negotiations. Simply put, the changing conceptualisation of being "Chinese" in the era of globalisation opens up new avenues for investigating the following question: what transformations has capitalist globalisation effected in contemporary Chinese social and cultural arenas.

Notably, Chinese-ness is a nebulous yet productive discourse that remains central to the agenda of constructing Chinese modernity and postmodernity. The single English word "Chinese" is both complicated and intriguing, for there is no single corresponding equivalent in the Chinese language that can encompass its denotations. There exist a cluster of terms in both spoken and written Chinese to reflect its different attributes: racial (*zhongguoren/huaren* or the Chinese people), cultural (*zhonghua/huaxia* or the Han/Huaxia civilisation), ethnic (*hanzu/hanren* or the Han people), and citizenry (*zhongguoji* or the Chinese citizenship). This multi-layered concept of "Chinese-ness" can serve as an entry point to the complications of Chinese identity.

In the relatively self-reliant "Middle Kingdom" of the past, such conceptual frameworks as "Chinese" or "Chinese-ness" were vague and insignificant. Chinese emperors upheld an ideology that they were the necessary rulers of the entire world. The modernist concept of "Chinese" and "Chinese-ness" were not developed until after the Sino-British Opium War (1839–42). In the face of this national crisis, Chinese intellectuals' two-fold mission of enlightenment and national salvation mandated a clearer definition of Chinese ethnicity or national identity. They were obliged to deal with such imported concepts as nation, state, sovereignty, citizenry, race, ethnicity, and national/cultural identity. The definition of Chinese-ness had therefore become part and parcel of the agenda of constructing Chinese modernity. The modernist notion of a unified, homogeneous, and unquestioned Chinese identity as represented by the People's Republic of China (PRC), the socialist party-state, was emblematic of the quest for Chinese modernity.

As China has been increasingly integrated into the capitalist world system in recent decades, the emergence of Chinese postmodernity has led to a rethinking and redefinition of the modernist notion of Chinese-ness. In this chapter, I will make a genealogical survey of the evolution of the concept "Chinese-ness", focusing on its socio-historical significance in the agenda of constructing Chinese modernity and postmodernity. By using mass media and popular culture as conceptual prisms, I would like to unravel how the media, in the context of cultural globalisation, have evoked a redefinition of Chinese-ness, or more precisely a transformation of identity politics in China. First, two theoretical models of redefining Chinese-ness will be considered, namely, "cultural China" advocated by a group of overseas Sinologists and "grand China" by some indigenous "post-ist" theoreticians. Second, in terms of mediating the changing conception of Chinese-ness, this chapter will address the following questions: (1) How has the trend toward globalisation transformed the media ecology and cultural topography in contemporary China? (2) In what ways is the ongoing "glocalisation" related to the reconstruction of identity politics in terms of class, gender, ethnicity, society, and culture? (3) How are global and local media mediating a pluralistic, dynamic and multi-dimensional Chinese-ness in the era of globalisation?

"Chinese-ness" as a Geopolitical and Cultural Concept: Encounters between Centre and Periphery

The question of Chinese-ness, as Kwang-chih Chang points out, first emerged in the "axial-age" half a millennium prior to the birth of Confucius in 551 BCE. The geopolitical centre of "the central plain" (*Zhong Yuan*), located in the areas near the Yellow River in North China, is generally acknowledged as the cradle of Chinese civilisation. Since ancient times, being Chinese always meant being at the centre, surrounded by culturally inferior "barbarians" at the geopolitical peripheries, namely, *Yi* in the East (*dong yi*), *Di* in the West (*xi di*), *Rong* in the North (*bei rong*), and *Man* in the South (*nan man*). Throughout history, Chinese-ness, as a geopolitical and cultural concept, has been constructed in the process of enforced population mobilisation, from the geopolitical centre to the remote, marginal frontier lands. To those inhabitants in the peripheral areas, acknowledging the authority of the geopolitical centre has always been an important prerequisite of being Chinese. This anthropocentric view is based upon a deep-rooted sense of belonging to a unified civilisation that boasts thousands of years of uninterrupted history.[1]

As Owen Lattimore puts it, the classical distinction between Chinese and "barbarians" is predicated upon two drastically different ways of life: the agrarian community of the Central Plain and the nomadic tribes of the steppes.[2] In this light, to be Chinese means not only to subjugate oneself to the authority of the geopolitical centre, but also to accept and learn the proper, civilised ways of dressing, eating, dwelling and travelling. In other words, any ethnic group, so long as they acknowledge their loyalty to the geopolitical centre, will be granted membership in the vaguely defined "grand Chinese family". Such a concept as "Chinese-ness" is therefore not emblematic of ethnicity *per se*, but rather of the particular cultural consciousness that is "occasioned by primordial ties defined in ethnic, territorial, linguistic, and ethical-religious terms".[3]

In one of the earliest scholarly surveys of Chinese nationalism, James Harrison defines the traditional Chinese self-image as "culturalism", "based upon a common historical heritage and acceptance of shared beliefs", not as "nationalism", "based upon the modern concept of the nation-state".[4] He argues that this self-image, or the traditional definition of Chinese-ness, does not evoke an acute awareness of racial distinction and ethnic identity. The primary Chinese identity is therefore "cultural", with no clear-cut definition or perception of the Chinese nation-state. Supreme loyalty is therefore attached to the culture *per se*, not to the state. Despite the changes of dynasties and emperors over the past four millennia, the cultural heritage of Chinese civilisation remains intact and unchallenged.

The "centre-peripheries" paradigm as such can also be applied to understand the press system in pre-modern China. Chinese media historians concur that the "court newsletter" (*di bao*) was the earliest form of newspaper in China, and perhaps in the world as well.[5] It served as a channel for the flow of information between the central, provincial and county governments. Obviously, the emperor himself, the centre of "cultural China", was the equivalent of a "gatekeeper" in the modern press system. All information was sent to the imperial court on a regular basis, and then his decrees were disseminated to the geopolitical peripheries so as to consolidate his ultimate authority. Though the mass-circulated tabloid newspaper did not become prevalent until the mid- fifteenth century, the Chinese press had been subjugated to heavy-handed imperial censorship for the a few centuries before that. Thus, the press system in pre-modern China cannot but reinforce this "centre-peripheries" model of Chinese-ness.

Historically, Chinese civilisation had seldom been challenged by an equal, if not superior, civilisation until the penetration by the West in the Sino-British Opium War (1839–42). In the Chinese historical imaginary, the coming of the West could have been viewed as a "de-centring" from the peripheries. Chinese ruling elites and intellectuals could not simply relinquish their deep-rooted conviction of "centre versus periphery". Their last-ditch efforts at maintaining the unchallenged omnipotence of the age-old "Chinese centre" ended up in vain.

The convulsive disturbances that China suffered since the Opium War made the geopolitical centre a bygone myth. To a significant extent, Chinese cultural consciousness was also inevitably influenced by Western discursive power. Modernisation, in this light, was considered as the panacea for China's national crisis. A total transformation of the conceptualisation of Chinese-ness was consequently the precondition for China's modernisation.

Chinese-ness and the Quest for Chinese Modernity: From Culturalism to Nationalism

With Western penetration in nearly all spheres of social life, the latter part of the nineteenth century and nearly the entire twentieth century saw the historical vicissitudes of China's nation-building and the quest for Chinese modernity. At different socio-historical junctures, the concept of Chinese-ness was defined and refined in line with the agenda of constructing Chinese modernity. In this process of modernisation, mass media loomed larger. The Western penetration into the Chinese social sphere is perhaps best exemplified in the flourishing of "foreign newspapers" (*wai bao*) after the Opium War. With Shanghai and Hong Kong as its major bases, this type of newspaper, owned by Christian churches and/or missionaries, accounted for over 60 per cent of the 76 titles of the newspapers and journals in nineteenth-century China.[6] More importantly, the dominance of "foreign newspapers" subverted the traditional dichotomy between centre and peripheries to one between China and West, thereby fomenting a social vogue of Westernisation, that is, a wholesale adoption of the Western political system, social institutions, science and technology. This media campaign for "Westernising China" culminated in the "One Hundred Days' Reform" in 1898, advocating that modern governmental institutions, such as bureaus of commerce, industry, and agriculture, be established to emulate Western political efficiency.[7] Despite the brevity of the abortive reforms, this political campaign helped introduce into China the new ideas and discourses of the modern Western humanities and social sciences. Chinese elite statesmen and intellectuals thus showed tremendous interest in such modern Western concepts as nation, state, race and ethnicity in the Chinese context.

The emergent modern mass media provided a platform for heated debate over the construction of Chinese-ness and Chinese modernity. Successive social movements and political campaigns provoked the rise of the modern press in China. The three peaks of Chinese modernisation, namely, the "One Hundred Days' Reform" in 1898, the 1911 Revolution and the May Fourth Movement in 1919, coincided with the peaks for the domestic press and publishing industry. By 1919, there were estimated to be over 1,000 titles of newspapers and journals circulated in China.[8]

Zhang Taiyan, one of the leading intellectuals of the time, was among the earliest to propose an authoritative definition of Chineseness in the mass media. He published over one hundred editorials and news commentaries about the Chinese people, or in his own term, "the people of the middle country" (*zhong guo ren*). He wrote that since ancient times, the ancestors of the Han nationality, led by Emperors of Yan and Huang, had lived in North China, which they considered as the centre of the world. They called themselves "Hua Xia", the combinations of the two kingdoms. Zhang concluded that "Hua", "Xia", or "Han" formed a unity, that is, an undifferentiated race and ethnic community that originated in North China, and emerged during the legendary Xia Dynasty (circa. twenty-second century to seventeenth century BCE). In this light, the words "Hua", "Xia" or "Han" can be used interchangeably to mean China as nation-state, as race (or ethnic community), and as geographic location.[9] Despite his vague and inclusive definition, Zhang's effort marks the beginning of constructing a modern concept of the Chinese nation-state and national identity. Accordingly, Chinese-ness is also transformed from a geopolitical and culturalist category to a modern nationalist conceptualisation.

Later efforts were made both in and out of China, through social movements and media discourses, to define Chinese-ness on the basis of Zhang Taiyan's nationalist view, which led to the birth of the Republic of China (ROC), the first modern nation-state in Chinese history. However, this new republic remained as a modern Chinese nation-state only, for its nation-building agenda had never been turned into reality. Domestic turbulence evoked by the conflicts between regional warlords and the colonisation of the Western imperial powers disrupted the Nationalist Party or the KMT's construction of a modern nation-state. By and large, the agenda of saving China by Westernisation bore little fruit.

During the Republican era (1911–49), the mass media seemed to have matured as it exerted significant influence on modern Chinese culture and society. Despite the ineffectiveness of political nation building, the nationwide media system created an "imagined community" throughout China. The KMT government achieved national unity, albeit on a nominal and imaginary level, with a centralised media system composed of the nationwide circulated newspaper, the *Central Daily* (*Zhongyang Ribao*), the Central News Agency (*Zhongyang Tongxunshe*) and the Central Radio (*Zhongyang Guangbo Diantai*). In his quasi-ethnographic narratives, Shen Congwen, one of the most renowned novelists and columnists in the 1930s, described how these media outlets penetrated into the public sphere of the remote interior such as northwestern Hunan, and helped build a mediated simulacrum of both "nation-state" and "world".[10] On the one hand, the mass media disseminated knowledge of science and technology as well as Western ideals of democracy, rule of law, and social equality, thereby subverting the traditional ideology of Confucianism and patriarchy. On the other, it also helped construct a shared experience of political and social events, thereby constructing a shared identity as ROC citizens. According to Shen's account, almost everyone in this township, be it the landlord, the president of the Trader's Union, or the clerks in the tea-house, could all attribute their consciousness of and belief in "nation-state" to the cultivation of such national newspapers as the *Central Daily* and the *Shanghai Daily* (*Shen Bao*).[11]

Chinese-ness as the Conceptual Framework for the National Popular Culture in Maoist China

The three decades from 1949 to 1976 are known as the Maoist era in modern Chinese history. For both China and the rest of the world, the Great Helmsman became asymbol of the Chinese nation-state. Mao himself, as the mythical prototype for the Chinese people, was endowed with unchallenged authority to define Chinese-ness as an all-encompassing category. Simply put, the Maoist definition of Chinese-ness is "national-popular". Associated with the concepts of hegemony and Jacobinism, the term "national-popular" was prominent in the writings of Antonio Gramsci, leader of the Italian Communist Party in the 1920s, as central to Gramsci's blueprint for his country's transition to modernity. Politically, the term "national-popular movement" reflects Gramsci's conceptualisation of the socialist revolution in Italy as a national movement to "fulfil under socialism the historical tasks which the bourgeoisie had abdicated after the Risorgimento".[12] Culturally, the term embraces the forms of media and culture that meet the needs of the socialist revolution. The Maoist definition of Chinese-ness remains the core of his revolutionary alternative to capitalist modernity. Notably, Mao distinguished himself from his predecessors by both his interpretation of Chinese ethnicity and his attitude toward the West.

Mao's definition of Chinese-ness is a reinscription of ethnicity in the Marxist, universalist discursive system. The conceptualisation of Chinese-ness should primarily serve to construct and consolidate the PRC, the unified, independent, multinational Chinese nation-state. In order to maintain a peaceful co-existence between the Han majority and the ethnic minorities, the Maoist definition of Chinese-ness therefore transcended Han chauvinism and aims to draw the subaltern groups, including the non-Han ethnic communities, into the party-state's alliance, or what he called a "unified battlefront" (*tongyi zhanxian*). Strategically, Mao elided the clear-cut demarcation of ethnicity between the Han and non-Han ethnic groups, and instead used an all-encapsulating category of "the oppressed" to represent the collective will of the Chinese people. The quantitatively dominant peasant class, be it ethnically Han or non-Han, had every right to represent and speak for the oppressed. In every respect, Mao's definition of Chinese-ness was therefore characterised by the sanctification of the collective interest of the peasant class. The overarching Marxian category of "class", in lieu of race and ethnicity, became central to the Maoist agenda of defining Chinese-ness.[13]

Secondly, Chinese-ness should be used as an effective Althusserian ISA (Ideological State Apparatus) to fight against all the existing and potential adversaries.[14] Mao therefore abandoned the May-Fourth intellectuals' enlightenment-oriented project of reconstructing Chinese-ness, or what they called "national character" (*guomin xing*), on the ground of the latter's suspect complicity with pro-Western standpoints. In Mao's political agenda, the West remained the most intimidating adversary to China's modernisation. Mao advocated a kind of indigenous, nativist, national form as the counter-discourse to the Western "master narrative" of modernity. His definition of Chinese-ness was deeply embedded in a self-conscious repositioning of China *vis-à-vis* the West in the course of constructing Chinese modernity.

The highly centralised media system in Maoist China effectively propagated and inculcated this Maoist definition of Chinese-ness. Print media (e.g. books, newspapers and magazines) and audiovisual media (e.g. film, radio, television, propaganda posters, pop music and choreography) were all used as the ideological state apparatus to expedite the party-state's political agenda. As one of the most articulate, if not the best, writers among his contemporaries, Mao personally wrote numerous

editorials and news commentaries for *People's Daily*, to instigate the
"Anti-Rightist Campaign" of 1957, the "Great Leap Forward" of 1958,
and the "Great Proletariat Cultural Revolution" (1966–76). During
Mao's reign, the media texts not only helped promulgate socialist cultural
hegemony, but also embodied the Chinese national-popular movement
to consolidate a homogeneous Chinese national identity.

The re-definition of Chinese-ness and the construction of Chinese
modernity in the Maoist era became a process of domination and coer-
cion through manipulative media and cultural policies rather than what
Gramsci called "consent and direction".[15] The identities mediated by the
Maoist mass media and popular culture were monolithic, unified, and
homogeneous. Women, for instance, were liberated by the party-state
to take up "half the sky" along with their male counterparts. They were
provided with access to politics, civil rights, education, and professional
development that had been considered unorthodox in the past four
millennia. What remained unchanged was the male-centred consciousness deep-rooted in the concept of Chinese-ness, which demanded an
unconditional uniformity. The Maoist heroines prevailing in the films,
novels, dramas and propaganda posters were strikingly identical to men,
exhorted, as Mao put it in his verses, "to throw away cosmetics and to
take up weapons" (*bu ai hongzhuang ai wuzhuang*). They were either
single or widowed, deprived of any reference to femininity, maternity,
and/or sexuality. Women were supposed to assume their social role
and gender identity as defined by their patriarch. In this vein, female
subjectivity was still suppressed by the male-centred culture under the
aegis of Maoist revolutionary hegemony.[16]

The monolithic conceptualisation of Chinese-ness can also be found
in media representation of ethnic minorities in the Maoist era. The
mid-1950s and the early 1960s saw an unprecedented boom of books,
news items, non-fiction reportage (*baogao wenxue*), dramas, films, and
pop songs about the life and experiences of the ethnic minorities. In
these media texts, heroes and heroines of the dominant Han nationality
were always portrayed as liberators, incarnations of the all-powerful
party-state, who condescend to emancipate the ethnic minorities in the
border villages from brutal slavery, serfdom and oppression. In return
the minority characters show their loyalty to the party-state and their
willingness to accept the Han (read Maoist) model of modernity, that
is, socialist revolutionary hegemony. In these media representations, the
melodramatic episodes reached their climax in a life-and-death struggle
between progressive forces (mostly the oppressed slaves or peasants

with a Han Communist mentor) and reactionary forces (mostly the slave owners or landlords in complicity with Western imperialists). In general, the ethnic stereotyping prevailing in the Maoist media texts was emblematic of hierarchic, latent Han-centrism that demands unconditional conformity at the expense of erasing ethnic and cultural diversity, thereby consolidating the modernist notion of a homogeneous Chinese identity.

The Maoist conceptualisation of Chinese-ness demanded uniformity, homogeneity and conformity at the expense of difference and diversity. In the name of maintaining national sovereignty as the top priority, the Maoist leadership succeeded in establishing and consolidating the PRC as an independent, unified, multi-national Chinese nation-state. Under the aegis of promoting the collective will of the peasant class, the Nietzschean "will-to-power" of the party-state, represented by Mao himself, became omnipotent and remained unchallenged in nearly all spheres of social and cultural life in Maoist China. The derogatory stereotype of "blue ants", as Western media labeled the Chinese people in their blue and gray "Mao suits", provided a quintessential symbol of Maoist cultural hegemony, which inevitably led to political conformity and aesthetic monotony.

Cultural China vs. Grand China: Revitalising the Centre-periphery Controversy in the Era of Capitalist Globalisation

Mao's death in 1976 marked the end of the Maoist era as well as the beginning of a "New Period" (*xin shiqi*). The different labels for the new period, "post-Mao", "post-socialist", or "post-revolutionary", reflect the ongoing conflict between the legacy of Maoist revolutionary hegemony and all-powerful global capitalism. The problem for post-Mao cultural politics lies in its vague definition of "Chinese-ness". Mao was never ambiguous in endowing the sanctified peasant class with a distinctive culture in content and form, and giving it hegemony in the Chinese cultural arena. The plurality and hybridity of post-Mao cultural sites make it almost impossible to detect any pure, uncontaminated "cultural dominant" in contemporary China.

On the one hand, popular culture is highly commercialised under the influence of global capitalism. On the other, the once-homogeneous category of "Chinese-ness" has become more pluralistic. For example, how is one able to incorporate the distinctive cultural phenomena of

Hong Kong, Taiwan, Tibet, and other geopolitical and cultural margins into the once-hegemonic mode of "Chinese culture"? In addition, the increasingly influential "Chinese diaspora" further dilutes any unified and unquestioned Chinese identity represented by the socialist state.[17] As Maoist cultural hegemony gives way to capitalist globalisation, the post-Mao cultural politics has proved unable to construct a new conceptualisation of Chinese national identity, or even to consolidate any cultural counter-weight to the all-powerful global capitalism. An intellectual, cultural, and moral vacuum becomes what one critic called one of the "pitfalls of China's modernisation".[18] Redefining Chinese-ness has become a challenging "mission impossible" which has attracted scholarly attention from within and without.

The geopolitical dominance of the mainland in the Chinese-speaking world does not translate into dominance over Chinese identity, once the isolation of Maoist China is breached. Socio-cultural diversification now leads to a disintegration of any hegemonic mode of Chinese-ness. What could be seen as peripheries from a Maoist perspective emerge as the major sources of redefining Chinese-ness in the era of globalisation. The economic miracle of the "mini-dragons"— Hong Kong, Taiwan, Singapore and Korea — not only attests to the potency of so-called "neo-Confucianism" (*xin rujia*), but also poses challenges to the legitimacy of the communist leadership in mainland China, the fountainhead of Confucian philosophy. Policies of economic reform and the open-door promoted by the rhetoric of "constructing socialism with Chinese characteristics" (*jianshe you zhongguo tese de shehuizhuyi*) have allowed economic and cultural regionalism to undermine the centralised uniformity of the past.

The "peripheries" have made significant contributions to economic and cultural reconstruction in post-Mao China. Overseas investment from Hong Kong, Taiwan and Chinese diasporic communities in the Southeast Asia have accounted for around half of foreign capital that has poured into mainland China since the 1980s. These financial resources are an important, even decisive, factor in spurring mainland China's economic boom in the past two decades.[19] The cultural impact of Hong Kong, Taiwan, and Singapore on mainland China, particularly in the arena of mass media and popular culture — has been equally profound. It will suffice to mention the following cultural phenomena: the craze for the martial arts fiction imported from Hong Kong and the romances by women writers in Taiwan, the thriving of pop music from

Hong Kong and Taiwan, infatuation with TV dramas imported from Hong Kong, Taiwan and Singapore. The idolatry of teenagers is — not to worship Mao, but the music and TV superstars outside the mainland. "Hong Kong-styled transformation", "Taiwanisation" or "Singaporisation" have been spoken of in sections of such metropolises as Beijing and Shanghai, in coastal provinces like Guangdong and Fujian, and selected social strata like white collars and urban teenagers. The age-old debate between centre and periphery, culturalism and nationalism, has been resuscitated among intellectuals at home and abroad.

There exist two major projects worth our attention: "cultural China", proposed by some overseas-based scholars, and "grand China", by some scholars based in the mainland. The idea of "cultural China" is not unfamiliar to those who still cherish the bygone glory of the Chinese Empire and the enduring impact of Confucianism. Not surprisingly, scholars who hold the belief in "cultural China" are those Sinologists, with or without a Chinese ethnic origin, in Euro-American academic institutions. They tend to visualise China as a perpetual "civilisation-state" rather than a modern nation-state. As historian Lucian Pye clearly puts it, "the fundamental problem of China's modernisation is that China is really a civilisation pretending to be a nation-state". By way of finding an analogy in Western terms, he characterises present-day China as "what Europe would have been if the unity of the Roman Empire had lasted until now".[20] Since China has never been disintegrated into separate nation-states like Europe, such distinctive phenomena as a "dynamic nationalism" and the goal of modernisation still remain "agreed-upon objectives[s] at all levels of Chinese society".[21] Like most Euro-American Sinologists, Pye also privileges models from the socio-geopolitical and cultural "peripheries", such as Shanghai in the 1930s, or Hong Kong, and the Chinese diaspora today. The numerous stories of business and intellectual miracles he finds here prove that Chinese as individuals can be "an outstanding success in the modern world". However, the intrinsic and unresolved conflicts between tradition and modernity, between nationalism and modernisation, restrict the development of a civil society, without which China cannot create a "vibrant form of nationalism" that would be required to modernize her time-honoured civilisations.[22]

Pye's vision of China as a civilisation-state provides a socio-historical and cultural foundation for Wei-ming Tu's project of "cultural China". As an overseas Chinese scholar based in the US, Tu also acknowledges that the geopolitical and cultural centre, despite numerous revolutions, wars, and reforms, has failed and is unlikely to resolve the inherent discrepancies between Chinese tradition and Western modernity. Lamenting the unfulfilled agenda of modernisation at the price of annihilated tradition in mainland China, he celebrated the coming of the so-called "Third Epoch of Confucian Humanism" in the overseas peripheries, where the agenda of integrating Western modernity with Confucian values has been proved to reinforce, rather than weaken, Chinese-ness.[23] Echoing a proposition by another leading America based Sinologist, Ying-shih Yu, "the centre is nothing, whereas the periphery is everything", Tu concludes that the mainland, as the traditional geopolitical and cultural centre, no longer has "the ability, insight, or legitimate authority to dictate the agenda for cultural China".[24]

A legitimacy crisis, as Jürgen Habermas puts it, is "directly an identity crisis".[25] In this light, the PRC as the centre seems to have lost its privilege of defining such all-powerful category as "Chinese-ness". In Tu's project of cultural China, it is precisely "the fruitful interaction among a variety of economic, political, social and cultural forces at work along the periphery" that will activate a dynamic redefinition of Chinese-ness.[26] By way of resuscitating the idea of the civilisation-state, he transcends the conception of the modern nation-state and highlights the continuous interaction among three "symbolic universes": the first consists of mainland China, Hong Kong, Taiwan and Singapore, "the societies populated predominantly by cultural and ethnic Chinese"; the second consists of Chinese communities scattered around the world or the members of Chinese diaspora; the third, perhaps the most interesting and controversial, consists of "individuals, such as scholars, teachers, journalists, industrialists, traders, entrepreneurs, and writers, who try to understand China intellectually and bring their conceptions of China to their linguistic communities".[27]

It is no coincidence that Tu uses the word "universe", also used to describe the Chinese Empire, to delineate his all-encapsulating project of "cultural China". To him, Chinese-ness is basically not a political question, but rather a human concern pregnant with ethical-religious implications. As one of the heralds of Neo-Confucianism, Tu cherishes the past glory of the Chinese Empire as a civilisation-state and endeavours to reinvigorate its timeless splendour through his "cultural China". Ironically however, he also advocates Westernisation through the leadership of the external forces. In his project of "cultural China", all the components of the symbolic universes except mainland China have socio-political or cultural connections with the West. His ambitious inclusion of non-Chinese individuals into his symbolic universe of "cultural China" is rooted in his confidence in the epistemic and discursive hegemony of the Western world (Japan included). Put bluntly in Tu's words, "for the last four decades, the international discourse on cultural China has unquestionably been shaped by the third symbolic universe more than by the first two combined". Writings in English and in Japanese have exerted a much greater impact on "the intellectual discourse on cultural China" than those written in Chinese.[28]

Tu's construction is predicated upon his presumption that mainland China as the centre refuses to communicate with the peripheries and the Western world. Thus, his construction of "cultural China" is still an intellectual variant of the Cold War mentality. As China is now endeavouring to integrate herself into the global world-system and the Chinese "diaspora" has become a worldwide phenomenon, the constant transgression between the three symbolic universes conduces to deconstructing any deep-seated dichotomy between centre and periphery. Tu's tripartite division of cultural China, as his own problematic identity evinces, has become all but irrelevant in the era of globalisation.

The twentieth century was a century of modernisation and nation building around the world. To secure her permanent membership in the global world-system, China had no choice but to establish and consolidate her own modern nation-state. A loosely connected civilisation-state would not do. The achievements of China as a civilisation-state occurred in an earlier context before competitive nationalisms and the modern nation-state had come to China. To resuscitate culturalism in contemporary China means to question the legitimacy of Chinese nationalism. In the era of capitalist globalisation, there is a hunger to redefine Chinese-ness as part of the quest for ethnicity, national identity and sovereignty. In this light, the project of "cultural China" cannot but transform "Chinese-ness" into an illusionary cultural signifier that will eventually force contemporary China off the track of globalisation and modernisation. As long as modernisation and nation-building remain central to Chinese intellectual discourse at home and abroad, the periphery as the centre, or the peripheralisation of the centre, will prove a utopian vision with little relevance to the relationship between China's national history and her complicated *status quo*.

In contrast to the culturalism argument of these overseas-based Sinologists, another group of scholars, most of who live in mainland, have been bearing the banner of nationalism in the revitalised centre/

periphery controversy since the 1990s. Interestingly enough, the rise
of nationalism in Chinese intellectual discourse is intertwined with
the thriving of Chinese "post-ist" theory or "postology" (*houxue*). Postmodernism and postcolonialism, as two major theoretical discourses
in Western academia, were not introduced into China until the mid-
1980s. By the mid-1990s, both had achieved what Edward Said calls
the "final outcome of traveling theory" or that "the now full (or partly)
accommodated (or incorporated) idea is to some extent transformed
by its new uses, its new position in a new time and place".[29] Adapted
for "the sole purpose of rejecting Western thought (socio-cultural as
well as political) as colonising, imperialist, and altogether unsuited to
Chinese realities", postmodern and postcolonial theories, as critic Ben
Xu correctly points out, are conveniently used to "affirm the value
of local and traditional elements and even the cultural and political
status quo".[30]

The project of "grand China" proposed by a group of Chinese
post-ist theorists led by Zhang Yiwu, a Peking University professor of
Chinese popular culture, aims to provide a new definition of "Chinese-
ness", a new "mode of knowledge" for the all around socio-cultural
transformation during the so-called "post-new-era" (*hou xin shjqi*), from
1989 till the present.[31] Alluding to the popular geopolitical category
of the Asia-Pacific Rim, they intend to construct a "rim" of Chinese
culture. Mainland China, or the authentic Chinese nation-state, remains
the core of the rim of Chinese culture; Hong Kong, Taiwan, and Macao
constitute its second ring; the third ring consists of overseas Chinese
communities scattered around the globe, or the Chinese "diaspora";
the outermost includes the East and Southeast Asian nations under the
influence of Chinese culture.[32]

In terms of component and structuring, the project of "grand
China" bears a resemblance to Tu's three "symbolic universes" in his
construction of "cultural China". Both projects are based on the traditional geopolitical and cultural topography of the centre and periphery.
Like the aforementioned overseas-based Sinologists and culturalists,
Chinese post-ist theorists also ground the socio-historical necessity of
building a Chinese community in two landmark events: the economic
miracle of the "mini-dragons" in East Asia and the emergence of a
Neo-Confucian model of socio-political construction in the geopolitical
periphery, Singapore in particular. Chinese post-ist theorists also insist
that Chinese communities, at home and abroad, must converge on a
common cultural ground, which they specify and classify into the fol-

lowing five aspects: the recognised Chinese *lingua franca* — Mandarin
Chinese (*putonghua*); common economic mode (e.g. the Asian-Chinese
mode of four mini-dragons); Chinese aesthetic style; Chinese way of
thinking and reasoning; and Chinese (mainly Confucian) ethics and
value system.[33]

In essence these two projects, "cultural China" and "grand China",
are constructed on the basis of two different, sometimes conflicting,
foundational beliefs, namely, culturalism and nationalism. Though
maintaining an all-inclusive Chinese rim of some sort, the native post-ist
theorists hold firmly to their nationalist standpoint. First, they highlight the importance of identity politics over those of culture and
civilisation. Chinese-ness, in this light, is not merely a cultural signifier,
but more importantly, a conceptual framework that encapsulates such
ideological and politico-cultural categories as ethnicity, national identity
and sovereignty. It is therefore on the ground of a unified, clear-cut
national identity that Tu's third symbolic universe, comprised of non-
Chinese who are related to Chinese culture in one way or another,
cannot be counted as a component of the "grand China" project. Second,
Chinese post-ist theorists adhere to the unchallenged authority of
China's geopolitical and cultural centre — the mainland. The relationship
between centre and periphery is thus defined as "centripetal". Cultural
diversity manifested in the mainland, the peripheral islands, and the
overseas communities, should accord with a distinctive Chinese cultural
subjectivity that is mandated by the centre. As Ben Xu points out, the
project of "grand China" will eventuate in the construction of the rim of
Chinese culture, which is reminiscent of the term "Asia-Pacific Rim", but
is far more "ideologically hegemonic" and "culturally homogeneous".[34]
Such culturalist viewpoints as "the periphery as the centre" and "the
peripheralisation of the centre", appear to Chinese post-ist theorists
to be wishful thinking with little regard to China's socio-political and
cultural subject-position.

The divergence between the overseas culturalists and the indigenous nationalists lies in their response to the fundamental question:
Who is able to speak for and represent China? If China can be seen
as a civilisation-state, as the culturalists steadfastly believe, the all-
encompassing Chinese civilisation *per se* can adequately speak for and
represent China. In this light, the historically fixed model of centre
and periphery no longer has potency and relevance in the domain of
"China studies", for "Chinese of all regions and communities may take
comfort in the vision that their boundaries will no longer close them

off; but instead crisscross each other to form interlocking networks in which there is no single centre".[35] One has to bear in mind that the nation-state remains the basic unit of the global world-system, and will continue to do so in the foreseeable future, The native nationalists in this vein have every reason to dismiss such crisscrossing and interlocking networks as a utopian vision, at least in the mainland where modernisation is yet to be fulfilled. As long as an idealistic, Habermasian "world republic" or "world community" does not turn into reality, ethnicity, citizenry, national identity and sovereignty should be foregrounded in any intellectual debate on the relationship between centre and periphery. However ethnically diverse, naturalised American citizens, including the overseas-based culturalist-Sinologists, are required to pledge their allegiance to their new nation. In the same vein, China can only attain her legitimate membership in the global community as a centralised nation-state, rather than as a loosely bound civilisation-state. The mainland, as China's authentic geopolitical and cultural centre, should be consolidated rather than weakened or peripheralised.

In the face of incipient capitalist globalisation since the early 1990s, the controversies over such binary issues as centre versus periphery, tradition versus modernity, and culturalism versus nationalism, is emblematic of the ongoing conflicts between global and local. The construction of two dichotomous discourses — "cultural China" and "grand China" — represents the endeavours made by Chinese intellectuals, at home and abroad, to alleviate and eventually eradicate the friction between Chinese nation-building and Western hegemony. However different their ideological bases and socio-political foundations, the two projects attest to the fact that Chinese-ness is far from a distinctive, fixed model of socio-historical and cultural experience. In the post-new-era of unstable and unpredictable socio-political and cultural scenes in all sectors of Chinese communities at home and abroad, any modernist, unified definition of Chinese-ness has proved futile. Chinese-ness cannot but be visualised as "an incomplete project whose historical content is to be continuously constructed and worked out".[36] A dynamic re-definition of Chinese-ness has become urgent in the Chinese intellectual and cultural arena, be it native or overseas-based.

Conclusion: Toward a Dynamic Chinese-ness in the Era of Globalisation

The historiographic evolution chronicled here points to the fact that redefining Chinese-ness remains the central task on the intellectual and cultural agenda of constructing Chinese modernity. As a signifier of socio-political and cultural identity, Chinese-ness was necessarily defined and redefined in China's incessant encounters with the external world. In pre-modern China, it was less a category of national identity or ethnicity *per se* than the geopolitical centre's (or Han's) cultural consciousness, adopted to conquer and/or assimilate the peripheral non-Han communities. In the modern era, Chinese-ness becomes much more pronounced in China's continuous direct and indirect encounters with the imperialist West's socio-political and cultural dominance and violence. It is exactly on the basis of the perpetual tension between China and the West that such imported Western theoretical discourses as postmodernism and postcolonialism gain their potency and relevance in the Chinese socio-historical context. Considering China's own socio-historical temporality and spatiality, one might have every reason to cast doubt upon the validity and immediate applicability of postmodern and postcolonial discourses in the Chinese context. Some critics are of the opinion that Chinese postmodernity does not make much sense as long as modernity still remains an unfulfilled and incomplete project in the present-day China.[37]

As for postcolonialism, Rey Chow, for instance, suggests that the two decisive criteria of postcolonial politics do not apply to China very well. The first is "the ownership of particular geographical areas, an ownership whose ramifications go beyond geography to include political representation as well as sovereignty over ethnic and cultural history". The second is the reclamation of "native cultural traditions that were systematically distorted by the colonial powers in the process of exploitation".[38] China, except for a few peripheral islands like Hong Kong, Macao, and Taiwan, was not territorially occupied or culturally distorted by Western (or Japanese) colonial powers. Even during the semi-feudal and semi-colonial era (1840–1949), China still maintained her national sovereignty, her own *lingua franca*, and her unique cultural tradition under the incessant intimidation, encroachment, and even invasion from the West (including Japan). At least theoretically speaking, China was never thoroughly modernised or colonised, therefore forestalling the problems raised by postmodernism and postcolonialism.[39]

To invalidate postmodernism and postcolonialism in contemporary Chinese intellectual discourse is as arbitrary and hegemonic as the Eurocentric diagnosis that China is a civilisation-state "pretending to be a nation-state". The modern West, as Ashis Nandy tells us, is less a geographical or temporal category than "a psychological space". In his words, "the West is now everywhere, within the West and outside: in structures and in minds". China, in this light, cannot "reclaim autonomy and seclusion from the space of world history and chronopolitics with the West as its central figure".[40] Since postmodernism and postcolonialism persistently hold a critical stance towards Western hegemony, it is fully grounded for Chinese indigenous intellectuals to adopt "post-" theories to deal with their own experience of oppression, domination, resistance, and liberation in global/local socio-political and cultural encounters.

In the context of globalisation Chinese-ness should be constructed on the basis of a dynamic relationship between China and the West. Dialogue and interaction have become both permissible and desirable in the post-Cold-War era. What Chinese intelligentsia should keep a critical eye on is any form of politico-economic and cultural hegemony, be it native or foreign, rather than Western culture and civilisation *per se*. Moreover, modernisation or globalisation is not identical to Westernisation. The reconstruction of more "globalised" Chinese identities also requires more intensive intercultural communications with China's allies in Asia, Africa and Latin America. The successful China-ASEAN and China-Africa summits in 2006 are emblematic of China's rising impact upon the non-West world. To redefine a dynamic Chinese-ness therefore plays an important, if not the decisive, role in the course of constructing Chinese modernity, an ongoing process of incessant global/local encounter, conflict, and negotiation.

Secondly, a dynamic Chinese-ness should transcend the binary model of geopolitical and cultural centre and periphery. From its outset, Chinese-ness was deeply rooted in the centre's superiority complex *vis-à-vis* the peripheries, which remained unchallenged till the rise of the peripheral islands and the emergence of a significant Chinese "diaspora" toward the end of the millennium. The aforementioned projects of "cultural China" and "grand China", among the most recent endeavours of redefining Chinese-ness, are both grounded in the uncompromising tension and unidirectional exchange between the mainland, the geopolitical and cultural centre of China, and the peripheries. Overseas-based culturalists believe in a centrifugal decentralisation, or the peripheralisation of the deteriorating centre, while native nationalists adhere to a centripetal re-centralisation, or what they call "revitalising the centre's indisputable authority over the peripheries".[41]

In the age of globalisation when cultural diversity and ideological pluralism are celebrated, the demarcation between centre and peripheries has been blurred, and the tension between them dissolved. For instance, it is not uncommon in recent years that a mainland director produces a film in Hong Kong with Taiwanese sponsorship, and that it receives its first acclaim from audiences in North America. Central to the agenda of mapping China's geopolitical and cultural topography is how to incorporate fluid interactions between the centre and peripheries into a more inclusive, dynamic discourse, rather than arguing whether the centre will continue to dictate to the peripheries or the peripheries will overpower the centre. A dynamic Chinese-ness should be able to unfold discrepancies and contradictions in a hybrid Chinese culture based on both intranational and international communication between the mainland, the peripheral islands, and the "diasporic" communities.

Thirdly, globalisation has brought restructuring, stratification, and diversification to contemporary China. A dynamic Chinese-ness should encompass the complex socio-historical specificities of class, race, gender, and ethnicity, and the intriguing relationships among them. Chinese-ness is not merely an abstract, vacuous signifier of national identity. By the same token, the endeavour to define Chinese-ness should not be restricted to such master discourses as "cultural China" or "grand China". Instead, Chinese-ness should be visualised as a hybrid entity of social, ethnic, gender, and cultural identities, so that the process of re-definition entails uncovering the dependencies, inequalities, and oppressions which the official or mainstream discourse intends to obscure in its celebration of a modernist, unified, and homogeneous national identity.

As my genealogical overview has shown, Chinese-ness remains a nexus of meaning whereby national identity and cultural subjectivity can be reasserted not merely as a discursive formation of radical other-ness, but also as a locale wherein difference, disjunction, and displacement between class, race, gender, and ethnicity can be coordinated into a dynamic, organic entity. It is precisely due to "dynamic" Chinese-ness as such that we can never settle into "being" but will be always "becoming" Chinese. As such peripheral colonies as Hong Kong and Macao have been handed over to the PRC, as the reunification with Taiwan may be accomplished by either military conquest or peaceful negotiation in a foreseeable future, as the Chinese "diaspora" all over the world (particularly in North America and Oceania) has become a significant socio-cultural phenomenon, the problematic of Chinese-ness will remain at the core of the prospering Chinese cultural studies wherein every "organic intellectual" will play an active part.

Notes

1   Kwang-chih Chang, *The Archaeology of Ancient China* (New Haven [CT]: Yale University Press, 1986), pp. 21–37.

2   Owen Lattimore, *Inner Asian Frontiers of China* (Oxford: Oxford University Press, 1940), pp. 15–40.

3   Wei-ming Tu, "Cultural China: The Periphery as the Centre", *Daedalus* 121, 2 (1992): 3.

4   James L. Harrison, *Modern Chinese Nationalism* (New York: Hunter, 1969), pp. 2–3.

5   Chinese media historian still disagrees with the date for the earliest "official newsletter". Some say that it occurred as early as in the Han Dynasty (circa. the first century BC), others would argue for Tang or Song Dynasty (circa the seventh or eighth century). For a detailed account, see Li Bin, *Zhongguo Xinwen Shehuishi* [A Social History of Chinese Journalism] (Shanghai: Shanghai Jiaotong University Press, 2007).

6   Zhuo Nansheng, *Zhongguo Jindai Baoye Fazhanshi* [History of Early Modern Chinese Press] (Beijing: Xinhua Press, 1994), pp. 25–30.

7   Hu Sheng, *Cong Yapian Zhanzheng dao Wusi Yundong* [From the Opium War to the May Fourth Movement] (Beijing: Renmin chubanshe, 1979), pp. 47–56.

8   Chow Tse-tsung, *The May Fourth Movement: Intellectual Revolution in Modern China.* (Cambridge [MA]: Harvard University Press, 1960), p. 28.

9   Zhang Taiyan, "Zhonghua Minguo Lun" [On the Republic of China], in *Zhonghua Minzuzhi* [Chinese Ethnography], ed. Hu Nai-an (Taipei: Tianxia chuban gongsi, 1964), pp. 4–18.

10   Shen Congwen, *Chang He* [The Long River] (Beijing: Renmin wenxue chubanshe, 1984).

11   For a detailed analysis of mass media's role in Shen's short stories, see Wu Xiaodong, "*Chang He zhong de Chuanmei Fuma: Shen Congwen de Guojia Xiangxiang he Xiandai Xiangxiang* [Media Codes in *The Long River*: Analyzing Shen Congwen's Imaginary of Nation-State and Modernity]", unpublished PhD dissertation, Peking University, 1992.

12   Antonio Gramsci and David Forgacs, ed., *A Gramsci Reader: Selected Writings from 1916–1935* (New York: Schoken Books, 1988), p. 426.

13   For a detailed elucidation on Mao's policy on ethnic minorities, see Gong Yuzhi, ed, *Mao Zedong, Deng Xiaoping he Jiang Zemin Lun Minzu Wenti* [Mao Zedong's, Deng Xiaoping's and Jiang Zemin's Viewpoints on Chinese Nationality] (Beijing: Renmin chubanshe, 1999).

14   The French Marxian philosopher Louis Althusser coined the term ISA, see Louis Althusser, *Lenin and Philosophy and Other Essays*, trans. Ben Brewster (New York: Monthly Review Press, 1971), pp. 245–51.

15   Gramsci and Forgacs, *A Gramsci Reader*, pp. 470–1.

16   For a detailed analysis of "the Maoist heroines", see Dai Jinhua and Meng Yue,

Fuchu Lishi Dibiao [Emerging out of the Surface of History] (Zhengzhou: Henan renmin chubanshe, 1990).

17   Arif Dirlik & Xudong Zhang, ed., *Postmodernism and China* (Durham [NC]: Duke University Press, 2000), p. 4.

18   He Qinglian, *Xiandaihua de Xianjing* [The Pitfalls of China's Modernisation] (Beijing: Jinri zhongguo chubanshe, 1996).

19   Ibid., pp. 17–38.

20   Lucien Pye, "How Chinese Nationalism is Shanghaied", in *Chinese Nationalism*, ed. Jonathan Unger (New York: M.E. Sharpe, 1996), pp. 109–10.

21   Ibid., p. 112.

22   Ibid., pp. 112–3.

23   Wei-ming Tu, "Toward a Third Epoch of Confucian Humanism: A Background Understanding", in *Confucianism: Dynamics of Tradition*, ed. Irene Eber (New York: Macmillan, 1986), pp. 3–21.

24   Wei-ming Tu, "Cultural China: The Periphery as the Centre", *Daedalus* 121, 2 (1992): 28.

25   Jürgen Habermas, *Legitimation Crisis*, trans. Thomas McCarthy (Boston: Beacon, 1975), p. 46.

26   Wei-ming Tu, "Cultural China: The Periphery as the Centre", *Daedalus* 121, 2 (1992): 29.

27   Ibid., p. 12.

28   Ibid., pp. 13–4.

29   Edward Said, *The World, the World and the Critic* (Cambridge [MA]: Harvard University Press, 1983), p. 227.

30   Ben Xu, *Disenchanted Democracy: Chinese Cultural Criticism after 1989* (Ann Arbor [MI]: University of Michigan Press, 1999), p. 111.

31   Zhang Yiwu *et al.*, *Da Zhuanxing: Hou Xinshiqi Wenhua Yanjiu* [Great Transformations: Studies on the Post-new-era Culture] (Harbin: Heilongjiang renmin chubanshe, 1995).

32   Ibid., pp. 20–1.

33   Ibid., pp. 24–36.

34   Ben Xu, *Disenchanted Democracy*, p. 116.

35   Leo Ou-fan Lee, "On the Margin of the Chinese Discourse: Some Personal Thoughts on the Cultural Meaning of the Periphery", *Daedalus* 121, 2 (1992): 224–5.

36   Ben Xu, *Disenchanted Democracy*, p. 118.

37   Sun Jin, "Hou Shenme Xiandai, Erqie Zhuyi?" [What the Hell Does "Post-Modern-Ism" Mean?], *Dushu* [Reading] 135 (1992): 34–9.

38   Rey Chow, "Between the Colonizers: Hong Kong's Postcolonial Self-Writing in the 1990s", *Diaspora* 2, 2 (1992): 158–9.

39   Ibid., pp. 160–1.

40   Ashis Nandy, *The Intimate Enemy: Loss and Recovery of Self under Colonialism* (New Delhi: Oxford University Press, 1983), pp. xii–xv.

41   Zhang Yiwu *et al.*, *Da Zhuanxing*, p. 25.

Chapter 9

Family and Friends:
China in Changing Asia

Wang Gungwu

Studies of modern China's foreign relations have noted the rupture between its structure of tribute and trade or "the Chinese world order" and the newer system of nation-states governed by international law. Chinese reluctance to accept the rules introduced by the Great Powers into Asia went through many stages and it is only recently that the government in Beijing is seen to be functioning comfortably in the dominant United Nations state-system. It is possible to explain that change as inevitable. After all, in the world of nation-states, China has no choice but play by the rules that guide the actions of all other states. But the fact that it took China so long to demonstrate that it accepted the key aspects of the system and the fact that some neighbouring states in Asia still have doubts about China's future intentions suggest that the issues remain less clear-cut than might have been expected.

On the one hand, the moralistic position that China insisted on in dealing with foreign rulers through the centuries was always accompanied by given sets of ritual, defined levels of hierarchy and agreed criteria of hegemonic authority. However, despite the sense of continuity that Confucian historians have given to the nature of Chinese dynastic rule, there was never any immutable structure of tributary relationships.[1] What seemed unchanging were the language of feudal condescension and the administrative rules drawn up by various Chinese courts to deal with power realities at different periods of history. Chinese rulers and mandarins had to be flexible in interpreting tribute relations according to the political, economic, security or cultural needs at any one time.

They employed terms that appealed to fealty, family or friendship and most of these were interchangeable depending on circumstances.

On the other hand, the practical position China took since the second half of the nineteenth century was guided by principles of law incorporated into the post-Westphalia system of nation-states. Despite this legal language that shaped modern international behaviour, the Chinese were painfully aware that much of that was subject to close examination and that, for each situation, there were always specific political, economic and security calculations to be made. There was always room for challenge and debate in concepts like equality, sovereignty, interest, pride, dignity, honour, morality, history, memory and leadership in inter-state relations.[2] In that context, successive Chinese governments during the twentieth century have accepted or rejected parts of the international law that the Great Powers have highlighted at different times.

Thus the Chinese have swung back and forth between the moralistic and practical positions, and these swings reflect their many struggles to emerge from a century of weakness towards the recent decades of growing strength. And, while a largely legalistic framework has replaced China's feudalistic approach, the reality for the modern Chinese state has never been either one or the other but the negotiable areas in between that directly influenced all power relations between nations. For the Chinese, navigating in those areas has been feasible and even reassuring because they have always found ways around the hard language of international law by continually using the more comfortable rhetoric of family and friendship.

During the second month of his Provisional Presidency in February, 1912, Sun Yat-sen told an American reporter that his people could not understand why the Great Powers were not prepared to recognise his government in Nanjing. He was extravagant in insisting that there was no government in Beijing and in claiming that the Nanjing government ruled over 350 million people and its writ reached to the borders of Burma. He had made several personal appeals to the Japanese government. His foreign minister, Wang Chonghui, the first graduate of Beiyang College in Tianjin, was using personal connections to negotiate with his former teacher and president of Beiyang College, Dr C.D. Tenney, the American "special representative". But there was no response from Japan and no agreement was reached with the United States. All the foreign embassies waited in Beijing to watch future developments. They eventually recognised the Republic of China more than a year after

Yuan Shikai took over as President. Sun complained, "The world was friendly, the Europeans were friends, we have friends everywhere, but we need recognition, you should recognise our government." Earlier, he had asked the French government "to establish friendly relations as two sister republics". But the law of nations was above family and friendship. None of the Great Powers made a move when they knew that Sun could not unite the country by force and that, in order to avoid a civil war that he could not be sure to win, he had to allow Yuan Shikai to take over the presidency from him.[3]

In the inauguration swearing-in speech he made early in January 1912, Sun had used more wishful traditional language. He spoke of combining the lands of the Han, Manchu, Mongol, Hui and Tibetan as one country and as one people. He described the five peoples as "one family" but urged all to work together so that the other states in the five continents would be more friendly and treat China as a fraternal state (*xiongdi zhi bang*) that was as close to them as lips and teeth. Elsewhere, he used more legalistic terms: in the new constitution of Sun's party, the Tongmeng Hui, promulgated in March 1912, its platform spoke of assimilating all the peoples of China into one nation and seeking equality among the nations of the world.[4]

Sun Yat-sen was the most modern Chinese political leader at the time and he had to struggle with a range of terms that mixed the familiar and the new in his addresses to his people. One can imagine how much more difficult it was for most other Chinese to envisage the position China was in with regards to the Great Powers and to its neighbours in Asia. But it was not a new problem. The problem had been there since at least the seventeenth century when officials who were tasked to write the history of the Ming dynasty (1368–1644) had included, in the section on foreign Asian countries, three European countries that had taken lands in Southeast Asia during the sixteenth and seventeenth centuries, like the Iberian states of Portugal and Spain (Folangji) and the Netherlands (Helan).[5] None of these could be said to have fitted into the tributary system that the Ming had designated as the basis for foreign relations.

In any case, Zhang Tingyu's final version of the *Ming History* was not published until 1739, almost a century after the fall of the dynasty. By that time, the Jesuits had worked at the Qing court and the English East Company had become a major player in Asia, and Manchu and Chinese mandarins were aware that the geography of China and Asia in the world was far more complex than they had once thought.[6] Although Qianlong Emperor's notorious words to Lord Macartney saying that China needed nothing from the West have been endlessly quoted to suggest that the dynasty was ignorant of what had changed in Asia, it would be wrong to think that the new developments had no impact on China's traditional tributary system. Although the framework and the official rhetoric were still in use, the key officials dealing with foreign relations had observed changing power relations in the maritime kingdoms and ports to China's east and south and were already aware of writings by travelers like Xie Qinggao, Wang Dahai and others.[7] Information gathered from foreigners meeting at the port of Guangzhou (Canton) in the early nineteenth century also enabled Lin Zexu, Wei Yuan, Xu Jiyu and others to prepare new studies concerning China's neighbours, like *Sizhou ji*, *Haiguo tuzhi* and *Yinghuan zhilue*. All these books incorporated new information about the rest of the world, but they did so with China's worldview still more or less intact.[8]

Nearly 200 years after the *Ming History* was completed, the loyalist former officials of the Qing dynasty published in 1927 the Draft History of the Qing dynasty (*Qingshi gao*) in which they outlined changes in the nature of international relations. A new section of eight chapters on the powers that had diplomatic relations with the Qing covered most of Europe and parts of the Americas but, where Asia was concerned, Japan was now listed with the other Great Powers. It had been loosely grouped with China's tributary states in the past. Only four chapters at the end dealt with the rest of Asia. In three of them were the kingdoms of Korea, Vietnam, Burma, Siam and Laos. But, of the scores of tributary maritime kingdoms and ports that filled past official histories, only the island states of Ryukyu (Okinawa) and Sulu remained. The seven in Asia that remained were listed under the title of *shuguo* (tributary states or colonies), but it was noted that none of them were China's *shuguo* by the end of the nineteenth century. They had become the colonies of powerful countries like Japan, France, Britain and Spain. Only Siam was depicted as a former *shuguo* that had achieved self-rule or independence (*zizhu*) in 1852 through diplomatic negotiations between Britain and France. It is noteworthy that Korea was not recorded as a *shuguo* of Japan, another Asian state, but as having been amalgamated (*hebing*) with it. Why *hebing* was used was unexplained. These loyalist historians were compiling their work in Manchuria under the shadow of Japanese power and it is understandable why they had to be careful in the language they used when describing what the Japanese after the Meiji Restoration had done to Qing China, including annexing the province of Taiwan and *shuguo* like Ryukyu and Korea.[9]

Chinese leaders of the late nineteenth century found it difficult to believe that what had been an enduring set of feudal-personal relationships between their Son of Heaven and the neighbouring kingdoms and chiefdoms in Asia was coming to an end. The regulation of tribute and trade, after centuries of loosely defined multi-layered relationships, had evolved into an elaborate institution during the Ming and Qing dynasties (fourteenth to nineteenth centuries). The mandarins thought that this was a proven system that had gained respect for China and ensured China's security. Now that new forces were active in global politics and their system was no longer effective, Chinese leaders recognised that they had to follow the set of international laws that the Western Powers applied to China. But their doubts about that framework remained for another century, especially when they found that these laws could not save China from continued threats of invasion and dismemberment and could even be used to thwart China's desperate efforts to reunify the country. What is more, they also learned that the laws were largely unenforceable when powerful states chose not to adhere to them. This confirmed that, in the end, China needed to regain wealth and power before it could count on the efficacy of law. In the meantime, to assist its survival as a unitary state, it would have to make use of informal appeals to friendship and familial ties among all states. Although these were not binding, they were more familiar to its Asian neighbours than the legal language of the West.

Immanuel Hsu, in his study of the years 1858–78, spoke of "China's entrance into the family of nations".[10] He did this in 1954 when the term "the family of nations" was taken to mean the group of nineteenth century Great Powers that had determined which countries were worthy to join their family and which were not yet ready. In the 1950s, China under the Chinese Communist Party was freely using family and friendship terms in certain contexts. Among revolutionaries, words like comrade were common but, echoing older usage, there were also phrases like the brotherhood of man that knew no borders and, in particular, the relations between transnational communist parties that were described as fraternal. These words pertaining to family and friend could be interchangeable in Chinese. Close friends were likened to siblings though it was recognised that, between friends, there was a distance that needed additional mental and spiritual bonds if set against the demands of blood and kinship.

The family metaphor was popularly used in European international relations as well, especially before the First World War when hopes for the peaceful resolution of Great Power conflicts were seriously disrupted. It remained among the other words that were used during the discussions leading to the Covenant of the League of Nations, including more formal and legally correct words like association, community, confederation, alliance, and society. The Chinese keenly followed this development. In their tradition, joining the family could be compared with joining the club in the English-speaking world, something China had not been asked to do. Both words conveyed warmth and intimacy and were appropriate in less formal celebratory occasions. But they also suggested tight-knit bonds that excluded those who did not belong.

When the Chinese Communist Party came to power in 1949, the People's Republic of China (PRC) was not able to join the family of the United Nations. Actually, Mao Zedong proclaiming at Tiananmen that the Chinese people had stood up was in a far superior position than Sun Yat-sen's 37 years earlier. He had, like the great empire-founders in Chinese history, won total victory on the battlefield and held the Mandate of Heaven although the mopping-up job was not complete. The rival regime under Chiang Kai-shek was far weaker than Yuan Shikai's in Beijing in 1912. But the Nationalist Government of the Republic of China was still a member of the family of United Nations, the new legitimising body, and it was supported by the United States and had a Treaty of Friendship and Alliance with the Soviet Union. Hence Mao Zedong had good reason to feel insecure in the larger world family and wanted as soon as possible to sign a Friendship Treaty with the USSR and get Stalin to break off with Chiang Kai-shek. He thus adopted the idea of a socialist *family* of nations (*shehuizhuyi guojia dajiating*) by going to Moscow and signing the Sino-Soviet Treaty of Friendship, Alliance and Mutual Assistance of February 1950, an act that made the two countries "brothers in arms".[11]

This was a fateful decision. Within months, it led Mao Zedong to fight on the side of the North Koreans against UN forces led by the United States. This consolidated his identification with the communist or socialist family of nations headed by the Soviet Union. By limiting that family to nations that shared the same ideology and revealing the exclusive and defensive position of the PRC, it underlined the possibility of more than one family of nations. Of course, as demonstrated in the course of a decade, this was illusory. After the Sino-Soviet quarrel became serious in the early 1960s, the Chinese did not find the phrase "family of nations" comfortable to use for relations between nations. In addressing the developing nations of Asia, Africa and Latin America, they turned to other phrases like, "within the Four Seas, all men are brothers", or special relationships that are "as close as lips and teeth", and made general appeals to old and new friendships. When eventually the PRC was admitted into the UN and took its seat in the Security Council, it still hesitated to speak inclusively of the family of nations. And, for the first decade of Deng Xiaoping's reforms, friendship between nations was the preferred term.

Since the 1990s, the term family of nations has reappeared but is still sparingly used for relations among states. Only in the context of the UN family have the Chinese been uninhibited in using it. Nevertheless, its current informal use reminds us that, more than a century earlier, the Chinese had been forced to acknowledge that the structure that John K. Fairbank called "the Chinese World Order" had become obsolete. My essay in the volume he edited focused on the institutionalising of the mature tributary system soon after 1368 (see note 1). Almost exactly 500 years later, in 1864, Henry Wheaton's *Elements of International Law* was translated into Chinese. That translation showed how complex the new power reality in Asia had already become. It was a landmark not only for the Chinese but also for the Japanese who immediately reprinted it and adopted it for all their future diplomatic dealings, not least in advancing their interests on the mainland at the expense of China. The rules were those used by the family of Western Great Powers at China's gates. In the state-system where nations were seen as autonomous moral and political entities, the underlying principles were based on philosophical and theological traditions rooted in the Mediterranean and Atlantic worlds. Romano-Germanic legalism or Judaeo-Christian ideas of natural law had little in common with Chinese ideas that stress moralistic, voluntaristic, familial and hierarchical understanding of power, part-Confucian and part-Buddhist, that China and Japan shared to different degrees and in different proportions. The Qing mandarins after 1864 struggled with the legal terminology used in *Elements* and tried to make the new words match those that they had invented for their ancient tribute-trade system. Some officials still thought that there could be more than one family in the world of nations. But after the Qing fell and dynastic China came to an end, the Republic of China from 1912 (on the mainland till 1949 and in

Taiwan since then), as seen above in the pleas by Sun Yat-sen, sought desperately to join "the international family", if only so that the new polity could use the family's rules to fight for China's sovereign rights and reject the "unequal treaties" that the Great Powers had imposed on them in the nineteenth century.[12]

The PRC after 1949 purported to scorn the system that excluded it for more than two decades. But, since its admission as the sole legitimate government of China into the inner circle of the United Nations Security Council in 1971, it has accepted that, whether called family or not, it could live with the United Nations structure around which the rest of the world turned. This did not mean that the Chinese agreed with all the assumptions that underpinned international law as understood in Europe and the United States. They had reservations about the universality of some of the assertions claimed in United Nations circles if only because they believed that some of them could lead to undue interference in what they considered to be a country's internal affairs. In addition, they knew their history and were conscious of alternative ways of dealing with the harsh realities in the power relations between polities.[13] For example, the loose term, family of nations, could provide more room for dealing with dynamic and unstable conditions while courts of international law could be appealed to as the last resort. They also recognised that there was room for improvement in the current international system and were ready to take part in moves to reform and improve that system as long as their views and interests were taken into account.

China has become deeply immersed in the UN processes since then, but many countries still ask what China really wants. Is it really committed to all the principles embodied in the UN Charter? Clearly the Chinese have learnt that nothing is absolute and immutable in power relationships. Therefore, international law can only be one of the means by which inequalities and uncertainties among nations are kept in check. Behind legalistic rules and practices have always been questions of humanity, morality and justice, and states dealing with one another needed to agree on the value systems that permitted constructive discourse before any rules could be seen as binding. In the meantime, the language of family and friendship helped to make the environment for negotiation and disputation less threatening. It is in that context that Chinese leaders and thinkers have abandoned the defined inequality of tributary relations in recognition of the dynamic realities of a globalised world. But, given the lack of enforceable laws, they have remained cautious about the fiction of equal sovereign states and have preferred the softer hierarchy implied in terms like family and friends among whom greater emphasis could be placed on ideas of reciprocity and moral responsibility. None of these have legal content, but they could enable necessary bilateral and multilateral relations, including those formalised by all varieties of treaties and agreements, to be conducted in a peaceful atmosphere while the international system was being improved. In short, nothing should be taken as final or sacred.

The Chinese world order described by John King Fairbank in the 1960s had been useful in Asia when all kingdoms and rulers believed in unequal relations and employed tribute-like feudal and personal language in their relationships. But the promise of the Westphalian state system to acknowledge the sovereign rights of nations trumped that decisively, especially for the smaller and weaker nations. When the Chinese were introduced to Wheaton's work on international law, they were greatly impressed by the way such law regulated the behaviour of the civilised nations and also justified the rights of a concert of powers that ruled over lesser peoples, including their imperial expansion and the acquisition of colonies. Dynastic officials compared these arguments with their own assumptions, centered on preserving the security and superiority of a single power. Where there was no such power centre but, instead, a number of competing powers, different rules and practices were needed. Hence the mandarins turned back to their ancient history, to the anarchic conditions in pre-Qin China during the period of the Warring States that were familiar to all Chinese scholars. They concluded that the modern global situation was a transitional state of affairs in which the challenge for hegemony could be bitter, painful and continuous, a view that still finds currency in Chinese analyses of the world situation today.[14] They also realised that China was in no position to join that challenge as long as it was technologically and economically inferior. When Japan not only defeated the Qing but also justified the war with the Wheatonian arguments that had guided the expansionist actions of other Great Powers, the Chinese were humiliated. By that time, Japan had been admitted into the family of nations as an equal while China was but a lowly family member with an "unequal" status that remained for another half-century.

In this context, family is an appropriate metaphor. There is generational inequality; there is stem and branch membership that mark degrees of relationships; and, among those of the same generation, there are older and younger siblings. Locating oneself within a family is something that the Chinese understood well. But they were alarmed when their country was treated as if it was a distant relative belonging to a weak branch, and in danger of being an older brother (possibly the eldest) only among the benighted natives of the European colonies. How they could recover the dignified position they once had and become a core member of the stem family of states became a matter that kept their best diplomats busy after 1895. But China's position continued to deteriorate despite their siding with the victorious allies during the First World War. Joining the League of Nations, too, did not save it from losing control of (Outer) Mongolia and Manchuria, nor from another war with Japan that it had little hope of winning. Fortunately, the United States came into the war and, after 1945, catapulted China to Great Power status by insisting on having the Republic of China as one of the five Permanent Members of the Security Council of the newly established United Nations. This provided the cockpit from which China could try to re-position itself. Ever since 1978, the PRC has systematically laid the foundations for Great Power status through determined economic reforms. Now that the reforms have proved successful and had their dramatic impact on the capitalist world, what does that do to its relations with its neighbours in Asia?

Two of the challenges China faced to its once-dominant position in Asia are pertinent to the question of family and friendship in foreign relations. The earlier challenge concerns what family and friend could mean to the Chinese when their country was weak. The later challenge evolved in stages as China recovered from war, civil war and the Cold War and reached its present position when wealth and power are accumulating but with enough unpredictability to arouse fears among some of its Asian neighbours.

The first challenge lasted for half a century till the reunification by the CCP in 1949. By the 1920s, most young Chinese had abandoned the traditional idea of a superior Chinese civilisation. Instead, there was the growing appeal of nationalism, whether directed against the Western empires or specifically against Japan, and this began to turn a civilisational concept — that of *tianxia* (All under Heaven) — into analogies with the national empires of the Great Powers. Adopting the rhetoric of nation-state expansionism and in response to actual encroachments on Chinese lands, for example, cession of territories like Hong Kong and Taiwan and the blurring of endangered borderland territories like Manchuria, Xinjiang and Tibet, the idea of Chinese sovereignty became sacred. The strong emotions generated found their way into nationalist textbooks from the 1920s to the 1950s in order to claim political rights over all lands that had a tributary relationship with imperial China, especially those in Southeast Asia like Vietnam, Laos and Burma. This was misguided. The ardent nationalists had little understanding of the tributary system. What had served as devices for trade, defense and diplomacy, as well as displaying cultural superiority, were re-interpreted by them to mean that these smaller neighbouring states were either territories owing allegiance to China, or were simply Chinese lands lost to foreign powers.[15] It was an example of the transfer of the language of international law and the rhetoric of national power to be used to assert the Chinese position towards its neighbours in Asia and is perhaps the most striking example of rationalisation of positions that had moved from one of strength and confidence to one of helplessness and victimhood.

But when China became disunited and weak and embraced nationalism, especially in the 1920s and 1930s, China found that it had neither family nor friend among its Asian neighbours. In any case, all were subject to foreign dominance (including Thailand, though it was formally independent) or actual colonial administration, so that, even if the indigenous nationalists in these colonies were sympathetic, they were unable to be of any help. The only exception was Japan, a Great Power that was newly aggressive on Chinese soil. Neither family nor friend, it was instead a dangerous enemy against whom China had to look outside Asia for help to defend itself. This was something that China had never had to do before. It had joined the family of nations on terms dictated by the West, and now it had to seek assistance as a feeble new member. There was, in fact, no country that China could call a friend. Even the help that it did receive from other members of the family of nations were clearly self-interested, and China could not count on having any of that help for any length of time.[16] Given these circumstances, it was understandable that some Chinese leaders should turn to the deliberate mobilisation of popular nationalism. In this, the nationalists were inspired by the successes of Japan and post-Bismarckian and Nazi Germany. They felt that they had no choice but to follow their example in order to fight off multiple threats to the country, most notably those of Japanese territorial ambitions, Soviet Russian ideological subversion and, not least, the total control of China's economy by foreign business interests from Europe and the United States.

Modern nationalism is a two-edged sword. At the positive end, it helps to build a loyal citizenry for national unity and this could receive sympathy. At the opposite end, however, it is spurred by a sense of inferiority to emphasise the restoration of former greatness, and the strong emotions aroused would recognise no family or friend outside the country's borders. China's primary goal was the difficult task of unifying its peoples and this led to anachronistic depictions of an ancient "world order" to match the colonial claims of Western powers in Asia and elsewhere. Thus Chinese leaders turned to unjustified territorial claims to remedy China's disunity and weakness. The most striking cases in the textbooks that I recall using as a schoolboy in the state of Perak (one of the Federated Malay States of British Malaya) in the 1930s listed Korea, Vietnam, Burma, Laos and Malaya as some of China's "lost *colonies*". It is a good example of how, in adopting a nationalistic response following successive humiliations, the Nanjing authorities came to speak the language, and thus acquire the face, of its worst enemies. Although understandable, this could be alarming to China's neighbours in Asia. Most Chinese, including those who were resident overseas, were new to such nationalism and their responses were uneven. As a result, both nationalist Guomindang (GMD) and CCP leaders and their fervent supporters both at home and abroad, when faced with Japanese expansion, intensified their propaganda against Japan to produce the patriotic commitment they needed. But there was an unavoidable contradiction in this position. The louder the nationalist calls to action, the greater the danger of rejection by other nations that did not share China's fears. The main remedy against the consequences of chauvinism and isolation was to use skilled diplomacy to make friends among those who had some common interests with China. This required acceptance and mastery of the prevailing international system. To do that, it was necessary to affirm China's membership in the family of nations and show commitment to its values in spite of the system's faults and weaknesses. In the end, China discovered that the narrow nationalist path was incompatible with any claim to represent a higher moral order in international affairs. That danger was not lost among GMD and CCP leaders during the Second World War. Both realised that they had to modify their nationalism if they wanted to win friends among the other powers and the only way to do that was to act as a good member of the family.[17]

The second challenge arose after the end of World War II when the reunited China under the CCP began to rebuild new strength from abysmal weakness. The Mao Zedong era from 1949 till 1976 was an idiosyncratic one that historians will continue to explore. But it left a

very strong impression on China's Asian neighbours. Offering support
to fraternal communist parties that tried but failed to overthrow postcolonial nationalist leaders did little to win friends for China. Standing
up to the Russians might have appealed to some Chinese nationalists,
but the ideological reasons for doing so were at best mystifying, not
least to those in Asia, including leftist political leaders in Japan, who
were friendly towards the Chinese revolution. In retrospect, the major
contribution of Mao's Cultural Revolution to later developments was to
have touched a diplomatic bottom where China had neither family nor
reliable friend to turn to for help. China's position during those years
served to show how dangerous it was to be almost totally isolated.[18]

During the Mao years, China was kept out of the United Nations
family for the first twenty-two years and had to be content with the
socialist family. Many had believed that revolutionary internationalism
would replace the failed nationalisms of the previous decades. But they
found that bending to the will of the Soviet Union was increasingly
unbearable. The socialist family permitted Big Brother to intervene in
another country's internal affairs in the name of ideological conformity. And fraternal differences could still lead to dangerous rival
nationalisms that cut across family feelings.[19] Fortunately for China,
the world outside was changing fast. Numerous international organisations were established out of the United Nations Organisation, scores
of new nations joined that UN family and continuous attempts were
made to refine and extend the writ of international law. With rapid
decolonisation in Asia and Africa, many new members were added
to the UN. With the help of many such members, China eventually
regained its position in the enlarged family. The Chinese then set out
systematically to master the rules and mores that guided the behaviour
of legally equal nations. Among the lessons they learnt was to substitute
friendly symbols between communist-socialist parties with those between family member states. Above all, they also learnt that international
laws were not as clear or absolute as they were made out to be and
that they could only be enforced with great difficulty. In that context,
formal alliances and partnerships offered no real advantage. Instead,
while laws were being disputed and debated, the cultivation of family
and friendly relations among nations remained invaluable in the new
international organisations.

Thus Deng Xiaoping, who had no illusions about international law,
reversed course after 1979. He turned to maximum pragmatism, and

set out to win friends in Asia and be a good citizen in the family of nations. He recognised that the economic development of China to restore health and strength to its devastated structures would need time and help from a peaceful environment that only the international system could provide. As a direct result, China's growth since the reforms after 1978 has been remarkable. A strong China now stands before its Asian neighbours for the first time in over a century. As these neighbours gaze at that phenomenal transformation, there is speculation whether China could some time in the future return to a modern and sophisticated version of tributary relationships, one that China might dress up in accordance with international relations theory. But the overall thrust so far is clear. China is proactive in economic relations and has given priority to making friends wherever it can, most notably and urgently in its neighbourhood. There is keen interest in a new regionalism that hinges on Southeast Asia, one that could also be called upon to help China deal with its sensitive relations with Japan and Korea as well as help its wish to bring Taiwan back into its fold.[20]

China's concerns today are practical. The danger is that, without ideals and ideology, the efforts to search for shared values that are rooted deeply in Chinese soil could, if crudely handled, lead its people back to the nationalism that left China without family and friends and thus damage the progressive image that China wants to project to the outside world. Now that China is seen to be strong again, it cannot afford to display the kinds of nationalism associated with expansionism and empires. The international system understands how national empires could lurk behind the rhetoric of national pride and it can normally check such developments among its smaller members. But the system cannot easily contain imperial urges when a country is strong. Thus the stronger China becomes, the more fearful its neighbours are. If that strength were accompanied by nationalism, China would find it difficult to convince them of its best intentions. Chinese leaders have protested that they eschew nationalism and have no intention to expand in any direction. Their credibility depends on their ability to convince all concerned that China encourages economic growth only to satisfy the people's needs and arms itself only for defense. With consistent displays of friendship and family feeling expressed through self-control, strong civic discipline and respect for other people's values, a powerful China may actually help strengthen the international system that it has so cautiously embraced.

Notes

1   John K. Fairbank, ed., *The Chinese World Order: Traditional China's Foreign Relations* (Cambridge: Harvard University Press, 1968); Morris Rossabi, ed., *China Among Equals: The Middle Kingdom and its Neighbours, 10th–14th centuries* (Berkeley: University of California Press, 1983); Wang Gungwu, "Early Ming Relations with Southeast Asia, a Background Essay", in *Community and Nation: Essays on Southeast Asia and the Chinese* (Singapore and Sydney: Heinemann and Allen & Unwin, 1981), pp. 28–57, and "The Rhetoric of a Lesser Empire: Early Sung Relations with its Neighbours", in *The Chineseness of China: Selected Essays* (Hong Kong: Oxford University Press, 1991), pp. 100–17.

2   There is a vast literature debating such concepts since the publication of Wheaton's *Elements of International Law* in 1836. Particularly influential has been Hedley Bull, *The Anarchical Society: a Study of Order in World Politics* (London: Macmillan, 1977); and Robert Jervis, *Perception and Misperception in International Politics* (Princeton: Princeton University Press, 1976). A useful survey of some new issues is Michael Cox, Tim Dunne and Ken Booth, eds., *Empires, Systems and States: Great Transformations in International Politics* (Cambridge: Cambridge University Press, 2001).

3   Fredrick McCormick, *The Flowery Republic* (London: John Murray, 1913), pp. 257–96. Duan Yunzhang, ed., *Sun Wen yu Riben shishi biannian.* 段云章. 孙文与日本史事编年 (Sun Yat-sen and Japan: a Chronological History) (Guangzhou: Guangdong Renmin Chubanshe, 1996), pp. 229–84; Li Jikui, *Sun Zhongshan yu Riben,* 李吉奎. 孙中山与日本 (Sun Yat-sen and Japan) (Guangzhou: Guangdong Renmin Chubanshe, 1996), pp. 286–303.

4   *Sun Zhongshan quanji* 孙中山全集 (The Complete Works of Sun Yat-sen) (Beijing: Zhonghua shuju, 1982), Vol. 2, pp. 1–19, 47–8, 94–7, 105, 160–7 and 316–29.

5   Zhang Weihua, *Mingshi Folangji Lusong Helan Yidaliya sizhuan zhushi* 张维华, 明史佛郎機呂宋和蘭意大里亞四傳注釋 (A Commentary of the Four Chapters on Portugal Spain Holland and Italy in History of Ming Dynasty) (Beijing: Hafo yanjing xueshe, 1934).

6   Fan Hong-ye, *Yesuhuishi yu Zhongguo kexue* 樊洪业, 耶稣会士与中国科学 (The Jesuits and Science in China) (Beijing: Zhongguo renmin daxue chubanshe, 1992). Fu, Lo-shu, ed., *A Documentary Chronicle of Sino-Western Relations, 1644–1820* (Tucson: The Association for Asian Studies by University of Arizona Press, 1966).

7   Xie Qinggao, *Hai Lu zhu* 谢清高, 海录注 (Annotated edition of Maritime Records) (Beijing: Zhonghua shuju, 1955); Wang Dahai, *Haidao yizhi jiaozhu.* 王大海, 海岛逸志校注 (Annotated Edition of Records and Anecdotes of the Island World) (Xianggang: Xuejin, 1992).

8   Lin Zexu, *Sizhou zhi* 林則徐, 四洲志 (Record of the Four Continents). Annotated by Zhang Man 張曼 (Beijing: Huaxia chu ban she, 2002); Wei Yuan, *Haiguo*

tuzhi 魏源, 海国图志. (Gazeteer and Maps of the Maritime World). Annotated by Chen Hua *et al.* 陈华等. 长沙：岳麓书社, 1998; Xu Jiyu, *Yinghuan zhilue jiaozhu.* 徐继余 [余 and 田], 瀛寰志略校注 (A Brief Description of the Ocean Circuit). Annotated by Song Dachuan 宋大川 (Beijing: Wenwu chuban she, 2007).

9   Zhao Ersun deng, *Qingshi gao.* 赵尔异等 [lacking the font, NUS library uses an alternate character for *sun*, the original name consists of the full form of 选 without running radical] 清史稿 (Draft History of the Qing Dynasty) (Changchun: Jilin chubanshe, 1995). On Korea, the edition stops with the Treaty of Shimonoseki (1895) and concludes by saying that Korea became fully independent. Other editions add that Korea was amalgamated with Japan. It also says that the Ryukyu kingdom ceased to exist. For Vietnam as for Laos, the sections conclude by saying that they came under the protection of the French. For Burma, the section notes that the British failed to send Burma's once-in-ten-years tribute due in 1898. For Siam, it points out how Siam remained independent between British and French colonies.

As for Sulu, it briefly mentions how the Spanish failed to subjugate the Muslim kingdom, and that it no longer sends tribute to the Qing emperor. Archival records show that that kingdom managed to sustain its tributary relations through the Qianlong emperor's reign (1736–95) despite several Spanish efforts to stop them; First National Archives, ed., *Qingdai zhongguo yu dongnanya geguo guanxi dang'anshiliao huibian.* 中国第一历史档案馆编, 清代中国与东南亚各国关系档案史料汇编. (A Collection of Archives on the Relations between China and Southeast Asian Countries in Qing Dynasty). *Volume Two, The Philippines.* 第二册, 菲律宾卷 (Beijing: International Cultural Publishing Co. 北京：国际文化出版公司).

10   Immanuel Hsu Chung-yueh completed his PhD thesis on China's entrance into the family of nations in 1954. This was subsequently published as *China's Entrance into the Family of Nations: the Diplomatic Phase, 1858–1880* (Cambridge: Harvard University Press, 1960).

11   Odd Arne Westad, ed., *Brothers in Arms: The Rise and Fall of the Sino-Soviet Alliance, 1945–1963* (Washington, D.C.: Woodrow Wilson Center Press and Stanford: Stanford University Press, 1998); Chen, Jian, *Mao's China and the Cold War* (Chapel Hill: The University of North Carolina Press, 2001).

12   Chinese diplomats had a very difficult time as the government visibly weakened after the Versailles Treaty in 1919. A good example of how the struggle to rid China of discriminatory parts of the Unequal Treaties was seen at the time is Zeng Youhao, *Zhongguo waijiaoshi* 曾友豪编, 中国外交史 (History of Chinese Diplomacy) (Shanghai: Commercial Press, 1926) (reprinted as No. 187 of Part Two, Jindai zhongguo shiliao congkan xubian 近代中国史料丛刊续编, 第十九辑, volume 19), pp. 386–458. This may be compared with the work of later historians of Chinese foreign policies, for example, Wu Dongzhi, ed., 吴东之编, *Zhongguo waijiaoshi: Zhonghua minguo shiqi 1911–1949* 中国外交史: 中

华民国时期, *1911–1949年* (Diplomatic History of China: Republican Period, 1911–1949) (Henan: People's Publishing House, 1990), in which the unequal treaties debates during 1920–28 are covered on pp. 69-185. After the Nanjing government was established by the Guomindang in 1928, the nationalists briefly asserted themselves, but their efforts were totally undermined by the Japanese takeover of Manchuria three years later; Hong Junpei, ed., 洪钧培编. *Guomin zhengfu waijiaoshi* 国民政府外交史 (Diplomatic History of the Republican Government) (Shanghai: Huatong Publishing, 1932), reprinted as no. 280 in Jindai zhongguo shiliao congkan 近代中国史料丛刊 (Taipei: Wenhai Publishers, 1968). For a broader perspective based on personal experience, see Gu Weijun, *Gu Weijun Huiyilu* 顾维钧回忆录. (The Memoirs of Wellington V.K. Koo) (Beijing: Zhonghua Publishing Co., 1983), Vol. One, pp. 316–65, 391–400 and 409–42.

[13]   Alastair Iain Johnston and Robert S. Ross, eds., *Engaging China: the Management of an Emerging Power* (London: Routledge 1999), especially the essay by Alastair Iain Johnston and Paul Evans, "China's Engagement with Multilateral Security Institutions", pp. 235–71.

[14]   Richard L. Walker, *The Multi-state System of China* (Hamden, Conn.: Shoe String Press, 1954).

[15]   See chapter by Zheng Yangwen in this volume.

[16]   The League's failure to deal with Japan's attack on Manchuria has left many documents and contemporary accounts. The most accessible record of the key issues is still W.W. Willoughby, *The Sino-Japanese Controversy and the League of Nations* (New York: Greenwood Press, 1968 [first published in 1935]). Willoughby's perceptive conclusions are in pp. 657–69. S.R. Smith, *The Manchurian crisis, 1931–32: A Tragedy in International Relations* (New York: Columbia University Press, 1948), pp. 225–62, captures the hopeless position of China most effectively.

[17]   The clearest turnaround in style and purpose may be found in the speeches and writings of Soong Mei-ling (Madame Chiang Kai-shek), *This is Our China* (New York: Harper, 1940). In comparison, Mao Zedong's story to Edgar Snow reflects an alternative voice of a tentative and tactical reconciliation, *Red Star over China* (London: Victor Gollancz, 1937).

[18]   Wang Gungwu, *China and the World since 1949: The Impact of Independence, Modernity and Revolution* (New York: St. Martin's Press, 1977), pp. 106–41.

[19]   Shen Zhihua, Yang Kuisong *et al.* 沈志华、杨奎松等编著, *Zhong Su guanxi shigang, 1917–1991* 中苏关系史纲 (A History of Sino-Soviet Relations, 1917–1991) (Beijing: Xinhua Publishers, 2007). The last straw was probably the Brezhnev doctrine as applied to Czechoslovakia in 1968. But as shown in Robert A. Jones, *The Soviet Concept of "Limited Sovereignty" from Lenin to Gorbachev: The Brezhnev Doctrine* (Basingstoke: Macmillan, 1990), the roots of that doctrine can be traced much further back.

[20]   The PRC closely studied the establishment of the ASEAN Ten, completed in 1999, and concluded that ASEAN represents a regionalism that China could not

only live with but also build on to enhance peace and stability in its southern neighbourhood. There was a major shift in policy from an emphasis on bilateral relations to an acceptance of multilateral diplomacy by treating ASEAN as a unitary organisation with which China wanted close economic ties. Within two years, Premier Zhu Rongji had moved quickly towards the China-ASEAN Free Trade Agreement. The ASEAN perspective on this development is sensitively described in Rodolfo C. Severino, *Southeast Asia in Search of an ASEAN Community: Insights from the Former ASEAN Secretary-General* (Singapore: Institute of Southeast Asian Studies, 2006). Also, Wang Gungwu, "China and Southeast Asia: the Context of a New Beginning", in *Power Shift: China and Asia's New Dynamics*, ed. David Shambaugh (Berkeley: University of California Press, 2006), pp. 187–204.

Bibliography

Unpublished Manuscripts and Documents

Directorate of Defence Services Intelligence Reports or DDSI Report (unpublished classified document: statements given by U Sai Aung Win on 29 June 1990).

Foreign Office Papers, Clifford to Colonial Secretary, 5 September 1895, Public Record Office, London.

National Library, Thailand (abbreviated as NL)

NL.CMH.R.IV: Administrative Records, the Fourth Reign (*Chotmaihet, Ratchakan thi si*)

National Archives of Thailand (abbreviated as NA)

NA.KT (L): Bound Volumes, Series for the Ministry of Foreign Affairs (*Ekkasan yep lem, chut Krasuang Kantangprathet*)

NA.KT: the Ministry of Foreign Affairs (*Krasuang Kantangprathet*)

NA.R.V.T.: the Fifth Reign, the Ministry of Foreign Affairs (*Krasuang Kantangprathet*)

NA.R.V.N.: the Fifth Reign, the Ministry of the Capital (*Krasuang Nakhonban*)

NA.R.VI.N.: the Sixth Reign, the Ministry of the Capital (*Krasuang Nakhonban*)

Printed Works

Acharya, Amitav, *Constructing a Security Community in Southeast Asia*. New York: Routledge, 2001.

Althusser, Louis, *Lenin and Philosophy and Other Essays* (translated from French by Ben Brewster). New York: Monthly Review Press, 1971.

Andaya, Barbara, *To Live as Brothers: Southeast Sumatra in the Seventeenth and Eighteenth Centuries*. Honolulu: University of Hawaii Press, 1993.

Anderson, Benedict, *Imagined Communities: Reflections on the Origin and Spread of Nationalism*. New York: Verso, 1991.

Angkinuntana, Polagool, "Botbat Chao Chin nai Prathet Thai nai Ratchasamai Phrabat Somdet Phra Chunlachomklaochaoyuhua" [The Chinese Movement in the Reign of King Rama V], MA thesis, Witthayalai Wichakansuksa, 1971.

Aoyama, Harutoshi, "Shincho Seifu ni yoru 'Nanyo' Chosadan Haken (1886–88nen) no Haikei: Shinmatsu 'Nanyo' Ryoji Setchi Mondai tono Kanrende" [The Background of Sending a Chinese Mission of Inquiry on the Overseas Chinese in 'Nanyang' (Southwest Asia) [*sic*] and Australia] by the Qing Government

[1886–88], *Bunkenkai Kiyo: The Journal of the Graduate School of Humanities, Aichigakuin University*, 13 (2002): 8–28.

_____, "Shincho Seifu ni yoru 'Nanyo' Chosa (1886–88nen): Kajin Hogo no Jisshi to Ryoji Setchi no Yobi Chosa" [The Inquiry on 'Nanyang' (Southeast Asia and Australia) by the Qing Government 1886–88], *Bunkenkai Kiyo: The Journal of the Graduate School of Humanities, Aichigakuin University*, 14 (2003): 1–24.

_____, "Shincho Seifu ni yoru 'Nanyo' Kajin no Hogo to Seiyo Shokoku tono Masatsu: 1886nen no 'Nanyo' Chosadan no Haken Kosho wo Chushin ni" [Protection of Nanyang Chinese by Qing Government and Friction between China and Western Countries], *Higashi Ajia Kindaishi* [*Modern East Asian History*] 6 (2003): 52–69.

Apornratana, Chariyavan, "Panha khong Ratthaban Thai nai Ratchasamai Phrabat Somdet Phra Chunlachomklaochaoyuhua thi kieo kap Khon Esia nai Bangkhap Angkrit lae Farangset" [The Problems of Thai Government Concerning the Asian British and the Asian French Subjects during the Reign of King Rama V], MA thesis, Chulalongkorn University, 1982.

Banno, Masataka, *China and the West 1858–1861: The Origins of the Tsungli Yamen*. Cambridge [MA]: Harvard University Press, 1964.

Baruah, Sanjib, "The Strange Career of Southeast Asian Studies in India", paper presented at *International Convention of Asia Scholars* (ICAS) Shanghai, China, 22 August 2005.

Bauer, Wolfgang, ed., *China und die Fremden: 3000 Jahre Auseinandersetzung in Krieg und Frieden* [China and the Foreign: 3000 Years of Engagement in War and Peace]. Munich: Beck, 1980.

Blue, Gregory 2000, "Opium for China: the British Connection", in *Opium Regimes: China, Britain, and Japan, 1839–1952*, ed. Timothy Brook and Bob Tadashi Wakabayashi. Berkeley: University of California Press, 2000, pp. 31–54.

Bowring, John, *The Kingdom and People of Siam*. Kuala Lumpur (reprint): Oxford University Press, 1969 (1857).

Brown, C.C., "Sejarah Melayu or Malay Annals", *JMBRAS* 25, parts 2 and 3 (1952): 55, 120 and 154.

Brunsson, N., *The Organisation of Hypocrisy: Talk, Decisions and Actions in Organisation*. Chichester: John Wiley, 1989.

Bull, Hedley, *The Anarchical Society: A Study of Order in World Politics*. New York: Palgrave, 1977.

Business Line Bureau, "India, China to Achieve $20-b Trade Target ahead of Schedule", *Hindu Businessline*, 10 September 2006.

Buzan, Barry and Little, Richard, *International Systems in World History — Remaking the Study of International Relations*. Oxford: Oxford University Press, 2000.

Ceng Mu Han Memorial Editing Committee, 曾慕韓先生遺著 [*Memorial Works of Ceng Mu Han*]. Chinese Youth Party Central Committee, 1954.

Ceng, Qi and Shen, Yulong, eds., 曾慕韓（琦）先生日記選 [*Ceng Mu Han (Qi)'s Diary*]. Taipei: Wenhai Publishing, 1971.

Chandra, Vipan. 1988. *Imperialism, Resistance, and Reform in Late Nineteenth-Century Korea: Enlightenment and the Independence Club*. Berkeley: Institute of East Asian Studies, University of California at Berkeley.

Chang, Hyong-won, "19 Segi Chosun ui Jukwon Kaenyum Suyong kwa Hyung-sung" [The Adoption and Development of the Sovereignty Concept in Nineteenth Century Chosun Korea], in *Sipgu Segi Chosun ui Keundae Kukje Jongchi Kaenyum Doipsa* [The History of Chosun Korea's Adoption of Concepts in Modern International Relations in the Nineteenth Century], ed. Ha Young-sun. Seoul: forthcoming, publisher unknown.

Chang, Kwang-chih, *The Archaeology of Ancient China*. New Haven [CT]: Yale University Press, 1986.

Chay, John, "The First Three Decades of American-Korean Relations, 1882–1910: Reassessments and Reflections", in *United States–Korean Relations, 1882–1982*, ed. Tae-Hwan Kwak *et al*. Seoul: Kyungnam University Press, 1982.

Cheah, Boon Kheng (compiler), *Sejarah Melayu: The Malay Annals*. Kuala Lumpur: MBRAS, 1998, pp. 124, 207 and 250.

Chen, Chi (Ciliang), *Yong Shu*. Shenji shuzhuang (location of this private publishing house is not indicated in the book], 1898.

Chen, Jian, *Mao's China and the Cold War*. Chapel Hill [NC]: The University of North Carolina Press, 2001.

Chen, Zhimin, "Nationalism, Internationalism and Chinese Foreign Policy", *Journal of Contemporary China* 14, 42 (Feb. 2005): 35–53.

Cheng, Zheng Mao, 曾琦先生文集 [*Articles on Ceng Qi*]. Taipei: Academia Sinica, 1993.

Ch'en, Kuo-tung Anthony, *The Insolvency of the Chinese Hong Merchants, 1760–1843*. Monograph Series, No. 45, Nankang, Taipei: Institute of Economics, Academia Sinica, 1990.

Choi, Byung Wook, *Southern Vietnam under the Reign of Minh Mang (1820–1841): Central Policies and Local Response*. Ithaca, NY: Cornell University Southeast Asia Program, 2004.

Choi, Dong-hi, "1880 Nyondae Choson ui Munje wa Kumiyeolkangkwaui Oigyokwankye", in *Hankuk Oigyosa* [The History of Korea's Foreign Relations], ed. Hankuk Jongchi Oikyosa Hakhoi. Seoul: Chipmundang, 1993.

Chow, Rey, "Between the Colonizers: Hong Kong's Postcolonial Self-Writing in the 1990s", *Diaspora* 2, 2 (1992): 151–70.

Chow, Tse-tsung, *The May Fourth Movement: Intellectual Revolution in Modern China*. Cambridge [MA]: Harvard University Press, 1960.

Chu, Liu *et al*. eds. *Taoyuan Wenlu Waibian*. Shenyang: Liaoning renmin, 1994 (first edition, 1983), p. 129.

Chun, Hae-Jong, "Sino-Korean Tributary Relations in the Ch'ing Period", in *The Chinese World Order: Traditional China's Foreign Relations*, ed. John K. Fairbank. Cambridge [MA]: Harvard University Press, 1968.

Chung, Chien-peng, *Domestic Politics, International Bargaining and China's Territorial Disputes*. London: RoutledgeCurzon, 2004.

Chung, Ok-ja, *Choson Junghwa Sasang Yongu* [A Study of the Ideology of Sinocentrism in Choson]. Seoul: Iljisa, 1998.

Chung, Yong-hwa, *Munmyung ui Jongchi Sasang: Yu Kilchun and Keundae Hanguk* [The Political Ideology of Civilisation: Yu Kilchun and Modern Korea]. Seoul: Munhak Kwa Jisongsa, 2004.

Colbert, Evelyn, *Southeast Asia in International Politics*. Ithaca [NY]: Cornell University Press, 1977.

Couling, Samuel, *The Encyclopaedia Sinica*. Shanghai: Kelly and Walsh, 1917.

Cox, Michael, *et al.*, eds., *Empires, Systems and States: Great Transformations in International Politics*. Cambridge: Cambridge University Press, 2001.

Cox, Robert W. *Approaches to World Order*. Cambridge: Cambridge University Press, 1996.

Cushman, Jennifer W., *Fields from the Sea: Chinese Junk Trade with Siam during the Late Eighteenth and Early Nineteenth Centuries*. Ithaca: Southeast Asia Program, Cornell University, 1993.

Dai, Jinhua and Meng, Yue, *Fuchu Lishi Dibiao* [Emerging out of the Surface of History]. Zhengzhou: Henan Renmin Chubanshe, 1990.

Day, Tony, *Fluid Iron: State Formation in Southeast Asia*. Honolulu: University of Hawaii Press, 2002.

Deuchler, Martina, *Confucian Gentlemen and Barbarian Envoys: The Opening of Korea, 1875–1885*. Seattle: University of Washington Press, 1977.

Deudney, Daniel, "Binding Sovereigns: Authorities, Structures, and Geopolitics in Philadelphian Systems", in *State Sovereignty as Social Construct*, ed. Thomas J. Biersteker and Cynthia Weber. New York: Cambridge University Press, 1996.

Di Cosmo, Nicola, *Ancient China and Its Enemies: The Rise of Nomadic Power in East Asian History*. Cambridge: Cambridge University Press, 2002.

Dirlik, Arif and Zhang, Xudong, eds. *Postmodernism and China*. Durham [NC]: Duke University Press, 2000.

Dittmer, Lowell and Kim, Samuel S., eds. *China's Quest for National Identity*. Ithaca [NY]: Cornell University Press, 1993.

Drakard, Jane, *A Kingdom of Words: Language and Power in Sumatra*. Kuala Lumpur: Oxford University Press, 1999.

Duan, Yunzhang v, ed., *Sun Wen yu Riben Shishi Biannian* 孙文与日本史事编年 [Sun Yat-sen and Japan: a Chronological History]. Guangzhou: Guangdong Renmin Chubanshe, 1996, pp. 229–84.

Duara, Prasenjit, *Sovereignty and Authenticity: Manchukuo and the East Asian Modern*. Lanham [MD]: Rowman and Littlefield, 2003.

Esherick, Joseph W., "How the Qing became China", in *Empire to Nation: Historical Perspectives on the Making of the Modern World*, ed. Joseph W. Esherick, *et al.* Lanham [MD]: Rowman and Littlefield, 2006.

Fairbank, John K. and Têng, Ssu-yü, "On the Ch'ing Tributary System", *Harvard Journal of Asiatic Studies* 6, 2 (June 1941): 135–246.

————, *Ch'ing Administration: Three Studies*. Cambridge [Mass]: Harvard University Press, 1960, pp. 193–8.

Fairbank, John K., "Tributary Trade and China's Relations with the West", *Far Eastern Quarterly* 1, 2 (February 1942): 129–49.

————, *The Chinese World Order: Traditional China's Foreign Relations*. Cambridge [MA]: Harvard University Press, 1968 and "A Preliminary Framework", in *The Chinese World Order: Traditional China's Foreign Relations*, ed. John K. Fairbank. Cambridge [MA]: Harvard University Press, 1968, pp. 1–19.

Fan, Hong-ye 樊洪业, *Yesuhuishi yu Zhongguo Kexue* 耶稣会士与中国科学 [The Jesuits and Science in China]. Beijing: Zhongguo renmin daxue chubanshe, 1992.

Farquhar, David M., "The Origins of the Manchus' Mongolian Policy", in *The Chinese World Order: Traditional China's Foreign Relations*, ed. John K. Fairbank. Cambridge [MA]: Harvard University Press, 1968, pp. 198–205.

Far Eastern Economic Review, 10 May 2001.

Feuerwerker, Albert, "Presidential Address: Questions about China's Early Modern Economic History that I Wish I Could Answer", *Journal of Asian Studies* 51, 4 (1992): 757–69.

First National Archives 中国第一历史档案馆编 (ed.), *Qingdai Zhongguo yu Dongnanya Geguo Guanxi Dang'anshiliao Huibian* 清代中国与东南亚各国关系档案史料汇编 [A Collection of Archives on the Relations between China and Southeast Asian Countries in Qing Dynasty]. Vol. 2, the Philippines 第二册菲律宾卷. Beijing: International Cultural Publishing Co., 1998.

Frank, Herbert and Twitchett, Denis, ed. *The Cambridge History of China*, Vol. 6: *Alien Regimes and Border States*. Cambridge: Cambridge University Press, 1994.

Fu, Lo-shu, ed. *A Documentary Chronicle of Sino-Western Relations, 1644–1820*. Tucson: The Association for Asian Studies by University of Arizona Press, 1966.

Fujii, Shozo, "孫文の‘大アジア講演’と日本 [Sun Yat Sen and his Speech on 'Pan-Asianism and Japan ']", in 海外事情 [*Foreign Affairs*], 26–8 (Aug. 1978): 41–8.

Fujimura, Michio, "Japan's Changing Views of Asia", *Japan Quarterly* 24, 4 (1977): 423–31.

Garver, John W., *Protracted Contest: Sino-Indian Rivalry in the Twentieth Century*. Seattle: University of Washington Press, 2001.

Gernet, Jacques, *A History of Chinese Civilisation* (translated by J.R. Foster). Cambridge: Cambridge University Press, 1982.

Gilpin, Robert, *War and Change in World Politics*. New York: Cambridge University Press, 1981.

Gong, Gerrit W, *The Standard of 'Civilisation' in International Society*. Oxford: Clarendon Press, 1984.

Gong, Yuzhi, ed. *Mao Zedong, Deng Xiaoping he Jiang Zemi Lun Minzu Wenti* [Mao Zedong's, Deng Xiaoping and Jiang Zemin's Viewpoints on Chinese Nationality]. Beijing: Renmin chubanshe, 1999.

Gramsci, Antonio. *A Gramsci Reader: Selected Writings from 1916–1935*, ed. David Forgacs. New York: Schoken Books, 1988.

Greenberg, Michael, *British Trade and the Opening of China 1800–42*. Cambridge: Cambridge University Press, 1951.

Gu, George Zhibin, "It Takes Two to Tango", *Asia Times Online*, 17 February 2005.

Gu, Weijun, *Gu Weijun Huiyilu* 顾维钧回忆录 [The Memoirs of Wellington V.K. Koo]. Beijing: Zhonghua Publishing Co., 1983, vol. 1, pp. 316–65, 391–400, 409–42.

Habermas, Jürgen, *Legitimation Crisis* (translated by Thomas McCarthy). Boston: Beacon, 1975.

Haboush, Ja Hyun Kim and Deuchler, Martina, "Introduction", in *Culture and the State in Late Choson Korea*, ed. JaHyun Kim Haboush and Martina Deuchler. Cambridge [MA]: Harvard University Asia Center, 1999.

Hahm, Chaibong, "Anti-Americanism: Korean Style", in *Anti-Americanism in Korea: Closing Perception Gaps*. Pacific Forum CSIS Issues and Insights 3, 5 (July 2003): 9–22.

————, "Civilisation, Race, or Nation? Korean Visions of Regional Order in the Late Nineteenth Century", in *Korea at the Center: Dynamics of Regionalism in Northeast Asia*, ed. Charles K. Armstrong *et al.* Armonk [NY]: M.E. Sharpe, 2006, pp. 35–50.

Hahm, Pyong-Choon, "The Korean Perception of the United States", in *Korea and the United States: A Century of Cooperation*, ed. Youngnok Koo and Dae-Sook Suh. Honolulu: University of Hawaii Press, 1984.

Hamashita, Takeshi, "The Intra-regional System in East Asia in Modern Times", in *Network Power*, ed. Peter J. Katzenstein and Takashi Shiraishi. Ithaca [NY]: Cornell University Press, 1997.

————, 近代中国の国際的契機：朝貢貿易システムと近代アジア [*International Moment of Modern China: Tributary Trade System and Modern Asia*]. Tokyo: Tokyo University Press, 1990.

Hao, Yen-ping, *The Commercial Revolution in Nineteenth Century China: The Rise of Sino-Western Mercantile Capitalism*. Berkeley [CA]: University of California Press, 1986.

Hara, Takemichi, "Korea, China, and Western Barbarians: Diplomacy in Early Nineteenth-Century Korea", *Modern Asian Studies* 32, 2 (1998): 389–430.

Hardt, Michael and Negri, Antonio, *Empire*. Cambridge [MA]: Harvard University Press, 2000.

Harrison, James L., *Modern Chinese Nationalism*. New York: Hunter, 1969.

Harootunian, Harry D., "The Functions of China in Tokugawa Thought", in *The Chinese and the Japanese: Essays in Political and Cultural Interactions*, ed. Akira Iriye. Princeton: Princeton University Press, 1980, pp. 9–30.

Haruyuki, Tono, "Japanese Embassies to T'ang China and Their Ships", *Acta Asiatica* 69 (Nov. 1995): 39–62.

Hart, Basil H. Liddell, *Strategy: The Indirect Approach*. London: Faber and Faber, 1941.

Hazama, Naoki, "序章 アジア主義とはなにか" [Introduction: What is Pan-Asianism?], 東亜 [*East Asia*], 410 (Aug. 2001): 68–77.

He, Qinglian, *Xiandaihua de Xianjing* [The Pitfalls of China's Modernisation]. Beijing: Jinri zhongguo chubanshe, 1996.

Healy, Brian, and Stein, Arthur, "The Balance of Power in International History: Theory and Reality", *Journal of Conflict Resolution* 17, 1 (March 1973): 33–61.

Hirano, Yoshitaro, 大アジア主義の歴史的基礎 [Historical Foundation of Pan-Asianism]. Kawaide Publishing, 1945.

Hla, Min, *Political Situation of Myanmar and Its Role in the Region*. Yangon: News and Periodical Enterprises, 2001.

Hobsbawm, Eric. *Nations and Nationalism since 1780*. Cambridge: Cambridge University Press, 1990.

Hong, Junpei 洪钧培编 ed., *Guomin Zhengfu Waijiaoshi* 国民政府外交史 [Diplomatic History of the Republican Government]. Shanghai: Huatong publishing, 1932 (reprinted and collected as Number 280 in *Jindai Zhongguo Shiliao Congkan* 近代中国史料丛刊 by Wenhai Publishers in Taipei in 1968).

Hong, Sŭn-ho, "Kaehang jon ui Daeoi Kwankye [Choson's Foreign Relations before Its Opening]", in *Hankuk Oigyosa* [The History of Korea's Foreign Relations], ed. Hankuk Jongchi Oikyosa Hakhoi. Seoul: Chipmundang, 1993, pp. 41–64.

Hsu, Immanuel Chung-yueh, *China's Entrance into the Family of Nations: The Diplomatic Phase, 1858–1880*. Cambridge [MA]: Harvard University Press, 1960.

Hu, Sheng, *Cong Yapian Zhanzheng dao Wusi Yundong* [From the Opium War to the May Fourth Movement]. Beijing: Renmin Chubanshe, 1979.

Huang, Dong Lan, "清末・民国期地理教科書の空間表象—領土・疆域・国恥" [Representation of Space in Late Qing and ROC Geography Textbooks], 中国研究月報 [*Monthly Chinese Studies*] 59, 3 (March 2005): 24–39.

Iijima, Akiko, "Tai ni okeru Ryojisaibanken wo Megutte — Hogomin Mondai no Shozai" [On the Consular Jurisdiction in Thailand: A Preliminary Note], *Southeast Asian Studies* 14, 1 (1976): 71–98.

Inoguchi, Takashi, "Korea in Japanese Visions of Regional Order", in *Korea at the Center: Dynamics of Regionalism in Northeast Asia*, ed. Charles K. Armstrong *et al.* Armonk [NY]: M.E. Sharpe, 2006, pp. 5–14.

————, "China's Intervention in Vietnam and Its Aftermath (1786–1802): a Re-examination of the Historical East Asian World Order", in *Rethinking New International Order in East Asia: United States, China and Taiwan*, ed. I Yuan. Taipei: Institute of International Relations, 2005, pp. 361–403.

Inthramontri, Luang, "Rayathang Ratchathut Thai Pai Krung Pakking Prathet Chin [Journey of the Royal Embassy to Visit Beijing, China]", in *Thalaeng-ngan Prawattisat Ekkasan Borannakhadi* [Journal of Historical Accounts and Documents] 8 (1974): 16–44.

Iriye, Akira, "Japan's Drive to Great-Power Status", in *The Cambridge History of Japan, Volume 5: the Nineteenth Century*, ed. Marius B. Jansen. Cambridge: Cambridge University Press, 1989, pp. 733–75.

Ito, Akio, "大アジア主義と三民主義－傀儡政権下の諸問題について－" [Pan-Asianism and Three Principles of the People — Problems under the Wang Jin Wei Administration], in 横浜市立大学論叢: 人文科学系列 [*Yokohama University Journal Humanities*] 40, 1 (March 1989): 225–47.

Jackson, Robert H., *Quasi-States: Sovereignty, International Relations, and the Third World*. New York: Cambridge University Press, 1990.

Jain, Girlal, *Chinese "Panchsheela" in Burma*. Bombay: Democratic Research Service, 1956.

Jansen, Marius B., *China in the Tokugawa World*. Cambridge: Harvard University Press, 1992.

Jensen, Lionel, *Manufacturing Confucianism: Chinese Tradition and Universal Civilisation*. Durham: Duke University Press, 1997.

Jervis, Robert, *Perception and Misperception in International Politics*. Princeton: Princeton University Press, 1976.

Johnson, Paul M., "The Subordinate States and Their Strategies", in *Dominant Powers and Subordinate States*, ed. Jan F. Triska. Durham [NC]: Duke University Press, 1986.

Johnston, Alastair Iain, *Cultural Realism: Strategic Culture and Grand Strategy in Chinese History*. Princeton: Princeton University Press, 1995.

Johnston, Alastair Iain and Evan, Paul, "China's Engagement with Multilateral Security Institutions", in *Engaging China: The Management of an Emerging Power*, ed. Alastair Iain Johnston and Robert S. Ross. London: Routledge, 1999, pp. 235–71.

Johnstone, William C., *A Chronology of Burma's International Relations 1945–1958*. Rangoon: Rangoon University Press, 1959.

Jones, Robert A, *The Soviet Concept of "Limited Sovereignty" from Lenin to Gorbachev: The Brezhnev Doctrine*. Basingstoke: Macmillan, 1990.

Kang, David, "Getting Asia Wrong: The Need for New Analytical Frameworks", *International Security* 27, 4 (Spring 2003): 57–85.

Kang, Dong-kuk, "'Zokuhou' no Seiji Sisousi: 19 Seikigo ni okeru 'Chousen Chi-I Mondai' wo meguru Gensetsu no Keifu" [The Political History of Zokuhou: the Discourse on the 'Choson Problem' in the Late Nineteenth Century], unpublished PhD Dissertation, University of Tokyo, 2004.

Kang, Etsuko Hae-Jin, *Diplomacy and Ideology in Japanese-Korean Relations: From the Fifteenth to the Eighteenth Century*. New York: St. Martin's Press, 1997.

Kang, Youwei, *Kang Youwei Quanji*. Shanghai: Shanghai guji, 1987.

Kataoka, Kazutada, "Shingai Kakumei Jiki no Gozoku Kyowaron wo Megutte" [Regarding the Theory of Five Races in the 1911 Revolutionary Period], in *Chugoku Kindaishi no Shomondai*, ed. Tanaka Masayoshi Sensei Taikan Kinen Ronshu. Tokyo: Kokusho Kankokai, 1984, pp. 279–306.

Katzenstein, Peter J., "Conclusion: National Security in a Changing World", in *The Culture of National Security: Norms and Identity in World Politics*, ed. Peter J. Katzenstein. New York: Columbia University Press, 1996, pp. 498–537.

Kawashima, Shin, 中国近代外交の形成 [*Formation of Modern Chinese Diplomacy*]. Nagoya: Nagoya University Press, 2004.

————, "支那, 支那国, 支那共和国 – 日本外務省の対中呼称政策" [China, State of China, Republic of China – Japanese Ministry of Foreign Affairs Policy toward the Name of China], 中国研究月報 [*Monthly Bulletin on Chinese Studies*] 571 (September 1995): 1–17.

Keegan, John, *A History of Warfare*. London: Hutchinson, 1993.

Kelley, Liam, "Vietnam as a 'Domain of Manifest Civility'" [Van Hien chi Bang], *Journal of Southeast Asian Studies* 34, 1 (Feb. 2003): 63–76.

Kierman, Frank A and Fairbank, John K, eds., *Chinese Ways in Warfare*. Cambridge [MA]: Harvard University Press, 1974.

Kim, C. I. Eugene and Kim, Han-Kyo, *Korea and the Politics of Imperialism, 1876–1910*. Berkeley [CA]: University of California Press, 1967.

Kim, Heaseung, *Hanguk Minjokjui: Balsaeng Yangsik kwa Chonkae Kwajong* [A Study on the Origins and Development of Korean Nationalism]. Seoul: Bibong, 1997.

Kim, Key-Hiuk, *The Last Phase of the East Asian World Order: Korea, Japan, and the Chinese Empire, 1860–1882*. Berkeley and Los Angeles: University of California Press, 1980.

Kim, Se-min, *Hankuk Keundaesa wa Mankukkongbop* [Modern Korean History and International Law]. Seoul: Kyongin munhwasa, 2002.

Kim, Yongkoo, *The Five Years' Crisis, 1866–1871: Korea in the Maelstrom of Western Imperialism*. Seoul: Circle, 2001.

Kim, Yong-jak, *Hanmal Naesyonollijum Yongu* [A Study of Nationalism in Late Choson Korea]. Seoul: Chong Gye Yonguso, 1989.

Kohno, Masaru, "On the Meiji Restoration: Japan's Search for Sovereignty?", *International Relations of the Asia-Pacific* 1, 2 (August 2001).

Koizumi, Junko, "Tai ni okeru Kokka Kaikaku to Minshu" [State Reform and the People in Thailand], in *Minzoku to Kokka: Zikaku to Teiko* [Nations and the State: Awakening and Resistance], ed. Rekishigaku Kenkyukai. Tokyo: University of Tokyo Press, 1995, pp. 327–51.

Kong Chotmaihet haeng Chat, Krom Sinlapakon, ed., *Samphanthaphap Thai-chin* [Thai-Chinese Relationship]. Bangkok: Krom Sinlapakon, 1978.

Krasner, Stephen D., *Sovereignty: Organised Hypocrisy*. Princeton: Princeton University Press, 1999.

————, "Organised Hypocrisy in Nineteenth-century East Asia", *International Relations of the Asia-Pacific* 1 (2001): 173–97.

————, ed., *Problematic Sovereignty: Contested Rules and Political Possibilities*. New York: Columbia University Press, 2001.

Kruger, Rayne, *All Under Heaven: A Complete History of China*. Chichester [Britain]: Wiley, 2003.

Ku, Dai Yeol, "Tongsoyang Kukjejilsokwanui Chungdol kwa Saeroun Jilsokwanui Hyongsong" [Clash of Eastern and Western Views of the International Order and the Formation of a New Worldview], *Kukjejongchi Nonchong* [International Politics Review] 28, 1 (1988): 3–21.

Kubo, Juntaro, "雑誌『新亜細亜』論説記事目録" [Records of Articles in the Magazine "New Asia"], in 神戸大学史学年報 [*Annual Journal of History Kobe University*] 17 (2002): 80–124.

Larsen, Kirk Wayne, "From Suzerainty to Commerce: Sino-Korean Economic and Business Relations during the Open Port Period (1876–1910)", unpublished PhD dissertation, Harvard University, 2000.

Lattimore, Owen, *Inner Asian Frontiers of China*. Oxford: Oxford University Press, 1940.

Ledyard, Gari, "Hanguk'in ui Sadaejui [Koreans and Sadae-ism]", *Sin Tonga* [a popular news magazine in Korea, somewhat like *Newsweek* but difficult to translate], October 1968.

Lee, Ki-baek, *A New History of Korea*. Seoul: Ilchokak, 1984.

Lee, Leo Ou-fan, "On the Margin of the Chinese Discourse: Some Personal Thoughts on the Cultural Meaning of the Periphery", *Daedalus* 121, 2 (1992): 207–25.

Lee, Yur-Bok, *Diplomatic Relations between the United States and Korea, 1866–1887*. New York: Humanities Press, 1970.

Leheny, David, *The Rules of Play: National Identity and the Shaping of Japanese Leisure*. Ithaca: Cornell University Press, 2003.

Lertpanichkul, Suparat, "Samakhom Lap Ang-yi nai Prathet Thai Pho.So. 2367–2453" [Triad Societies in Thailand 1824–1910], MA thesis, Chulalongkorn University, 1981.

Levenson, Joseph, *Liang Ch'i-ch'ao and the Mind of Modern China* (second edition). Berkeley [CA]: University of California Press, 1959.

Li, Bin. *Zhongguo Xinwen Shehuishi* [A Social History of Chinese Journalism]. Shanghai: Shanghai Jiaotong University Press, 2007.

Li, Chien-nung, *The Political History of China, 1840–1928*. Princeton: Princeton University Press, 1956.

Li, Da Zhao, "大亜細亜主義与新亜細亜主義" [Great Pan-Asianism and New Pan-Asianism], 国民雑誌 [*People's Magazine*] 1, 2 (1919) and 李大釗全集 [Complete Edition of Li Da Zhao]. Beijing: Renmin chubanshe, 1959.

Li, Jikui 李吉奎, *Sun Zhongshan yu Riben* 孙中山与日本 [Sun Yat-sen and Japan]. Guangzhou: Guangdong Renmin Chubanshe, 1996.

Li, Shucheng, "Xuesheng zhi Jinzheng", in *Xinhai Gemin Qian Shinianjian Shilun Xuanji*, ed. Zhang, Dan and Wang, Renzhi. 2 vols., Hong Kong: Sanlian shudian, 1962, vol. 1, pp. 452–9.

Li, Yumin, *Zhongguo Fei Yue Shi*. Beijing: Zhonghua Shuju, 2005.

Liang, Qichao, 飲冰室合集 [Collected Works of Yinbingshi]. Shanghai; Zhonghua Shuju, 1936.

Liao, Min Shu, "互市から見た清朝の通商秩序" [*Trade Order during the Qing Dynasty Seen from the Mutual Market Trade System*], unpublished PhD dissertation, School of Law and Politics, Hokkaido University, 2006.

Lin, Biao, "Renmin Zhanzheng Shengli Wansui" [Long Live the Victory of the People's War], *Renmin Ribao* [People's Daily], 3 September 1965.

Lin, Zexu 林則徐, *Sizhou Zhi* 四洲志 [Record of the Four Continents, annotated by Zhang Man 張曼] Beijing: Huaxia chubanshe, 2002.

Liu, Jian Hui, "日本でつくられた中国の自画像" [Self Portrait of China that was created in Japan], 中国 21 [*China 21*], 22 (June 2005): 85–104.

Ma, He Tian, 関於 "大亜細亜" 与 "新亜細亜" 題名的廻憶 [Consideration on "Pan-Asianism" and "New Asia"], *新亜細亜* [*New Asia*] First Issue, First Term (Oct. 1930): 139–40.

Mabbett, Ian, ed., *Patterns of Kingship and Authority in Traditional Asia*. London: Croom Helm, 1985.

Mahajan, Sneh, *British Foreign Policy, 1874–1914: The Role of India*. London: Routledge, 2002.

Mancall, Mark, *China at the Center: 300 Years of Foreign Policy*. New York: Free Press, 1984.

Marsden, William, *The History of Sumatra* (reprint of 1811 edition). Kuala Lumpur: Oxford University Press, 1966.

Martin, W.A.P., *The Awakening of China*. New York: Doubleday, 1907.

Maruyama, Masao, *Studies in the Intellectual History of Tokugawa Japan* (translated by Mikiso Hane). Princeton: Princeton University Press, 1974.

Masao, Mori, "The Tu-chüeh Concept of Sovereign", *Acta Asiatica* 41 (December 1981).

Masuda, Erika, "The Last Siamese Tributary Missions to China, 1851–1854 and the 'Rejected' Value of *Chim Kong*", in *Maritime China in Transition 1750–1850*, ed. Wang Gungwu and Ng Chin-keong. Wiesbaden: Horowitz Verlag, 2004, pp. 33–42.

McCormick, Fredrick, *The Flowery Republic*. London: John Murray, 1913, pp. 257–96.

Mende, Tibar, *South-East Asia between Two Worlds*. London: Turnstile Press, 1955.

Mitani, Hiroshi, *Escape from Impasse: The Decision to Open Japan* (translated by David Noble). Tokyo: International House of Japan, 2006.

Mori, Etsuko , "孫文と朝鮮問題" [Sun Yat Sen and the Issue over Korea], in 孫文研究会会報 [Journal on the Research on Sun Yat Sen], 13 (1991): 1–21.

Morrison, Charles E. and Suhrke, Astri, *Strategies of Survival: The Foreign Policy Dilemma of Smaller Asian States*. New York: St. Martin's Press, 1978.

Mote, Frederick W., *Imperial China, 900–1800*. Cambridge [MA]: Harvard University Press, 1999.

Motegi, Toshio, "変容する近代東アジアの国際秩序" [*Transition of the International Order in Modern East Asia*]. Tokyo: Yamakawa Publishing, 1997.

Mungello, D.E., *Curious Land: Jesuit Accommodation and the Origins of Sinology*. Honolulu: University of Hawaii Press, 1989.

Myanma Alin (state-published newspaper in Myanmar), 1 January 2007.

Myoe, Maung Aung, "The Peacock and the Dragon: Myanmar's Relations with China in the Monarchical Era", forthcoming, publisher unknown.

Nakami, Tatsuo, "A Protest against the Concept of the 'Middle Kingdom': the Mongols and the 1911 Revolution", in *The 1911 Revolution in China: Interpretive Essays:*

International Conference in Commemoration of the Seventieth Anniversary of the 1911 Revolution, ed. Eto Shinkichi and Harold Z. Schiffrin. Tokyo: Tokyo University Press, 1984), pp. 129–49.

Nahm, Andrew C., *Korea: Tradition and Transformations*. Elizabeth [NJ]: Hollym International Corp, 1988.

Nandy, Ashis, *The Intimate Enemy: Loss and Recovery of Self under Colonialism*. New Delhi: Oxford University Press, 1983.

Nelson, Frederick M., *Korea and the Old Orders in Eastern Asia*. Baton Rouge [LA]: Louisiana State University Press, 1946.

Newbold, Thomas J., *Political and Statistical Account of the British Settlements in the Straits of Malacca, viz. Pinang, Malacca, and Singapore: With a History of the Malayan States on the Peninsula of Malacca*. Vol I. London: J. Murray, 1839.

Nguyen, The Long, *Chuyen Di Su-Tiep Su Thoi Xua* [Diplomatic Stories from the Past]. Hanoi: Van hoa Thong tin, 2001.

Nguyen, Trai, *Bingh Ngo Dai Cao* (1428) as translated by O.W. Wolters, "Historians and Emperors in Vietnam and China: Comments arising out of Le Van Huu's History, Presented to the Tran Court in 1272", in *Perceptions of the Past in Southeast Asia*, ed. Anthony Reid and David Marr. Singapore: Heinemann, 1979, p. 88.

Okamoto, Takashi, "属国と自主のあいだ" [*Between Tributary State and Autonomy*]. Nagoya: Nagoya University Press, 2004.

"ONGC-CNPC Wins Bid for 38 per cent in Syrian Oil Fields", *Times of India*, Wednesday, 21 December 2005.

Pak, Chŏng Sŏk, "Hanil Yang-guk ui Gukje Jilsogwan e daehan Bigyo Yongu —Tukhi 19 Segi Joongyup ui Byun-yong ul Jungsim uro [A Comparative Study of the Korean and Japanese Worldviews — with Special Reference to the Transformation of the Hwa-i Ideology in the Mid-Nineteenth Century]", *The Journal of Asiatic Studies* 23, 2 (July 1980).

————, *Hankuk Chongchi Sasangsa* [The History of Korean Political Thought]. Seoul: Sanyoungsa, 1982.

Palmujoki, Eero, *Vietnam and the World: Marxist-Leninist Doctrine and the Changes in International Relations, 1975–93*. London: Macmillan, 1997.

Perdue, Peter *China Marches West: The Qing Conquest of Central Eurasia*. Cambridge, Mass.: Harvard University Press, 2005.

Perkins, Dorothy, *Encyclopedia of China: The Essential Reference to China, its History and Culture*. New York: Facts on File, 1999.

Pettman, Ralph, *China in Burma's Foreign Policy*. Canberra: Australian National University Press, 1973.

Pillsbury, Michael, *China Debates the Future Security Environment*. Washington DC: National Defense University Press, 2000.

Pittau, Joseph, *Political Thought in Early Meiji Japan, 1868–1889*. Cambridge [MA]: Harvard University Press, 1967.

Prachum Prakat Ratchakan thi 4 [Collected Proclamations of the Fourth Reign], 4 volumes. Bangkok (reprint): Khurusapha, 1985.

Promboon, Suebsaeng, "Sino-Siamese Tributary Relations, 1282–1853", PhD dissertation, University of Wisconsin, 1971.

Pye, Lucian W., "How Chinese Nationalism is Shanghaied", in *Chinese Nationalism*, ed. Jonathan Unger. New York: M.E. Sharpe, 1996, pp. 86–112.

Pyle, Kenneth B., "Meiji Conservatism", in *The Cambridge History of Japan*, ed. John Hall *et al.* New York: Cambridge University Press, 1989, pp. 674–720.

Qian, Shifu, ed., *Qingdai Zhiguan Nianbiao* [Chronological Tables of Offices and Officials during the Qing Dynasty], 4 volumes. Beijing: Zhonghua shuju chuban, 1980.

Ramachandran, Sudha, "India Embraces Myanmar on its Own Terms", *Asia Times Online*, 28 June 2006.

Ramesh, Jairam, *Making Sense of Chindia: Reflections on China and India*. New Delhi: India Research Press, 2005.

Ramo, Joshua Cooper, *Beijing Consensus*. London: The Foreign Policy Centre, 2004.

Rao, Huaimin, ed., *Yang Yuling Ji*. Changsha: Yuelu shushe, 2001.

"Raya Thang Ratchathut Thai Pai Krung Pakking Prathet Chin" [Journey of the Royal Thai Embassy to Visit Beijing, China], *Thalaeng Ngan Prawattisat Ekkasan Borannakhadi* 8 (1974): 16–44.

Reid, Anthony, *Southeast Asia in the Age of Commerce 1450–1680*. New Haven: Yale University Press, 2 vols., 1988–93.

———, "Political 'Tradition' in Indonesia: The One and the Many", *Asian Studies Review* 22, 1 (Feb. 1998): 23–38.

———, "Flows and Seepages in the Long-term Chinese Interaction with Southeast Asia", in *Sojourners and Settlers: Histories of Southeast Asia and the Chinese*, ed. Anthony Reid. Sydney: Allen & Unwin, 1996, pp. 22–6.

———, "Hybrid Identities in the Fifteenth-Century Straits of Malacca", in *Southeast Asia in the Fifteenth Century: The Ming Factor*, ed. Geoffrey Wade and Sun Laichen. Singapore: NUS Press, 2009.

Reischaur, Edwin O. and Fairbank, John K., *East Asia: The Great Tradition*. London: Allen & Unwin, 1960.

Rossabi, Morris, ed., *China among Equals: the Middle Kingdom and its Neighbors, Tenth to Fourteenth Centuries*. Berkeley: University of California Press, 1983.

Roy, Subir, "How to Sustain 8 Percent Growth", *The Economic Times*, New Delhi, 30 November 2005.

Said, Edward W., *The World, the World and the Critic*. Cambridge [MA]: Harvard University Press, 1983.

Schmid, Andre, *Korea Between Empires, 1895–1919*. New York: Columbia University Press, 2002.

Schroeder, Paul W., "Historical Reality vs. Neorealist Theory", *International Security* 19, 1 (Summer 1994): 108–48.

Severino, Rodolfo C., *Southeast Asia in Search of an ASEAN Community: Insights from the Former ASEAN Secretary-General*. Singapore: Institute of Southeast Asian Studies, 2006.

Shen, Congwen, *Chang He* [Long River]. Beijing: Renmin Wenxue chubanshe, 1984.

Shen, Zhihua, Yang, Kuisong *et al.* 沈志华、杨奎松等编著, *Zhong Su Guanxi Shigang, 1917–1991* 中苏关系史纲 [A History of Sino-Soviet Relations, 1917–1991]. Beijing: Xinhua Publishers, 2007.

Shi, Anbin, *A Comparative Approach to Redefining Chinese-ness in the Era of Globalisation.* New York: Edwin Mellen Press, 2003.

————, "The Taming of the Shrew", *Global Media and Communication* 1, 1 (2005): 33–6.

Shusawat, Sonsak, "Phukpi: Kanchatkep Ngoen Kharaeng Thaen Kan ken Raeng-ngan chak Khon Chin nai Samai Rattanakosin" [Pookpee: The Poll Tax Collection from the Chinese during Bangkok Period], MA thesis, Chulalongkorn University, 1981.

Sima, Qian, *Records of the Grand Historian* (translated by Burton Watson). New York: Renditions-Columbia University Press, 1993.

Simons, Geoff, *Korea: the Search for Sovereignty.* New York: St. Martin's Press, 1995.

Snow, Edgar, *Red Star over China.* London: Victor Gollancz, 1937.

Smith, S.R., *The Manchurian Crisis, 1931–1932: a Tragedy in International Relations.* New York: Columbia University Press, 1948, pp. 225–62.

Sun, Jin, "Hou Shenme Xiandai, erqie Zhuyi?" [What the Hell Does "Post-Modern-Ism" Mean?], *Dushu* [*Reader Magazine*] 135 (1992): 34–9.

Sun, Laichen, "Suzerain and Vassal, or Elder and Younger Brothers: The Nature of the Burmo-Chinese Historical Relationship", paper presented at the 49th Annual Conference of the Association of Asian Studies, Chicago, 1997, pp. 17, 43.

Soong, Ching Ling, *Good Neighbours Meet.* Peking: Foreign Languages Press, 1956.

Soong, Mei-ling (Madame Chiang Kai-shek), *This is Our China.* New York: Harper, 1940.

Spence, Jonathan, *Chinese Roundabout.* New York: W.W. Norton, 1992.

Stuart-Fox, Martin, *A Short History of China and Southeast Asia: Tribute, Trade and Influence.* New South Wales [Australia]: Allen and Unwin, 2003.

Su, Min, "Chairman Liu Shao-chi Visits Burma", *Peking Review* 6, 17 (26 April 1963): 7–8.

Suganami, Hidemi, "Japan's Entry into International Society", in *The Expansion of International Society*, ed. Hedley Bull and Adam Watson. Oxford: Clarendon Press, 1984, pp. 185–99.

Sun, Yat Sen, "大亜洲主義" [Pan-Asianism], in 国父全集 [*Founding Father Complete Works*]. Taipei: Central Books Publishing, 1957, pp. 507–19.

Sun, Zhongshan (Sun Yatsen), *Sun Zhongshan Quanji* 孙中山全集 [The Complete Works of Sun Yat-sen]. Vol 2, Beijing: Zhonghua shuju, 1982, pp. 1–19, 47–8, 94–7, 105, 160–7, and 316–29.

Swartout, Robert R. Jr., *Mandarins, Gunboats, and Power Politics.* Honolulu: The University of Hawaii Press, 1980.

Takeuchi, Yoshimi, "解説アジア主義の展望" [Commentary on the Development of Pan-Asianism], in アジア主義 [*Pan-Asianism*], ed. Takeuchi Yoshimi. Tokyo: Chikuma Shobo, 1963, pp. 15–8.

Tan, Chung, *China and the Brave New World*. Bombay: Allied Publishers, 1978.

Tanaka, Masaaki ed., 松井石根大将の陣中日誌 [*Diaries of Iwane Matsui during Wartime*]. Tokyo: Fuyo Publishing, 1985.

Tao, Jing-shen, *Two Sons of Heaven: Studies in Sung-Liao Relations*. Tucson: University of Arizona Press, 1988.

Tennant, Roger, *A History of Korea*. London: Kegan Paul, 1996.

The Chinese People's Institute of Foreign Affairs (compiler-editor), *A Victory for the Five Principles of Peaceful Co-existence*. Peking: Foreign Languages Press, 1960.

Thiphakorawong, *Chaophraya, Phraratchaphongsawadan Krung Rattanakosin Ratchakan thi 4* [The Dynastic Chronicles, Bangkok Era, the Fourth Reign], Bangkok (reprint): Cremation Volume for Anong Thiankharat, 1964.

————— (Thiphaakorawong), *The Dynastic Chronicles, Bangkok Era, the Fourth Reign, B.E. 2394–2411 (A.D. 1851–1868)*, 5 vols. (translated by Chadin Kanjanavanit Flood). Tokyo: The Centre for East Asian Cultural Studies, 1965–74.

Toby, Ronald P., "Reopening the Question of Sakoku: Diplomacy inn the Legitimation of the Tokugawa Bakufu", *Journal of Japanese Studies* 3, 2 (Summer 1977): 323–63.

—————, *State and Diplomacy in Early Modern Japan: Asia in the Development of the Tokugawa Bakufu*. Princeton: Princeton University Press, 1984.

Toyama, Shigeki, "Independence and Modernisation in the Nineteenth Century", in *Meiji Ishin: Restoration and Revolution*, ed. Nagai Michio and Miguel Urrutia. Tokyo: The United Nations University, 1985, pp. 29-42.

Trager, Frank N., "Sino-Burmese Relations: The End of the Pauk Khaw Era", *ORBIS* 11, 4 (1968): 1034–54.

Tran, Quoc Vuong, "Dan Gian Va Bac Hoc [Popular and Scholarly]", in Tran Quoc Vuong, *Trong Coi* [Inside the Realm]. Garden Grove [CA]: Tram Hoa, 1993), pp. 159–95.

Tsiang, T.F., "China and European Expansion", *Politica* 2, 5 (March 1936): 1–18.

Tu, Wei-ming, "Toward a Third Epoch of Confucian Humanism: A Background Understanding", in *Confucianism: Dynamics of Tradition*, ed. Irene Eber. New York: Macmillan, 1986, pp. 3–21.

—————, "Cultural China: The Periphery as the Center", *Daedalus* 121, 2 (1992): 3–31.

Twitchett, Denis, ed., *The Cambridge History of China*, Vol. 3: *Sui and T'ang China, 589–906*, Part I. Cambridge: Cambridge University Press, 1979.

Tyabji, Badruddin, *Indian Policies and Practice*. Delhi: Oriental Publishers, 1972.

United Nations, *Charter of the United Nations*, Chapter 1, article 2.

Van de Ven, Hans, "Introduction", in *Warfare in Chinese History*, ed. Hans van de Ven. Leiden: Brill, 2000, pp. 1–32.

Van de Walle, Nicolas, *African Economies and the Politics of Permanent Crisis, 1979–1999*. New York: Cambridge University Press, 2001.

Vatikiotis, Michael, "China, India and the Land Between", *Asia Times Online*, 4 March 2006.

Viraphol, Sarasin, *Tribute and Profit: Sino-Siamese Trade, 1652–1853*. Cambridge [MA]: Harvard University Press, 1977.

Vital, David, *The Inequality of States: A Study of the Small Power in International Relations*. Oxford: Clarendon Press, 1967.

Vliet, Jeremias van, "Description of the Kingdom of Siam (1636)" (translated by L.F. van Ravenswaay), *Journal of the Siam Society* 7, 1 (1910): 93.

Vuving, Alexander L., "The References of Vietnamese States and the Mechanisms of World Formation", *Asien* 79 (April 2001): 62–86.

————, "The Two-Headed Grand Strategy: Vietnamese Foreign Policy since Doi Moi", paper presented at the conference "Vietnam Update: Strategic and Foreign Relations" in Singapore on 28 November 2004.

Walker, Richard L., The *Multi-State System of China*. Hamden [CT]: Shoe String Press, 1954.

Waltz, Kenneth N., *Theory of International Politics*. New York: Random House, 1979.

Wang, Dahai 王大海, *Haidao Yizhi Jiaozhu* 海岛逸志校注 [Annotated Edition of Records and Anecdotes of the Island World]. Hong Kong: Xuejin, 1992.

Wang, Dong, *China's Unequal Treaties: Narrating National History*. Lanham [Maryland]: Lexington Books, 2005.

Wang, Gungwu, *China and the World since 1949: The Impact of Independence, Modernity and Revolution*. New York: St. Martin's Press, 1977.

————, "Early Ming Relations with Southeast Asia, a Background Essay", in *Community and Nation: Essays on Southeast Asia and the Chinese*. Singapore and Sydney: Heinemann and Allen & Unwin, 1981, pp. 28–57.

————, "The Rhetoric of a Lesser Empire: Early Sung Relations with its Neighbours", in *The Chineseness of China: Selected Essays*. Hong Kong: Oxford University Press, 1991, pp. 100–17.

————, "China and Southeast Asia: The Context of a New Beginning", in *Power Shift: China and Asia's New Dynamics*, ed. David Shambaugh. Berkeley [CA]: University of California Press, 2006, pp. 187–204.

Wang, Tao, *Taoyuan Wenlu Waibian*. Shanghai: Shanghai shudian, 2002.

Wang, Yang Chong, ed., 胡漢民先生政論選輯: 遠東問題与大亜細亜主義 [*Collected Works of Hu Han Min on Far East Issues and Pan-Asianism*]. Guangzhou: Guangzhou Minzhi Publishing, 1935.

Watanabe, Manabu, "The Concept of *Sadae Kyorin* in Korea", *Japan Quarterly* 24, 4 (1977).

Watson, Adam, *The Evolution of International Society*. London: Routledge, 1992.

Wei, Yuan 魏源, *Haiguo Tuzhi* 海国图志 [Gazeteer and Maps of the Maritime World, annotated by Chen Hua *et al.* 陈华等]. 长沙：岳麓书社, 1998.

Westad, Odd Arne, ed., *Brothers in Arms: The Rise and Fall of the Sino-Soviet Alliance, 1945–1963*. Washington DC: Woodrow Wilson Center Press and Stanford [CA]: Stanford University Press, 1998.

Willoughby, W.W, *The Sino-Japanese Controversy and the League of Nations*. New York: Greenwood Press, 1968 (first published in 1935), pp. 657–69.

Wilz, John Edward, "Did the United States Betray Korea in 1905?", *Pacific Historical Review* 54, 3 (Aug. 1985).

Win, Kyaw Zaw, "The Asian Socialist Conference in 1953 as Precursor to the Bandung Conference in 1955", paper presented at the 15th Biennial Conference of the Asian Studies Association of Australia, Canberra, 29 June–2 July 2004.

Winichakul, Thongchai, "The Quest for 'Siwilai': A Geographical Discourse of Civilisational Thinking in the Late Nineteenth and Early Twentieth Century Siam", *Journal of Asian Studies* 59, 3 (Aug. 2000): 528–49.

Wolters, W.O., "Historians and Emperors in Vietnam and China", in *Perceptions of the Past in Southeast Asia*, ed. Anthony Reid and David Marr. Singapore: Heinemann, 1979, pp. 69–89.

Womack, Brantly, *China and Vietnam: The Politics of Asymmetry*. Cambridge: Cambridge University Press, 2006.

Woo-Cumings, Meredith, ed., *The Developmental State*. Ithaca [NY]: Cornell University Press, 1999.

Woodside, Alexander Barton, *Vietnam and the Chinese Model: A Comparative Study of Vietnamese and Chinese Government in the First Half of the Nineteenth Century*. Cambridge [MA]: Harvard University Press, 1971.

————, "The Relationship between Political Theory and Economic Growth in Vietnam", in *The Last Stand of Asian Autonomies: Responses to Modernity in the Diverse States of Southeast Asia and Korea, 1750–1900*, ed. Anthony Reid. Basingstoke: Macmillan, 1997, p. 246.

Working People's Daily editorial, 6 March 1985 and 3 September 1991.

Wu, Dongzhi 吴东之, ed., *Zhongguo Waijiaoshi: Zhonghua Minguo Shiqi 1911–1949 nian* 中国外交史:中华民国时期, 1911–1949年 [Diplomatic History of China: Republican Period, 1911–1949]. Henan: Renmin chubanshe, 1990.

Wu, Xiaodong, "*Changhe* zhong de Cuanmei Fuma: Shen Congwen de Guojia Xiangxiang he Xiandai Xiangxiang" [Media Codes in *The Long River*: Analyzing Shen Congwen's Imaginary of Nation-State and Modernity], unpublished PhD dissertation, Peking University, 1992.

Xie, Bin, *Zhongguo Sangdishi* [China's Lost Territories]. Shanghai: Zhonghua shuju, 1936.

Xie, Qinggao 谢清高, *Hai Lu Zhu* 海录注 [Annotated Edition of Maritime Records]. Beijing: Zhonghua shuju, 1955.

Xu, Ben, *Disenchanted Democracy: Chinese Cultural Criticism after 1989*. Ann Arbor: University of Michigan Press, 1999.

Xu, Jiyu 徐继余, *Yinghuan Zhilue Jiaozhu* 瀛寰志略校注 [A Brief Description of the Ocean Circuit, annotated by Song Dachuan 宋大川]. Beijing: Wenwu chubanshe, 2007.

Yao, Huaimin, ed. *Yang Yuling Ji*. Changsha: Yuelu shushe, 2001.

Yasenev, Vladimir and Stepanov, Yevgeny, *China's Frontiers: From Traditional Expansionism to Hegemonism Today*. Moscow: Novosti Press Agency Publishing House, 1981.

Yi, Ki-baek, *Minjok kwa Yoksa* [The Nation and History]. Seoul: Iljogak, 1994.

Yu, Bin, "The Study of Chinese Foreign Policy: Problems and Prospect", *World Politics* 46, 2 (January 1994): 235–61.

Yu, Dingbang, "1852–1890 nian de Zhong Tai Jiaowang [Contacts between China and Siam from 1852 to 1890]", *Journal of Sun Yatsen University Social Science* 3 (1992): 58–65.

Yu, Insun, "Le Van Huu and Ngo Si Lien: A Comparison of Their Perception of Vietnamese History", in *Viet Nam: Borderless Histories*, ed. Nhung Tuyet Tran and Anthony Reid. Madison: University of Wisconsin Press, 2006, pp. 45–71.

Yu, Keun-ho, "Hanmal Daeoikwan ui Tukjil [The Characteristics of Late Choson Korea's Worldview]", in *Chosonjo Chongchi Sasang Yongu* [A Study of Political Thought in Choson Korea]. Seoul: Pyongminsa, 1987, pp. 203–20.

Yunnansheng Lishi Yanjiusuo (compiler/editor), '*Qing Shi Lu' Yuenan Miandian Taiguo Laowo Shiliao Zhaichao* [Extracts from Qing Shi Lu regarding Vietnam, Burma, Thailand, and Laos]. Kunming: Yunnan renmin chubanshe, 1985.

Zeng, Youhao 曾友豪, *Zhongguo Waijiaoshi* 中国外交史 [History of Chinese Diplomacy] Shanghai: Commercial Press, 1926 (it is collected in *Jindai Zhongguo Shiliao Congkan Xubian* 近代中国史料丛刊续编, Part Two, Number 187, 第十九辑, volume 19, pp. 386 to 458).

Zhang, Taiyan, "Zhonghua Minguo Lun [On the Republic of China]", in *Zhonghua Minzuzhi* [Chinese Ethnography], ed. Hu Nai-an. Taipei: Tianxia chuban gongsi, 1964, pp. 4–18.

Zhang, Weihua 张维华, *Mingshi Folangji Lusong Helan Yidaliya Sizhuan Zhushi* 明史 佛郎機呂宋和蘭意大里亞四傳注釋 [A Commentary of the Four Chapters on Portugal Spain Holland and Italy in History of Ming Dynasty]. Beijing: Hafo yanjing xueshe, 1934.

Zhang, Yiwu, *et al.*, eds., *Da Zhuanxing: Hou Xinshiqi Wenhua Yanjiu* [Great Transformations: Studies on the Post-New-Era Culture]. Harbin: Heilongjiang renmin chubanshe, 1995.

Zhang, Yongjin, "System, Empire and State in Chinese International Relations", *Review of International Studies* 27 (2001): 43–63.

Zhao, Ersun deng 赵尔异等, *Qingshi Gao* 清史稿 [Draft History of the Qing Dynasty]. Changchun: Jilin chubanshe, 1995.

Zhao, Shugui and Zeng, Liya, ed. *Chen Chi Ji*. Beijing: Zhonghua shuju, 1997.

Zhuo, Nansheng, *Zhongguo Jindai Baoye Fazhanshi* [History of Early Modern Chinese Press]. Beijing: Xinhua Press, 1994.

Contributors

Prasenjit Duara is Director of Research in Humanities and Social Sciences at the National University of Singapore and Emeritus Professor of History at the University of Chicago. He is the author of several books on Chinese and East Asian history including *Culture, Power and the State: Rural North China, 1900–1942* (1988), which won the Fairbank Prize of the AHA and the Levenson Prize of the AAS. His other books are *Sovereignty and Authenticity: Manchukuo and the East Asian Modern* (2003), *Rescuing History from the Nation* (1995), *The Global and the Regional in China's Nation-Formation* (Routledge, 2009) and an edited volume on Decolonization (Routledge, 2004). His work has been widely translated into Chinese, Korean and Japanese. Duara has also contributed to volumes on historiography and historical thought including "Transnationalism and the Challenge to National Histories", in *Re-thinking American History in a Global Age*, ed. Thomas Bender (2002). At present he is working on *Religion and Citizenship in Asia* and *Hong Kong during the Cold War*.

Junko Koizumi is a Professor at the Center for Southeast Asian Studies, Kyoto University, Japan. She received her PhD in agricultural economics from the University of Tokyo. She is interested in the Early Bangkok Period of Siam (Thailand) and has published several articles in English including "From a Water Buffalo to a Human Being: Women and the Family in Siamese History", in *Other Pasts: Women, Gender and History in Early Modern Southeast Asia,* ed. Barbara Watson Andaya (2000). Over the last few years, she has also been conducting research on Sino-Siamese relations in the late nineteenth and early twentieth centuries and the historiography of overseas Chinese in Thailand, and has started a historical study of Chinese-style shrines in towns along the Gulf of Thailand.

Maung Aung Myoe was a Postdoctoral Fellow at the Asia Research Institute, National University of Singapore (2004–6) when this chapter was written, and now resides in Myanmar. He holds a PhD in Political Science and International Relations from the Australian National University. He was a visiting fellow at the Institute of Defence and Strategic Studies, Singapore, where he produced a monograph titled *Neither Friend Nor Foe: Myanmar's Relations with Thailand since 1988*. He has published articles on security and foreign policy issues of Myanmar. He is currently working on a manuscript entitled "In the Name of Paukphaw (Kinfolk): Myanmar's China Policy since 1948".

Seo-Hyun Park is Acting Instructor and Research Fellow at Stanford University's Shorenstein Asia-Pacific Research Center (APARC). She specialises in International Relations and Comparative Politics, with a focus on the East Asian region. She received her PhD in Government (Political Science) from Cornell University. Her research interests include issues of sovereignty and national identity, globalisation and regionalisation, and East Asian security. She has been a recipient of the Japan Foundation Dissertation Fellowship, the Cornell University Einaudi Center's Carpenter Fellowship, and the Center for International Security and Cooperation Fellowship at Stanford University.

Anthony Reid is an historian of Southeast Asia, now again (2009) at the Research School of Pacific and Asian Studies at the Australian National University, where he worked 1970–99. Most recently he was founding Director in turn of the Centre for Southeast Asian Studies at UCLA (1999–2002) and of the Asia Research Institute of the National University of Singapore (2002–7). His books include: *The Contest for North Sumatra: Atjeh, the Netherlands and Britain, 1858–1898* (1969); *The Indonesian National Revolution* (1974); *The Blood of the People: Revolution and the End of Traditional Rule in Northern Sumatra* (1979); *Southeast Asia in the Age of Commerce, 1450–1680* (2 vols., 1988–93); *Charting the Shape of Early Modern Southeast Asia* (1999); *An Indonesian Frontier: Acehnese and Other Histories of Sumatra* (2004) and *Imperial Alchemy: Nationalism and Political Identity in Southeast Asia* (2009).

Anbin Shi is Associate Professor of media/cultural studies and assistant dean of pedagogy in School of Journalism and Communications, Tsinghua University, Beijing, China. His research interests include media/cultural studies, global communication and intercultural communication. He has published *Crisis Communication and Media Relation* (Guangzhou: South China Journal Press, 2004), *A Comparative Approach to Redefining*

Chineseness in the Era of Globalization (New York: Edwin Mellen Press, 2003), co-authored *Media on the Move: Global Flow and Contra-Flow* (London: Routledge, 2006), six Chinese translations of academic cannons in journalism and communication studies, as well as thirty Chinese and English articles in *Global Media and Communication, Social Semiotics* and nationwide academic journals.

Kawashima Shin is Associate Professor at the University of Tokyo who specialises in history of international relationship. His major works include: *Formation of Modern Chinese Diplomacy* [中国近代外交の形成] (Nagoya University Press, 2004, awarded Suntory Academic Prize); *Modern and Contemporary International History in East Asia* [東アジア国際政治史] (co-editor and author, Nagoya University Press, 2007); *Chinese Diplomacy* [中国の外交] (editor and co-author, Yamakawa Shuppansha Press, 2007); *History of Relations between Japan and Taiwan in 1945–2008* [日台関係史 1945–2008] (co-author, University of Tokyo Press, 2009) and *Recognition of History around 1945* [1945 年の歴史認識] (co-editor and author, University of Tokyo Press, 2009).

Alexander L. Vuving was Research Fellow at Harvard University's Belfer Center for Science and International Affairs when his chapter was written. Currently he is Associate Professor at the Asia-Pacific Center for Security Studies. He holds a PhD in Political Science and an MA in Political Science, Economics, and Sociology from the Johannes Gutenberg University, Mainz, Germany. His publications and invited presentations cover topics such as how long American primacy can last, the grand strategies of major powers after the Cold War, the emerging Asian international order, the transformation of China's and Japan's foreign policy, the trajectory of state-building in Vietnam, and Vietnam's foreign policy. Major areas of his research interests include grand strategy making, foreign policy change, historical and contemporary international relations of Asia, and international relations theory.

Wang Gungwu is University Professor, National University of Singapore and Emeritus Professor of the Australian National University. His books in English include: *The Chinese Overseas: From Earthbound China to the Quest for Autonomy* (2000); *Don't Leave Home: Migration and the Chinese* (2001); *Anglo-Chinese Encounters since 1800: War, Trade, Science and Governance* (2003); *Diasporic Chinese Ventures*, edited by Gregor Benton and Liu Hong (2004). He recently edited *Nation-building: Five*

Southeast Asian Histories (2005).   Professor Wang received his BA and MA degrees from the University of Malaya in Singapore, and his PhD at the University of London (1957).   His career took him from the University of Malaya (Singapore and Kuala Lumpur, 1957–68, Professor of History 1963–68) to the Australian National University (1968–86), where he was Professor of Far Eastern History and Director of the Research of Pacific Studies. From 1986 to 1995, he was Vice-Chancellor of the University of Hong Kong.

Zheng Yangwen teaches Chinese history at the University of Manchester. She received her PhD from the University of Cambridge and taught/researched at the University of Pennsylvania and National University of Singapore (Asia Research Institute) before joining Manchester. She is the author of *The Social Life of Opium in China* (Cambridge University Press, 2005) and co-editor of *Personal Names in Asia: History, Culture and Identity* (with Charles J-H MacDonald) (NUS Press, 2009), and *The Body in Asia* (with Bryan S. Turner) (Berghahn Books, 2009).

Index